GW00497929

Behavioural Social Work

Also by Barbara L. Hudson

Social Work with Psychiatric Patients

Behavioural Social Work
An Introduction

Barbara L. Hudson

and

Geraldine M. Macdonald

MACMILLAN

First published 1986

Published by
MACMILLAN EDUCATION LTD
Houndmills, Basingstoke, Hampshire RG21 2XS
and London
Companies and representatives
throughout the world

Filmsetting by Vantage Photosetting Co Ltd
Eastleigh and London

Printed in Hong Kong

British Library Cataloguing in Publication Data
Hudson, Barbara L.
Behavioural social work : an introduction.
1. Social case work
I. Title   II. Macdonald, Geraldine M.
361.3′2   HV43
ISBN 0–333–36132–6
ISBN 0–333–36133–4 Pbk

For Kenneth and Ezra Macdonald

Contents

Preface

Behavioural social work has much to offer from both an ethical and a practical standpoint. This is not to suggest that behavioural theories and methods will suffice to cope with all of the issues and tasks that confront social workers. We need a wide range of knowledge from the contributory disciplines besides psychology, and from psychology we need other knowledge, such as an understanding of normal development and abnormal functioning. And we require additional skills, such as obtaining material resources and finding our way through the maze of bureaucracy and political power structures. Nevertheless, a behavioural approach can help with a large chunk of our day-to-day work, from assessing situations and writing reports to intervening with individuals and groups and seeking to modify the behaviour of other people who exert an influence on our clients' lives.

This book will give you a basic understanding of the theories from which behavioural procedures have been derived, and of how the procedures are applied in practice. In the latter part of the book we illustrate some of the uses of behavioural procedures with several client groups and problem areas taken separately. We hope to demonstrate the applicability of the behavioural approach to the breadth of problems encountered by social workers. Some areas are not covered in any depth, such as the work of hospital and residential workers, as this book is aimed primarily at those 'in the field'. However, many of the interventions discussed, and the chapters on learning theory and assessment, should be useful to social workers in all settings.

A word about our use of references. Since this is an introductory text, we have not cited references for every statement for which there is research evidence available; in the main we have given key references on important topics and references where statements in the text may give rise to controversy.

In order to avoid accusations of sex discrimination, *and* to avoid the clumsiness of 'she/he', etc., we have used male and female pronouns randomly to denote workers, clients and others.

BARBARA L. HUDSON

University of Oxford   GERALDINE M. MACDONALD

Acknowledgements

Parts of the manuscript were read by Michael Crowe, Clive Hollin, Derek Johnston, Roger McAuley, Kenneth Macdonald, Pauline McDonnell, Ilona McDowell, Roger Morgan, Mike Noble, Ann Nursey, Brian Sheldon and Christine Stevens. We had permission to use case material (suitably disguised) from some of the aforementioned, and from Ian Mathews, Sarah Ainsworth and Howard Lomas. We are grateful to them all, and errors and omissions that remain are our own responsibility.

Much of the typing was done by Rachael Lawrance fast and expertly.

We thank the Macmillan Press, Pergamon Press, Roger McAuley, Judy Hutchings and Sheldon Rose for permission to reproduce published material.

B.L.H.
G.M.M.

University of Oxford

Introduction

Betty is leading a women's group on a council housing estate. The members are sharing their dissatisfaction about their accommodation: damp walls, peeling paint and expensive heating systems.

John is attending a social security tribunal with the parents of a mentally handicapped teenager. They are appealing against a social security decision to cut their benefit.

Ann is visiting the home of five year old Mary, who has been in care as a result of non-accidental injury. Ann has been explaining the legal position, and is having a game with the child while her mother makes them a cup of coffee.

Betty, John and Ann are all behaviourally-oriented social workers. Betty is helping her group to undertake a detailed assessment of their problems, their feelings, and their skills in a role-played interview with a housing official. Week by week the group will practise, assess their own and each other's progress, and take on homework assignments. John has used role-play too, to help his clients prepare for the tribunal; he is also working with them on a programme of rewards and sanctions to teach their son to do more things for himself and to reduce the frequency of his temper tantrums. Ann is helping the little girl's mother to develop her 'child management skills', to control her feelings of anger, and to play with her daughter in a way that gives pleasure to them both.

Behavioural social work is social work first and foremost, with its special concerns and diverse tasks and roles, together with its own education and training background distinguishing it from the other helping professions. But to these tasks behavioural social work brings to bear skills which mark it off from other social work approaches:

Behavioural social work applies the principles of learning and social learning theories to the analysis and modification of behaviour. These principles are derived from empirical research into how behaviour is learned, maintained and unlearned.

It is informed and guided by the findings of empirically-based research studies. This emphasis on empirical research is the hallmark of the behavioural approach. Because scientifically-based bodies of knowledge do not stand still, the behavioural approach is constantly changing as old hypotheses are discarded or refined, and new ideas are added. There is no room for theories constructed out of untested and untestable hypotheses, such as those of Freud and Klein. But there is room for well-founded ideas of other schools and disciplines: for example, the value of empathy, warmth and genuineness in the client–worker relationship and of cohesion in work with groups; the key role of social factors in depression, and of family interaction in schizophrenia; the stages of child development; the rules and sequences of social interaction.

Another aspect of the behavioural worker's empirical stance: the emphasis placed on evaluating progress and the outcome of each individual intervention. The worker always attempts to ascertain whether this particular intervention (rewarding desirable behaviour with attention, ignoring tantrums, tracking and disputing unconstructive thoughts) has a measurable impact on the particular problem of this individual or group.

It is difficult to test whether a problem has changed for the better unless you can reliably measure it before and after intervention begins, and for this reason – rather than because of some philosophical notion that people are simple or mechanical objects – the behavioural approach is characterised by a strong preference, wherever feasible, for identifying, measuring and working on discrete and observable bits of behaviour.

Behavioural workers focus on the present rather than the past. This is because the person's current reality can often be modified, whereas past events are over and cannot be changed. This is not to deny that past events have led up to present troubles; but it does mean that the current or contemporary causes of behaviour are of more practical significance: the events that trigger off problem behaviours, the consequences that make behaviours likely to occur more frequently. Behavioural workers have no need to delve deeply into people's earlier lives.

This concern with the present and interest in evaluating one's work are in fact shared with other modern social work approaches such as Perlman's problem-solving approach, task-centred work and crisis intervention. Additional shared features include dividing a broadly defined problem into smaller units to be tackled one by one; the tendency for intervention to be short-term and time-limited; and the establishment of a clear-cut working agreement with clients, rather than an open-ended and non-specific relationship.

Task-centred work, whilst perhaps the nearest relative, is both narrower and wider than behavioural work. It is narrower in the sense that it is generally recommended for a narrower range of problems, has a fixed time limit, and always requires tasks to be done at regular intervals between sessions. It is wider in the sense that it welcomes a variety of theories, some of which lack empirical support, and permits a looser approach to the evaluation of outcomes. Crisis-intervention shares these characteristics. Task-centred work can be behavioural work, but this is not necessarily the case. Similarly, people in crisis can be helped using a behavioural approach, but 'crisis-oriented behavioural work' is one application of a broader, very flexible approach, rather than a separate specialism.

So, whilst there are continuities and similarities between behavioural work and other social work approaches, the behavioural approach differs in its use of learning theories, its firm empirical stance and the specifically behavioural methods of intervention that derive from these two features.

However, rarely are these aspects of theory and method the basis for the view held by some that behavioural social workers are somehow (and pejoratively) 'different'. Rather it has to do with alleged differences in the philosophy, goals and general view of people in trouble believed to be held by behavioural workers. Such differences are far less substantial than is sometimes suggested.

Part of the difficulty stems from the fact that the learning theories are firmly research-based, and the original research began with studies of animal behaviour. It is now safe to claim that we must look mainly to the environment to decipher the factors that influence behaviour; behaviour is sandwiched between two sets of influences: antecedents and consequences. This is true of people as well as animals. But no behavioural practitioner would recommend dealing with a human being as if he or she were just a large rat or pigeon; nor would he conceptualise a person in such simple terms. The interaction between a person and his environment is infinitely varied and complex; people have a huge repertoire of behaviours and react to stimuli in idiosyncratic ways; they can, and do, exercise 'countercontrol', in part determining what stimuli will influence their behaviour and invalidating the stimuli used by another person trying to influence them. For these reasons, amongst others, the behavioural practitioner, by contrast with the animal experimenter, is concerned with many more and longer term antecedents and consequences, and many more and more subtle types of behaviour.

Furthermore, behavioural practitioners, despite their interest in discrete and measurable phenomena, do not neglect overall 'umbrella' goals of concern to all helping professionals and their clients. Such ends can, with benefit, be translated into behavioural language for the purpose of behavioural intervention. Thus 'improve self-esteem' might become (depending on the individual case) 'increase the number of activities the client considers worthwhile; increase the skills the client would like to develop; decrease the frequency of the client's self-critical responses'.

The main differences between the behavioural and other social work approaches are not in the goals themselves, but in the way they are specified and expressed. And, of course, in the methods by which the goals are pursued. The same ethical constraints apply in behavioural as in other approaches: both ends and means must meet equivalent standards of ethical acceptability to the client, to the social work profession and to society. Indeed, as we argue in the following chapter, behavioural social work can claim ethical superiority over many other social work strategies on a variety of issues.

In this introduction we have sketched in some of the key features of behavioural social work and identified some of the similarities and differences *vis-à-vis* other social work approaches. The rest of the book will elaborate on the scientific theories that underpin the behavioural approach; on its detailed assessment and evaluation procedures; and on the numerous behavioural techniques, the majority of which enjoy far better empirical support than those associated with any other social work approach.

Part 1

We begin with a general overview of behavioural social work, its ethical stance and theoretical underpinnings, and the basics of assessment and intervention.

1

Why Behavioural Social Work?

A behavioural approach is well suited to the multiplicity of tasks presented to social workers. It is rich and adaptable and, if we were to take the research evidence seriously, would be the intervention of choice for many problems. Before demonstrating this, let us defuse the charge that, as a particular solution to the social work task, behavioural social work is, in contrast to other approaches, somehow 'unethical'.

The social work task and the change agent role

There is little agreement on what is 'the social work task'. Opinions vary according to the agency, the setting, the theoretical orientation of the practitioner, her ethical stance and political outlook, to name but a few. And this is surely appropriate. Social work encompasses a wide range of activities which are rendered even more diverse by the unique constellation of circumstances each client presents.

But there are some common denominators. Whether the client is simply asking for advice or has asked for social work help with a wide range of complex problems, most requests fall into one of two categories.

The first is that some change be effected in a situation, when the request for help is equivalent to the request that something be different. For example:

—that my husband stop drinking/battering me/being impotent
—that my child/this pupil attend school/stop being delinquent
—that I receive what I am entitled to
—that I have relief from caring for my elderly relative.

The second type of request is that something be done to prevent change, usually, though not exclusively, in the form of deterioration or separation. For example:

—that my marriage not break down
—that my daughter not be taken into care
—that we are not made homeless
—that things don't go from bad to worse.

These 'maintenance' aims very often entail acting in ways that alter what would otherwise be the 'natural' course of things. They also, therefore, require the worker to act as an agent for change. This description of social workers as change agents extends to the statutory obligations placed on social work agencies, as well as to social workers' numerous non-statutory functions, ranging from advocacy to resource finding and creating.

A third category of social work function is assessment, which we would also maintain has an important change-related aspect. Social workers are called upon to make assessments of people and their situations which are then used by others to effect changes – often dramatic and with far-reaching consequences – in clients' lives. These others include the judiciary, adoption and foster panels, and social services committees.

Supervisory functions often straddle these categories: often a matrimonial supervision order will entail not simply monitoring and assessing the family's progress but actively helping the family to function satisfactorily and to adjust to the changes that caused the present situation. Juvenile supervision orders result in similar juxtapositions of roles in which you might find yourself working to improve family relationships, to effect changes in the young person's lifestyle and, at the same time, having to act as an agent of the court for whom you might have to produce a further report.

These aspects of our work require the ability to analyse people's behaviour, and the nature and effects of their interactions with others; the ability to form testable hypotheses about the probable consequences of particular kinds of action; and a repertoire of effective intervention methods. All of these requirements are met by the behavioural approach.

Effectiveness: the central ethical issue

In general the available empirical evidence suggests that the behavioural approach is an effective one and, where comparative data
exist, often more effective than competing approaches (see for
example, the reviews by Agras *et al.*, 1979; Rachman and Wilson,
1980; Thomlison, 1984; Reid and Hanrahan, 1982; Fischer, 1981;
Giles, 1983).

   The issue of effectiveness is, we would argue, the central ethical
criterion to be met by any interventionist discipline or profession. Of
course social work must attend to the ordinary moral constraints
affecting any human activity; we have no intention of devaluing these
and no grounds for believing that behavioural social work, properly
done, violates any defensible constraints. Our concern in this chapter
is with the question 'what are the ethical issues peculiar to an
interventionist profession?'. Being 'a social worker' is different from
being 'a friend', and it is important to locate the additional ethical
constraints imposed by the social work role. And in our view the
central such constraint is 'effectiveness'. If we do not meet this
criterion, we surely fall foul of the 'peculiar repulsiveness of those
who dabble their fingers self-approvingly in the stuff of other people's
souls' (Wootton, 1959, quoting Virginia Woolf). Those who think
the above quotation overstates the case or doubt that effectiveness is
a central ethical issue are invited to consider the following points
about the 'right to intervene'. We begin by considering those clients
who cannot be said to have invited social work intervention.

Involuntary clients

In some situations social workers are said to have a right to intervene
by reason of statute (e.g. child care legislation). However, they have
these powers in order that the interventions they permit will effect
desirable consequences that might not otherwise occur, such as the
protection of children, long-term planning for children, provision for
the elderly and so on. It is often the perceived absence of these
outcomes (or the occurrence of unexpected ones) that leads to
revisions and change. This is seen clearly in legislative changes which,
in endeavouring to get the 'right' balance, apparently favour first the
rights of natural parents, then the child or the substitute family, and
so on.

Voluntary clients

In this context a medical analogy is helpful. The doctor's right to treat his patient is conferred on him by dint of his having demonstrated his ability and effectiveness during and at the end of his training. Further, his competence depends in part on his familiarisation with techniques of proven effectiveness with which he can treat his patients. If he had failed his qualifying exam, or if ten years into his practice he continued to use what you the patient knew to be an outmoded and ineffectual form of treatment, you would not want to continue as his patient. Doctors have a responsibility to keep abreast of research findings because the grounds for authorising men and women to intervene in people's lives continue to be their individual competence in applying optimal strategies: their effectiveness. Some of what they learned during their training will be of continuing use, but some will not. The same applies to social work.

Competence

That social workers are required to undergo a certain amount of training and to demonstrate their knowledge in some way or another suggests that at the end of such training they should be able to offer help which other, untrained people in the main cannot, and that what they have to offer is of use; otherwise why the training and why the role? Much could be said about the paucity of evidence that most present day training courses do *demonstrably* equip people with such skills. What is pertinent here is that training courses should keep abreast of – and teach skills for keeping abreast of – the most effective methods of intervention, and that social workers should act following their training to maintain their initial level of competence.

Neither social workers nor doctors can personally research methods of intervention in the rigorous ways necessary to justify their adoption, but they can be trained to critically assess the research findings that become available, and decide which methods are likely to be most effective with which problems in which circumstances.

Too often social workers continue their practice using methods which they 'prefer' – 'it's what I know and feel at home with'; 'it's what I was taught'. Often the method used is the same regardless of the client, the problem or the constraints. This is tantamount to a GP recommending aspirin regardless of his patient's complaint. If your marriage was on the verge of breakdown, your child was causing your family major problems, or your aged parent had had a stroke, would you want help from a social worker who knew only what she had learned five, ten or maybe twenty years ago, especially if what she learned then is less effective than other methods of which she is unaware? Or, equally as bad, would you want help from a social worker who had been enthusiastically caught up in a new 'method' that had not been shown to be effective?

Social workers earn the 'right' to intervene in people's lives when they qualify, but with that right comes – or in our opinion should come – a responsibility to maintain the standards of understanding and practice competence recognised as essential then. This will mean adopting new knowledge and skills, and dropping old ones, as research evidence accumulates. This is acknowledged in the BASW and NASW codes of ethics but gets rather swallowed up by the wealth of oratory concerning the dignity of the individual and so on. The dignity of the individual is best preserved and enhanced by giving him the best possible help for the problems he faces.

Effectiveness is an important ethical concern not only for in-dividual workers but for the agencies in which they work. There is a disproportionate unconcern within agencies with self-evaluation (*qua* agency), and many of the social work catastrophes (e.g., children killed by their parents) are as much, if not more, about the failure of agencies to exercise effective monitoring and evaluation of their work as about individual error. Because of its concern with clarity and goal setting, and its emphasis throughout intervention on evaluation, the behavioural approach is particularly conducive to facilitating such institutional evaluation: it certainly provides an appropriate model and rationale for much of the work done in social work agencies, by planners and practitioners alike.

It is because of the effectiveness of so many behavioural techniques (this is shown in ensuing chapters), and because there are many indications that even when not wholly successful a behavioural approach is more effective than available alternatives, that we think it is unethical *not* to teach behavioural methods on qualifying courses and for social workers *not* to have them in their repertoire of skills. We agree with Martin Herbert that it is now time to ask the question: 'Why not behavioural social work?' rather than simply to defend its use (Herbert, 1979).

Behavioural work not a special case

In advocating this approach so strongly we are not denying that behavioural interventions pose ethical problems. Some have argued that people's overconcern with the ethical issues surrounding behavioural intervention is a direct consequence of its effectiveness: because it works it is potentially more threatening to the client; anything that can be used for good can usually be used for ill. This is a reasonable concern, but one which is generally overstated. Certainly we have to be particularly careful about whether and how to influence clients who have limited control over their own lives, such as children and people in institutions (prisoners, young offenders, the mentally ill and the mentally handicapped). With such clients it is particularly important to scrutinise the methods to be used and the goals to be pursued with regard to their acceptability to the clients, their families, and society as a whole. But these concerns are not peculiar to behavioural social work. They are brought more sharply into focus, because of the effectiveness of behavioural techniques; because the process of intervention is more readily open to scrutiny; and because the end results are more clearly related to the means than is the case, say, with some psychodynamic methods. We would argue that the ethical concerns surrounding behavioural social work are not distinct from those concerning social work practice in general.

Because behavioural interventions seem to effect more changes in people's overt behaviour than most other approaches they are assumed to be more controlling and manipulative and therefore less likely to encourage client autonomy or self-determination, regarded by many as intrinsically good. There are two major misunderstandings here. First, whilst it is important to guard against its abuse, control, properly understood, is an essential and therefore desirable prerequisite of change. Second, it is a fallacy that less technical, less avowedly or overtly directive approaches accord more importance to, or work more effectively towards, client self-determination.

Control

Behavioural methods do offer stronger potential means of control than most other approaches, but there are two uses of 'control' that need to be separated.

First there is control of one individual (or group) by another. This is what is commonly meant when issues of control and manipulation and the 'vulnerability' of the client *vis à vis* the behavioural worker are discussed. It is certainly possible to depict potential abuses of behavioural methods used purely for control, and instances of these have occurred. What differentiates these instances, however, is not the control element but the reasons and goals of the controllers – for example when interventions are used to ease the burden of caretakers in prisons and mental hospitals, with little or no reciprocal benefit to the people concerned. A fieldwork example would be assisting a mother to 'control' her very normal child's behaviour for her own ends, producing very abnormal levels of compliance and probably unhappiness, rather than working towards change in the mother's attitudes. These are problems of concern with any approach.

'Control' has another usage however. 'Bringing under control' is an essential element of change, even when an individual is trying to solve a personal problem such as finding a job, resolving marital conflict or coping with depression. In order to achieve the ends we want we need to be able to effect changes in our own behaviour and in that of others, whether our kin, our social worker, or the local Social Security officers. The effectiveness of our change endeavours entails gaining control over as many of the factors influencing the situation as is possible. Whenever possible this means placing such control in the hands of the client himself, otherwise the results of the intervention will terminate with the departure of the worker (that it so often does is one of the issues of concern to behavioural practitioners today).

'Client self-determination' is best served by using a behavioural approach

It is the case that behavioural methods are technical and directive. However, unlike many other approaches, behavioural social work requires that one works *overtly* towards goals stated and agreed on between clients and between clients and workers. Often the behavioural worker is aiming to help the client achieve a level of functioning that both increases his range of options and the probability of his achieving what he wants; that is to say, increasing the client's potential for self-determination. Equally important, the behavioural worker indicates to the client what improvement or change will look like, thereby increasing that client's ability to assess the effectiveness of the help given – and to choose to withdraw!

There is no room in behavioural work for covert goals or covert strategies on the worker's part. Indeed, we question the ethical status of covert worker strategies, such as the use of 'paradoxical injunction' or viewing Mrs Jones' request for help with problem X as really a request for help with problem Y and acting accordingly (that is, representing interventions aimed at solving Y as intended to solve X). For example:

X (presenting problem)	Y ('real' problem)
marital problem	'oedipal problem'
depression	'introverted anger'
enuresis	'symbolic weeping'

Further, behavioural workers do not assume the existence of hidden agendas on the part of the client. If for any reason the behavioural social worker believed there to be something else the client would like help with, he would endeavour to elicit it. This would be identifying other agendas, but by definition not hidden ones.

What, then, is the status of non-technical and avowedly non-directive approaches with regard to client self-determination? One could argue that they are more likely to foster client self-determination because they effect no change in the client's situation. Clearly this is not the position defended by those non-directive therapists who wish to claim effectiveness. Second, it might be argued, their interaction with their clients offers nothing prescriptive, or offers a number of alternatives each of which is presented without any particular value-judgment or recommendation. Consider this last possibility.

The simplest (most apparently straightforward) example of a non-directive approach would be helping a person to make up their own mind about something. Certainly one can take care not to sway a client deliberately one way or the other, but this is not sufficient to eliminate the possibility of worker influence. Giving the client information and directing him to various alternative courses of action not hitherto considered may have a direct effect on possible outcomes. It requires considerable skill not to indicate, even non-verbally, one's own preferences and biases. Even with considerable skill, one cannot control for the client's 'second guessing' and misinterpretation, for instance his taking a reminder about one particular consequence (which he may be consistently forgetting) as indicative of the worker's preference or dislike. And the situation with regard to control is similarly complex.

One famous (his critics would say 'infamous') behaviourist, B. F. Skinner, has debated the issue of control with an equally famous humanist therapist, Carl Rogers. In fact both agreed that therapists aimed to influence their client. Rogers stated:

> We are deeply engaged in the prediction and influencing of behavior, or even the control of behavior (Rogers and Skinner, 1956)

Rogers' contention, however, is that this is best and most appropriately done via a process which he describes as self-actualisation. Intervention aims to increase clients' ability to make optimum choices and to achieve the goals they set themselves. Skinner, on the other hand, maintains that this is naïve. As we shall demonstrate in the next chapter, learning theorists contend that what a person thinks, does and feels is in large part a consequence of his learning history; and the consequences of his behaviour play a determining role in what he 'chooses' to do. Of course, what he does has an effect on that very environment that influences him, so he is not merely a pawn in a game over which man has no control.

Skinner's contention is that one of the effects of behavioural analysis (indeed one of its aims) is to highlight as many of these controlling factors as possible and to manipulate them in the client's best interest. Skinner advocates that social policies should be formulated upon behavioural principles in order to maximise people's chances of such 'goods' as happiness and fulfilment. Contrary to his critics' views, Skinner is concerned that this is the only way we can ensure the compassionate treatment of groups with little or no power such as the poor, the elderly and the handicapped. The crux of the matter is that people are subject to all sorts of control, some structured and explicit (the law), others arbitrary and unpredictable (income, resources, health). What Skinner wishes to do is alter the balance, bringing more of the arbitrary factors of control 'under control'.

And this seems to summarise the most significant difference between directive and non-directive approaches to intervention.

Research on client-centred therapies such as that of Rogers has demonstrated quite categorically that workers do respond to clients' statements in ways which indicate approval or disapproval, enthusiasm or distance *and* that these responses affect the clients' subsequent behaviour, as we suggested above. And of course, most social work activities are considerably more complex than helping people to make decisions, and the opportunities for exerting a determining influence on clients' lives considerably greater. At one extreme, social workers can and do provide services (including their own time) contingent on their client's behaviour, although this may not be spelled out to the client – or even done wittingly by the worker.

It is a fallacy that less technical, less directive approaches influence the client less. What they may do is influence the client in less predictable and therefore less useful ways (possibly in ways more undermining of the client). More 'overtly' influential approaches are in a position to control these influences most effectively – or at least be aware of their effects and to use them in a planned way to achieve goals determined by the client.

To equate client self-determination with non-directiveness is to fall into several muddles. It is to misperceive the worker influence inherent in all approaches; it is to equate directiveness with telling the client to do something or not to do something (at best this is only a very small part of the most directive approach); and it is to overestimate the likelihood of the most co-operative client putting aside his own critical and decision-making apparatus in favour of blindly following the suggestions of a social worker. It also demonstrates a misplaced worry. The concerns of social workers are more appropriately focused on their *lack* of effectiveness and their *failure* to effect desired changes whatever approach they use. Much wringing of hands and shaking of heads is caused by the over-determination (apparently) of many of our clients to carry on regardless. . . . Outside of 'ethical debates proper' the majority of social workers would be only too glad to be in a position to influence their clients more. And, even within these debates, it is our contention that an effective and 'open' approach, however 'directive', is in the strongest position to promote client self-determination.

Finally, as a central ethical criterion, effectiveness helps to define usefully an often spurious and at best muddled distinction between 'task' and 'process'. Research has identified certain interpersonal 'process' skills, namely warmth, empathy and genuineness, that are correlated with successful task outcome. Further, these are skills that can be taught and learned. 'Process' is not, or should not be regarded as, an entirely individual, even rather mystical affair in which the worker endeavours to crystallise out his unique style. Rather, the individual worker develops his 'style' so that his communication of these three things is maximised. No other such factors have been shown to be correlated with effectiveness.

'Respect for persons' is enhanced by using a behavioural approach

Basic to the profession of social work is the recognition of the value and dignity of every human being . . . BASW Code of Ethics 6

He [the social worker] will respect his clients as individuals and will seek to ensure that their dignity, individuality, rights and responsibility shall be safeguarded.   BASW Code of Ethics 10:2.

This code is based on the fundamental values of the social work profession that include the worth, dignity and uniqueness of all persons . . .   NASW Code of Ethics

The allegation is often made that behavioural social work is incompatible with these aims because of its 'instrumental' nature and its relative disattention (compared with other approaches) to 'life-story' narrative. People's problems, indeed their lives, it is said, are reduced to so many behaviours (that could be anyone's) to be manipulated: how can such an approach safeguard or even recognise and acknowledge the unique 'value and dignity of every human being'?

Discussions within social work about the value of humanity and respect for persons have been, at best, woolly and exhortatory and the time is long overdue for an informed and thoughtful examination of the ethical problems inherent in and facing the social work task. It is our contention that behavioural social work would score well in such an examination. We shall confine ourselves here to answering those particular allegations that are held to be illustrative of the general point, leaving a full analysis until another time, perhaps when someone ventures a meaningful definition of what global terms like 'respect for persons' are actually intended to mean.

We have already suggested that providing the client with the best service possible is tantamount to acknowledging his importance and, *ipso facto*, his worth and his dignity, although these concepts add little. Behavioural social work does focus primarily on the client's present situation, but by no means exclusively (see p.63). The very success of interventions which are focused primarily on the present suggests that in fact past history is not an integral part of the 'presenting problem'.

Behavioural social work does break down problems into identifiable and manageable proportions: behaviours, their antecedents and consequences. Certain problems do have features commonly complained of by the sufferer: for instance it is often the case that a depressed person will complain of sleep disturbance. But to identify and itemise these is not to depersonalise the problem. On the contrary, any behaviour identified by the behavioural worker is described in a very precise way as it is exhibited or experienced by this particular client. The end result is a very detailed and personalised assessment leading to equally personalised intervention plan.

The choice of behavioural intervention will vary from client to client, and so will the minutiae of the procedure, reflecting the client's uniqueness. 'Instrumental' is not the same as 'the mindless and heedless application of techniques', as we hope this book will demonstrate. The behavioural social worker takes the client very seriously throughout their involvement, constantly bearing in mind what impact each move will have on him and on others concerned. Whenever practicable everything is explained, and nothing is done without the client's agreement: surely this is incompatible with a lack of regard for the client's importance?

Another positive point, in the debate about respect for persons, is that behavioural social workers are in the business of giving their clients generalisable skills. In so doing they hope to equip people with the means of solving other and future problems. The professional is no longer the owner of some incommunicable mystique, but of communicable skills. Conversely of course this justifies her privileged position: she has skills to pass on.

Behavioural social work is compatible with the ethical and efficient allocation of resources

Social work is not just a caring profession and social work agencies do not have the subtitle 'rent-a-friend', even though befriending and caring may be important aspects of social work. In a world of scarce resources ineffective care is a psychological luxury that is difficult to justify. By ineffective care we mean 'caring' that effects no change or only effects those changes that, it could be argued, should not be the responsibility of social workers e.g. providing the client with a friendly face and a sympathetic ear (although it may be appropriate that they should work towards establishing another source of that care). BASW's exhortation not to lose concern for the client's suffering even if unable to help him, is morally bankrupt. All measures of care are consequentialist: whilst the sentiment may be a worthy one in private relationships, it is misleading to suggest that 'caring' and 'concern' are intrinsic goods that can or should be allocated like other resources.

Social work is a very costly resource, and a scarce one. In order to make rational decisions about its allocation, effectiveness – demonstrable effectiveness – is a bottom-line requirement. If social work is not *effective* – however one wishes to define that – then the money spent on it would be better spent on interventions of demonstrated effectiveness, such as chiropody and the home-help service.

Conclusion

We have argued that the ethical concerns regarding behavioural interventions are no different to those of social work as a whole, and that behavioural interventions perform better than most when judged against a variety of criteria deemed 'ethical'. Effectiveness is the lynchpin of ethical social work intervention, and behavioural work has much to offer towards meeting this criterion.

The behavioural approach has another important contribution to make to the development of social work practice generally. Some recent research in the UK suggests that, while social workers are adept at making a thoughtful assessment of a problem, and at recognising the need for change, they seem reluctant to be the initiators of that change (see, for example, Fisher *et al.*, 1984). A thorough grasp of the behavioural approach can go some way to redressing this imbalance by equipping the social worker to assess and implement change procedures in a wide range of client groups. We are not suggesting that social work clients do not need very skilled help, merely that many of the requisite skills are well within the competence of social workers who, minimally, should be encouraged to adopt a more active role, rather than leaving 'direct treatment' to other professionals. Often they are the ones who know the client best, who visit at the home and who are uniquely equipped via their training to view the situation in the broad context increasingly recognised as essential. Even when referral to other agencies is necessary the social worker can be an active partner in change-related procedures. The alternative is rather bleak, with social workers increasingly finding themselves left with a co-ordinating and monitoring role (for instance, in child abuse cases). Whilst crucial this is not always a particularly rewarding task and is one which, in more cynical moments, workers might feel would be better done by a good administrator. Social work is a difficult enterprise with few built-in rewards. We suggest that effective, change-directed interventions provide important and much needed sources of job-satisfaction.

We begin our exposition of such interventions with a review of the theories informing the behavioural approach, aware that there is debate as to whether or not theory is a necessary prerequisite to effective intervention. At present the evidence is weighed in favour of the usefulness of theory informing practice. An understanding of the theory of behaviour change is both a way of ensuring that behavioural work does not deteriorate into a hotchpotch of techniques and a necessary means of furthering the understanding of the processes of human behaviour.

Ethical Guidelines of the Behavioural Social Work Group (UK)

Codes of ethics are notoriously difficult to write; their prose must be both generalised and precise; the form invites a focus on individual, not organisational, responsibility; and there is a school of thought which would say that without a clear enforcement mechanism they are empty ('words without the sword are but breath'). In this Annex to Chapter 1 we reprint the Ethical Guidelines of the Behavioural Social Work Group (UK), partly as a substantive starting point for discussion (it meets some, though not all, of the points we have raised), partly as an indicator of the ethical stance of behavioural social workers.

(1) A social worker should endeavour to use procedures which are in the best interests of the client or clients, minimising any

possible harm and maximising benefits for them over both the short and long term, while at the same time balancing these against any possible harmful effects to others or society as a whole.

(2) Choice of intervention should always be justified by the available evidence, taking into account possible alternatives or styles of work, the degree of demonstrated efficacy, discomfort, intervention time and cost of alternative intervention.

(3) The social worker should make exhaustive attempts to discuss and agree the goals and methods of intervention with the client, family and group. We recognise that these may have to be renegotiated from time to time, or intervention terminated.

(4) We also recognise that in situations where consent is impossible to obtain, the worker may not always be able to fulfil these criteria. These situations may include work with e.g. clients with severe mental handicap, very young children and elderly mentally infirm clients. In these situations reference should be made to the guardians/appointed or responsible care-givers.

(5) It is considered an integral part of the social worker's approach that he or she plans and implements all intervention in such a way as to allow its effectiveness to be evaluated. This should apply to casework, group work and community work. Such evaluations should be both qualitative and quantitative.

(6) The social worker should continually reappraise his or her competence both from formal training and from his or her experience. If he or she is faced with a situation in which his or her level of skill is in doubt, he or she should consult with a colleague so that either the case is taken on with adequate supervision and training, or it is appropriately referred elsewhere.

(7) The social worker should develop his or her expertise after formal training is finished, and take reasonable steps to keep up to date with current research and practice by, for example, reading current research or by attending appropriate courses.

2

Theories of Learning

RESPONDENT CONDITIONING

Dogs see food and salivate.
Dogs hear the sound of a tuning fork just before seeing food.
Dogs salivate at the sound of the tuning fork alone.

After a quite short period of time the dogs learned to associate one phenomenon with another: the sound with the food. This form of learning is not a function of the conscious brain, like learning to write or use a word processor, but of the autonomic nervous system which functions largely outside its control. Pavlov had set out to study the digestive system of dogs, one aspect of which is salivation. In the process he stumbled across the phenomenon of respondent conditioning when he found his experiments sabotaged by the dogs salivating ahead of schedule, that is, at the sound of the approaching assistant rather than when they got the food he was bringing. They had quickly learned to associate the food with the feeder. Before proceeding further let us pause to introduce some basic terms and notation. Salivation is a behaviour that is automatically elicited by the presentation of food. As such it is a *response* to a *stimulus*, and this finds notational representation as follows:

$$S \longrightarrow R$$

Further, salivation is reliably elicited by this stimulus: all dogs respond in the same way regardless of their learning history. Salivation in response to the sight of food is an involuntary or reflex behaviour, and it is said to be *unconditioned*, i.e. not learned. The stimulus is similarly labelled:

Unconditioned stimulus (UCS) → *Unconditioned response (UCR)*
(sight of food)   (salivation)
Other examples of unconditioned stimuli and responses are:
Loud noise   Increased heartrate/adrenalin
Flash of light   Eye blink

The majority of respondent behaviours are of this 'reflex' nature and largely outside our conscious control, although in certain conditions we can exercise some degree of control over them e.g. if we know someone is going to make a loud noise we can, with varying degrees of success, circumvent our normal startle response.

Let us return briefly to dogs and tuning forks. What Pavlov did in fact was to isolate a dog from all extraneous stimuli within a sound-proofed laboratory. Those conducting the experiment stood behind a one-way screen. A tuning fork was struck and half a second later the dog was fed, through a tube leading to its mouth, with food powder. In this experiment therefore the dog could not see the food and initially the dog salivated only when the food was inside its mouth. However, as tone and food continued to be paired, the dog salivated earlier and earlier until salivation eventually occurred *before* the dog was fed, but *after* the tone. The same results occurred using a variety of stimuli including bells, lights and shapes.

Pavlov termed this associative learning 'conditioning'. Today it is referred to as *respondent conditioning* (or classical or Pavlovian conditioning). Dogs do not ordinarily salivate at the sound of tones. Tones are *neutral stimuli* (ones which do not reliably elicit any particular response). However, when a neutral stimulus is regularly paired with an unconditioned stimulus (food) and itself begins to elicit the same response as that unconditioned stimulus, it is termed a *conditioned stimulus* and the response a *conditioned response*. Thus:

Conditioned stimulus (CS) ——→ *Conditioned response (CR)*
(Tone)   (Salivation)

What follows is an example of a conditioned fear response.

Joan was 34, mentally handicapped, and lived with her parents. In her early teens she was nearly knocked down by a lorry which was reversing near to the school-bus Joan had just left. Since that time Joan experienced an incapacitating degree of anxiety every time she saw a lorry or a bus. Her fear generalised to cars and even parked vehicles. As a result Joan would not go out alone and even in the company of another adult it was sometimes impossible to get Joan to cross the road.

In addition to the learning process just described respondent conditioning results in other associated phenomena. These are listed below and briefly described.

Higher order conditioning

Respondent conditioning can also occur when yet another neutral stimulus is paired with an already conditioned response. If, as a result of conditioning, you regularly experience feelings of anxiety at the sight of flowing water, then bridges, which are usually paired with water, may begin to alarm you even when they span roads or railway lines. This process is known as higher order conditioning.

Stimulus discrimination

This refers to the learned ability to discriminate between similar stimuli. Pavlov showed that it was possible to condition dogs to differentiate between tones which signified the arrival of food and those which did not, even when these were very similar in pitch. The baby cooing in an aunt's arms who then screams for food when his breast-feeding mother comes into the room is demonstrating early stimulus discrimination.

Stimulus generalisation

Pavlov found that having once conditioned his dogs to salivate in response to the tone of one tuning fork (or bell or noise) the same response occurred 'spontaneously' when the animals were presented with other, slightly different, tones. This phenomenon is known as stimulus generalisation. Once conditioned, a response can often be elicited by other stimuli which resemble the original conditioned stimulus. Thus the conditioning process creates more than one conditioned stimulus, the effectiveness of each in eliciting the conditioned response depending upon the degree of resemblance perceived by the subject.

Because of the high degree of similarity in actual appearance in groups like policemen, it is all too easy for feelings elicited as a result of a bad experience at the hands of one policeman to generalise to the rest.

Extinction

Learning is not an irreversible process and responses that have been learned can be unlearned. Thus, when Pavlov's dog hears the tone but this is not followed by the presentation of the food he is not doomed, nor will he continue to respond by salivating. Gradually the amount of salivation will decrease and eventually cease. When this happens salivation as a conditioned response is said to have been extinguished. The process is known as respondent extinction.

Importance of respondent conditioning

Initially the simple account of respondent conditioning outlined in preceding paragraphs was thought to account adequately for the development of many emotional responses, particular attention being paid to anxiety, phobias and sexual arousal. On the basis of this model a number of intervention strategies were developed aimed at resolving the problems which resulted from maladaptive emotional responses, i.e. those responses which handicap the individual (e.g. agoraphobia) or which result in unpleasant consequences for himself or others (e.g. some forms of sexual deviance). Often these interventions were generally – and sometimes strikingly – successful and many are still used today (see Chapter 5).

The following case example illustrates how a little girl developed and later lost a particular fear.

> Eighteen-month-old Melanie was battered by her stepfather. On admission to hospital she screamed and became very distraught whenever a male nurse or doctor approached her cot. The closer the man's resemblance to her stepfather (hair-colour and build) the greater her distress and the longer it took to calm her down. Melanie required many encounters with men whose presence did not signify pain before her conditioned response (fear) subsided and eventually disappeared.

The problem is that such an apparently clear example of the respondent conditioning of a fear response is extremely rare and it is no longer possible to retain this simple paradigm of learning as an adequate model of human behaviour (even of so-called respondent behaviours). The majority of fears do not originate from the pairing of the now feared stimulus (then neutral) with some sort of anxiety-provoking stimulus. Many spider phobics have never actually had a traumatic experience with a spider which could have resulted in the spider's acquiring the status of a conditioned stimulus. Many snake phobics have never encountered a snake in any circumstances. Further, laboratory experiments, and our own experience, establish quite clearly that even when neutral stimuli are repeatedly paired with fear evoking ones, it by no means follows that those neutral stimuli will become conditioned stimuli. Indeed, there are remarkably few things which become the subject of fears and phobias and this is not what one would expect from a model which embraces simple, contiguous pairing as its core explanatory concept. Similarly there are an enormous number of dangerous stimuli that evoke little or no fear, despite unpleasant experiences that are often associated with them e.g. electrical appliances.

The discussion about how respondently-derived treatment strategies work is equally controversial. Many theorists and researchers have endeavoured to account for both the phenomenon of respondent conditioning and the success of respondent interventions in terms of *operant* conditioning, and even the casual reader will be struck by the similarity of some of the learning processes identified above with those described in the next section on operant conditioning. Others have pointed out the apparent importance of thought in both paradigms; for instance, experiments have demonstrated that extinction is speeded up when subjects are *told* that the conditioned stimulus will no longer herald the unconditioned one. For example, when subjects are told that the red light which had been associated with a small electric shock will no longer be followed by shock they stop producing an anxiety-related skin reaction more or less immediately rather than gradually. Also, if one can exercise some kind of control over such behaviours when given advance warning, clearly 'the mind' is playing a significant role. We shall discuss these issues again later. Suffice it to say here that the paradigms of operant and respondent conditioning do not describe learning processes that work entirely independently, nor are they sufficient accounts of learning, either separately or jointly. But there does not yet exist a model of learning that adequately replaces both them and the other learning processes (modelling and cognition) discussed later in this chapter. In the absence of such a synthesis (or radical restructuring of the whole of learning theory) it remains pedagogically useful to maintain the models as we present them, pointing out the weakness of each and the inter-relationship and overlap between them. This we hope to do.

OPERANT CONDITIONING

Mrs Davies takes her five-year-old daughter Julie shopping. In the newsagent's shop Julie asks her mother for a bar of chocolate. Mrs Davies refuses as she has already had sweets and it is nearly lunchtime. Julie begins to cry and then to scream and stamp her feet. After nearly five minutes of this Mrs Davies gives in to her daughter's demand and buys a bar of chocolate which she gives to Julie, who immediately stops screaming.

Julie's behaviour is one example of a temper tantrum. It is also an example of operant behaviour.

The operant paradigm of learning is particularly associated with the name of B. F. Skinner (e.g. 1938). Operant behaviour is typically described as emitted behaviour (i.e. not reflexive) which effects change in the environment (operates on it) and which is, in turn, affected by that environment. The effect Julie's temper tantrum had on the environment in which it was performed or operated (the shop, with the presence of mother and others) was to secure for herself a bar of chocolate. Receiving a bar of chocolate makes it very likely that Julie will 'do' that behaviour again. Operant behaviours are the main focus of the bulk of social work attention, and the theory of operant conditioning has been described as the 'ABC' of behavioural work:

A	→B	→C
Antecedents	*Behaviour*	*Consequences*
'No'		
Shop	Temper tantrum	Receives a bar
Mother		of chocolate

Operant conditioning is the study of how behaviour changes with changes in the environment. The antecedents of behaviour – the setting in which it occurs and, quite literally, the things which happen beforehand (usually immediately before) – are important and are discussed on pp.30–2. We begin with the core of operant conditioning, the effect on behaviour of the consequences of that behaviour: the 'BC' of the 'ABC'.

A note on terminology

When looking at other behavioural literature you are likely to come across the notational representation of operant conditioning which is as follows:

$$R \longleftarrow\! S$$

Response   *Stimulus*
Behaviour   *Consequence*

It is unfortunate that the same terms, stimulus and response, have been used in both the respondent and operant paradigms of learning. Quite understandably the use of these terms in the operant paradigm causes confusion because one naturally thinks of stimuli as preceding responses whereas, in this model, the terms refer to the consequences of behaviour which *follow* the 'response' with which they are associated. Similarly the term 'response' is something of a misnomer. Do not be exercised over this, simply think of them as different animals, having a familiar meaning in the respondent paradigm (stimulus eliciting response) and an unfamiliar one in the operant paradigm (the association of a behaviour with a consequence).

Reinforcement and punishment

What someone does has a variety of effects on the environment. Some of these effects serve to strengthen behaviour and to increase the likelihood that it will happen again; this is known as *reinforcement*. In all probability Mrs Davies reinforced Julie's temper tantrum by buying her that bar of chocolate. Similarly, some consequences that follow behaviour make it less likely to recur. When this happens the process is called *punishment*. If Julie continues to 'throw a tantrum' when out shopping every time her mother refuses her requests, then one possible consequence is that Mrs Davies might curtail the number of times she takes Julie shopping. If this were to happen, then, in operant terms, we might say that Mrs Davies' 'shopping with Julie' behaviour has been punished.

This highlights one pitfall for the newcomer to a behavioural approach. In learning theory the terms reinforcer and punisher (and reinforcement and punishment) have very precise meanings which are subtly different from the meanings attached to them in everyday speech. It is tempting to think that there exist two groups of things: reinforcers and punishers. In actual fact nothing is by dint of its own intrinsic nature a reinforcer or punisher. Both are defined simply in terms of the *effect* they have on the behaviour they follow, and are therefore descriptions of the effect that things have rather than of the things themselves. One man's meat is another man's poison.

You have a problem. Several of your clients are frequently very late for appointments. You tell three of them that if they arrive on time you will take them out for coffee at the end of their appointment. After two months you review the situation and the results are as follows:

Client A who usually turned up on time for one in every three appointments, turned up on time every time. Conclusion: going out for coffee reinforced this client's punctuality.

Client B who usually turned up on time for one out of four appointments continued to do so. Conclusion: going out for coffee neither acted as a reinforcer nor a punisher for this client.

Client C usually turned up one in four times on time. He arrived on time for his next appointment but did not keep any subsequent appointments. Conclusion: going out for coffee with you acted as a punisher for this client: not for his time-keeping, but for his appointment-keeping, period. A warning to those social workers who see themselves and their company as their primary resource!

In behavioural terms then, reinforcers and punishers are defined as follows:

a *reinforcer* is anything which follows a behaviour and which increases the probability that the behaviour will be repeated a *punisher* is anything which follows a behaviour and which decreases the probability that the behaviour will be repeated.

The nature of the relationship between consequences and behaviour

Consider the following:

> If after strenuous efforts on your part you secure a scarce resource for your client, and win his undying gratitude, you will probably be more likely to make such efforts again, both for this particular client and for others. If you fail or your client changes his mind about wanting the resource in question, you will probably think twice before expending your energies again.

Neither outcome will *make* you act one way or the other, in the sense that on being presented with food Pavlov's dogs were made to salivate. They simply affect the probability of your doing one rather than the other. This is not to deny that reinforcers and punishers can provide the worker with very powerful determinants of behaviour and one has always to be sensitive to the vulnerability of certain groups. In particular, it is often tempting to select children as targets for change, when closer examination might indicate that the more appropriate (and more difficult) set of target behaviours are those of the parents. Similar problems have arisen with some behavioural programmes set up in institutions where the goal has really been to ease the management problems of staff rather than to help the residents. These are not faults in the techniques themselves but in the ways they are sometimes used.

Let us turn now to the antecedents of behaviour: more particularly to those antecedents which act as cues for the occurrence of certain behaviours.

Stimulus discrimination

One of the things we gradually learn in the course of our interaction with the environment is that certain behaviours are only reinforced in certain circumstances, and indeed when performed in other circumstances may be punished. For instance, dressing up as Mother Goose for a fancy dress party may bring lots of reinforcement in the form of laughs, admiration and possibly a prize. Wearing the same outfit to work would have quite different consequences. How many people would take your social enquiry report seriously (if indeed at all) if you sported so much as a red nose or a green wig? A party setting tells us that riotous behaviour is likely to be rewarded (alcohol is as much a cue as an intoxicant). The Courtroom and the Museum, on the other hand, signal that such behaviour will not be reinforced (and may well be punished by expulsion); they signal that decorous dress and quiet and respectful behaviour will be reinforced.

The socially competent amongst us quickly learn what behaviours are likely to be reinforced in what settings, and behave appropriately. This learning is designated as stimulus discrimination and is a part of the process we normally refer to as socialisation. It is therefore not surprising that children – at the beginning of this road – often 'get it wrong' and behave inappropriately, treating the Museum and the Courtroom as well as the playground as opportunities for loud and physical play (shouting 'race you, Daddy!' in the Museum corridor to the embarrassment of a father displaying 'cultural appreciation').

People can act as discriminative stimuli also. Policemen, spouses, teachers all elicit different behaviours from us because each will reinforce different behaviours (perhaps law-keeping, affection, and good work respectively). Individuals as well as groups can function in this way. For instance I may be more forthcoming in a meeting when someone is present who I know will support my views and reward me for contributing. The process is at work when social workers tailor the style and vocabulary of their court reports to the enthusiasms of particular magistrates. Some children will do a lot of work for one teacher and no work for another. It may be that the one teacher provides the student with a cue that reinforcement will be forthcoming, whereas the other teacher does not engage in any feedback other than critical feedback and may simply cue the student to the probability of punishment for his perhaps average performance. His solution is to do nothing; it is probably less painful to be harangued for being lazy than being stupid.

For the social worker it is important to attend to the settings in which behaviour occurs – the 'A' of the 'ABC' – as this can be the most appropriate and the most efficient point at which to intervene.

Jane was the despair of her mother, Mrs C. Every day after school she came home, took her coat off and left it on the floor. Every day her mother made her go back and hang it up (always a long

protracted battle). Eventually Mrs C hit on a different solution.
When Jane came home the next day (and left her coat on the floor),
Mrs C made her put her coat back on, go out of the house and come
in again, hanging the coat up as she took it off. After several days of
this the battle was won and the coat hung up regularly. Coming in
the door had replaced her mother's nagging as the discriminative
stimulus for hanging up the coat.

Operant conditioning experiments have demonstrated that reinforcers, punishers and discriminative stimuli can be systematically
manipulated to achieve changes in behaviour. It is this fact which
spawned the practice of behaviour modification as a means of
planned behaviour change. The next section examines the processes
of strengthening and weakening behaviour in greater detail.

Types of reinforcement

In receiving that bar of chocolate following her behaviour, Julie's
temper tantrum was positively reinforced. So far we have talked of
reinforcement as a process of positive reinforcement whereby
someone's behaviour results in the occurrence of something pleasing
to the person concerned. For example:

Behaviour	*Consequences*
Julie throws a temper tantrum	→receives chocolate
John helps his wife wash up	→wife tells him how good he is
Jean helps lady off bus	→lady gives Jean 10p

Assuming that these consequences do strengthen the behaviours they
follow (a matter for empirical observation) then the behaviours are
said to have been positively reinforced. But consider the following:

Behaviour	*Consequence*
Mother buys Julie chocolate	→Julie stops screaming
John yells at his wife	→Wife stops nagging
You agree to write to DHSS	→Client stops phoning you

The consequences of these behaviours also make it likely that these
behaviours will recur, but now the 'pay-off' is not the occurrence of
something pleasant but the termination of something unpleasant.

This process is called *negative reinforcement*. It is this process that maintains many of the maladaptive coping strategies exhibited by clients with child management problems i.e. immediate, albeit short-term, relief from the quarrels and the shouting.

Extinction

This is another way of weakening behaviour. Like respondent extinction, operant extinction refers to the process by which some behaviour can be terminated or 'unlearned'. Operant extinction involves the severing of the link between a behaviour and the reinforcer(s) which follow and therefore maintain it. The rationale is that a behaviour is being performed because there is a 'pay-off', and if that pay-off is removed its absence will dramatically affect the probability of the behaviour's continued occurrence to the point that it will probably cease. Reinforcers keep behaviour going: cut them off and the behaviour ceases. When someone ceases to do something they have hitherto done apparently as a matter of course, one possible reason is that the 'pay-off' is no longer there. If your spouse stops thanking you for keeping the house well and stops commenting on any changes you may make, you may stop making the effort. Similarly, the death of a spouse can have an immediate impact upon a number of behaviours, particularly those for which she or he was the main source of reinforcement. The bereaved person who asks 'why bother?' is not exceptional.

How to reinforce and when to do so

The number of times a behaviour is performed is known as the *rate of responding*. The quickest way to increase the rate of a particular behaviour ('behaviour' and 'response' will from now on be used interchangeably) is to reinforce the behaviour every time it occurs. Most behavioural interventions begin with this pattern of reinforcement, technically called a *continuous schedule of reinforcement*. Alternatively one can reinforce behaviour only some of the time. One can do this by reinforcing the behaviour either after certain intervals of time have elapsed, or after a predetermined number of occurrences of the behaviour. These are known as *intermittent schedules of reinforcement*. Whilst continuous schedules of reinforcement produce rapid increases in the rate of performance, these increases are not very durable. When reinforcement is terminated the rate of behaviour usually increases for a short period (in an effort to 'regain' reinforcement) and then extinguishes. This is known as the *extinction burst*.

In order to establish a behaviour in an individual's repertoire and make it resistant to extinction it is important, as work progresses, to move from a continuous to an intermittent schedule of reinforcement. For our purposes there are four specific schedules of reinforcement, each of which has a different effect on the rate of responding, and on making behaviour more or less resistant to extinction. It is worth taking the trouble it undoubtedly takes to familiarise oneself with these, since not only does this make the construction of intervention easier and more likely to succeed, but it is also important for assessment purposes.

Fixed ratio schedules

These are like continuous schedules of reinforcement, but instead of reinforcing every occurrence of a behaviour, you reinforce a certain number of occurrences, say every three or every four. These schedules produce high rates of responding (the more times you do X the more reinforcement you get) which are quite stable – so long as reinforcement is forthcoming. But, as with continuous reinforcement, withdrawal of reinforcement soon leads to extinction. Piece-work in factories is a good example of this.

Fixed ratio schedules are useful as a first stage away from continuous reinforcement. Once a behaviour appears to be established one can then 'thin out' reinforcement so that it is provided only every so often, say after every fifth time it occurs.

Fixed interval schedules

Here, reinforcement is provided after predetermined, regular periods of time. The weekly wage is the most obvious social example of a fixed interval schedule of reinforcement. The typical pattern of responding brought about by this schedule is a lull in performance immediately after reinforcement. This is because the individual knows that reinforcement will not occur again for a while. Then, towards the end of the period, the rate of responding increases again, in anticipation of reinforcement. Fixed interval schedules usually produce low rates of responding; the longer the interval the lower the rate of behaviour. When reinforcement is withdrawn, however, the behaviour continues to be performed at a fairly steady rate for a period.

Variable schedules

As with the previous schedules the ratio of reinforcement to number of behaviours or passage of time is again decided upon in advance, but it is an average one. Let us consider an example of a variable ratio schedule. An employer is trying to do something about his high rates of absenteeism and lateness and decides that each worker who arrives for work on time will be given a lottery ticket and so have a chance of winning a cash bonus if his ticket is drawn at the end of the week. The allocation of the lottery tickets is done on a continuous schedule of reinforcement, but the giving of a prize (which one assumes to be the more powerful reinforcer) is provided on what, for any individual, is a very sparse ratio of reinforcement indeed. Such an experiment was in fact carried out by Pedalino and Gamboa (1974) with notable success. A variable schedule of reinforcement underpins such gambling activities as the 'pools'.

Variable schedules of reinforcement produce very high rates of responding, with no post-reinforcement lull, and which are very resistant to extinction because the individual never quite knows when the next reinforcement is likely, and takes a long time to decide that it has in fact, stopped. The crucial factor, then, is the unpredictability of when reinforcement will occur. Before withdrawing from a case it is important to ensure that the behaviour targeted for change is at least on a schedule of variable reinforcement and preferably one that is operating naturally in the person's environment (perhaps due to your endeavours).

All these schedules (and various permutations of them) are already operating in the natural environment. Identifying what schedules are presently at work maintaining the behaviour you are trying to change is an important part of assessment. For example, because behaviour that is reinforced intermittently is resistant to extinction, problem behaviour that is only reinforced some of the time can take longer to modify; the individual concerned will continue his behaviour in the hope or expectation that next time, or tomorrow, he might receive the reinforcement he has found in the past. Social workers dealing with a single mother (or any client who has a lot to manage and is perhaps tired, or unwell) may find their treatment plans not working, because *sometimes* she simply hasn't the energy to do the 'right thing', for this, at least initially, is invariably more taxing than the 'wrong thing' which led to the problem in the first place. Giving little Julie that bar of chocolate she has been screaming for for thirty minutes or more is much easier than telling her 'No', and then ignoring her, and it is easy for the parent to think that 'just this once' does not matter. Sadly, to 'give in' intermittently is to establish a variable reinforcement schedule: next time little Julie (whose screams are not little) will probably scream for longer than thirty minutes and with more determination. Supporting and reinforcing mediators of change (such as parents) is an essential ingredient of effective behavioural intervention.

In sum, change endeavours will probably need to begin with a continuous or fixed schedule of reinforcement (consistency is the word to remember) and, in order to ensure that the behaviour will continue to be performed at a reasonably high rate, will need to end on some sort of variable schedule. The nature of the latter is also important if the behaviour is going to continue long after your programme has ended. It is crucial to make sure that by the end of your intervention sources of reinforcement are firmly established in the individual's natural environment. Better still is to make use of existing sources of reinforcement throughout your programme. Unfortunately social workers often face situations in which there is little such material to work with and it is a great challenge to teach the necessary skills of reinforcement to the client's significant others (and to programme for the reinforcement of those skills).

Punishment

When the consequences of a behaviour make it less likely that the behaviour will recur then the behaviour is said to have been punished. It is important to remember that in this technical sense the word 'punishment' excludes, by definition, things intended to remove a behaviour which do not in fact have this effect, such as adults' reprimands or spankings which fail to stop children's misbehaviour.

As with reinforcement there are two kinds of punishment. One kind entails the withdrawal of something pleasant following the performance of the target behaviour. Examples would be loss of privilege or removal of a toy from the child who was refusing to share it with his sister. This is known as *negative punishment*. Alternatively punishment can be the occurrence of something unpleasant following the target behaviour, such as a smack or verbal abuse. This is known (confusingly) as *positive punishment* or *punishment by application*.

Used with care and in small amounts (used carefully it should only be needed in small amounts) punishment can be a useful procedure. Used haphazardly, punishment is a very dysfunctional method of controlling behaviour as will be apparent to most of us who work with so-called 'problem families', where it is not unusual to find very high levels of quite severe forms of punishment coupled with high levels of 'bad behaviour' in the form of aggression and non-compliance. It is then, clearly ineffective in these situations, other concerns aside. Why punishment can become such a risky and undesirable method of behaviour control is neatly summed up in the following quotation:

> It [punishment] is likely to be administered in ways which are ill-timed, extreme, inconsistent, retaliatory, and without any accompanying choices and encouragement of more acceptable substitute behaviours. It has a nasty way of escalating. Because its effects are short-lived, the child repeats the undesirable behaviour; parents repeat the punishment, somewhat more forcefully; soon the child is back on the same misdemeanour . . . and there comes about another turn of the screw . . . harsher measures, and so on and on.
>
> (Herbert, 1981, pp. 119–20)

Why, if it is so unprofitable, do parents continue with these methods? Firstly, although the effects of punishment are very short-lived, they are immediate. Kate and Mary may well resume their quarrelling fairly shortly after their mother's intervention, but when she screamed at them to 'stop or else . . .!' they stopped. Mother's screaming behaviour was, in effect, negatively reinforced when the girls stopped quarrelling (removal of an aversive stimulus) and so she is quite likely to try screaming at them again in similar situations. This analysis of a mother's screaming, incidentally, reminds us that the behavioural approach provides us with tools for understanding what maintains (and hence what might change) the behaviour of *all* the actors in a situation (including the social worker's). Secondly, for most of us, punishment is easier (more 'natural') than reinforcement. This may be from a variety of reasons, among them our socialisation (ours is a very punitive culture) and the belief that 'bad behaviour should be punished'. Interestingly, it is a perennial problem for behavioural workers that the corollary of this last assertion is not deemed to be true; it is felt rather that good behaviour should not be rewarded as it is after all 'no more than should be expected'. This attitude is deeply engrained in many of our clients, as the following example indicates:

Mrs M was a single parent with two daughters aged seven and three. Her usual methods of controlling the girls were punitive ones, largely verbal abuse, nagging and shouting, but also some smacking. When the girls behaved themselves she simply ignored them and used the opportunity to do things about the house. She had never established a bedtime, or bedtime routine, for either daughter, and indeed the elder was often left downstairs whilst Mrs M went to bed, after numerous unsuccessful efforts to get her to bed.

As part of an intervention programme a star chart was set up for both the girls. Besides hoping that this would have an effect on the girls' behaviour *per se*, it was seen by the worker as providing the girls with an opportunity to receive some positive reinforcement from mother, who was given detailed instructions on how and when to award the stars, and about the importance of also using praise. Behavioural rehearsal was used to ensure that Mrs M had understood everything. Imagine the horror when the social worker called on Mrs M the next day to find that she had actually cut one star in half, because although the younger daughter had done as she was asked, Mrs M thought her manner was such that she didn't deserve a whole star!

Punishment is not always physical, nor is it confined to the dealings of adults with children. A vicious circle similar to the one outlined by Herbert can be identified in the dealings of adults. The wife who resorts to nagging her husband about his late arrival home in an endeavour to get him home on time may find that gradually he comes home later more often. Her nagging becomes the aversive stimulus which his staying away from home avoids (negative reinforcement). Rather than punishing his coming home late, her nagging becomes a punishment for coming home at all.

Similarly, people's experiences at the hands of bureaucracies like the Department of Health and Social Security and Social Services can be punitive. Requests for help which bring unexpected and unwanted or aversive responses, can have the effect of suppressing other potential requests for help. Alternatively they may result in people adopting very counterproductive stances such as aggressive and demanding behaviour, in anticipation of similar treatment, which as a consequence, they are more than likely to receive. One of the tasks social workers often have is of breaking into this cycle.

Other disadvantages of punishment

(1) Experimental evidence suggests that unless physical punishment is intense and immediately follows the behaviour it is unlikely to achieve more than a temporary cessation of behaviour.

(2) Particularly if punishment is dealt out non-contingently i.e. not following the behaviour it is intended to punish, one possible consequence is that the person punished will associate the punishment not with the behaviour but with the person delivering the punishment. This has obvious serious consequences. From the point of view of intervention it can make it extremely difficult to initiate change based on positive reinforcement.

(3) When punishment succeeds in eliminating one behaviour, its effects may spread ('generalise') to other behaviours as well, and/or to other situations: compliance becomes over-compliance; not interrupting becomes social withdrawal.

(4) If mild punishment is used, and even if it later becomes more severe, people tend to habituate themselves. Initially the rate of behaviour slows down but gradually the person 'acclimatises' and the behaviour returns to its previous rate.

Having said all this there is a role for the clearly defined and limited use of certain kinds of punishment. Sometimes inappropriate or noxious behaviour occurs at such a high frequency that it is not possible to begin intervention by simply reinforcing occurrences of appropriate responses: these are simply not occurring. In these situations it is helpful to suppress a behaviour in order to establish a desirable behaviour that is incompatible with it.

Effective use of punishment

The elements of the effective use of punishment are as follows:
—Extreme care is essential in order to select a form of punishment

that will be effective from the very start (particularly when punishment is physical) and yet is no more severe than is absolutely necessary.

— Punishment should be delivered immediately the target behaviour occurs.

— The same response should be made every time the target behaviour is performed and by all concerned i.e. including grandmother and aunt. If this does not happen, the chances are that the behaviour is being reinforced on an intermittent schedule of reinforcement which, as we have indicated, makes behaviour very resistant to modification.

— The person administering the punishment should be encouraged to adopt a matter-of-fact attitude and manner. This will minimise the possibility of the person punished perceiving the punishment and the punishment-giver as one and the same thing. It also helps to keep the latter calm in an otherwise fraught situation.

— Punishment should always be used in conjunction with a programmed opportunity to learn alternative ways or responding. If this is done the punished behaviour is less likely to reappear when punishment ceases. These issues will be taken up again in Chapter 5.

SOCIAL LEARNING THEORY

Fortunately for most of us the two theories just discussed are not the whole of the learning story. Much of what we learn falls outside the scope of respondent and operant conditioning, and this section deals with the third main area of learning theory from which the techniques of behaviour modification are drawn: modelling.

Operant learning says that what we learn to do is determined by the consequences of our behaviour. Clearly if this were the whole story we would learn very little, very slowly and very happenstansically. Learning would also be a very dangerous process if each of us, for instance, had to rely on our own experience to teach us that fires burn and driving the wrong way up a one-way street can be catastrophic. Much of what we learn we learn by dint of other people's experiences or learning which are communicated to us in various ways, sometimes verbally but often by watching how others behave in various situations. We then use the information thus obtained to determine, to some extent, our own behaviour. Essentially, it is this process of observation and subsequent imitation that comprises the modelling process.

Whilst the respondent and operant paradigms seem, on some interpretations, to adequately account for the continued occurrence of behaviours, it is modelling that appears best fitted to account for the way in which most behaviour is learned in the first instance. Modelling accounts for the acquisition of a vast range of very different behaviours: skills simple and complex, from washing dishes to brain surgery, from social good manners to conducting a philosophical debate; and also those kinds of behaviours we do not designate as skills, such as reacting with anxiety to thunderstorms or being brave in the face of danger. Numerous experiments have shown that skills, attitudes and emotional responses can all be acquired through modelling. Whilst complex skills will also require physical practice for good performance, simple skills can often be acquired on the basis of one example (one-trial learning), making it an economical and efficient mode of learning. Modelling is a key factor in a 'grand theory' of learning put forward by Albert Bandura known as Social Learning Theory. In this section we shall introduce the question of the need to include cognitive factors to explain learning. We shall then discuss their role in Bandura's theory (particularly as these inform the conceptualisation of modelling) and finally, we outline the process of modelling and identify its uses in behavioural work.

The role of cognition

The respondent and operant paradigms of learning confine themselves to the interaction of two things: a person's behaviour and his environment. The actions of either one, it is said, have an observable impact on the other and can be manipulated in predictable ways. How behaviour and environment come to form the relationship they do can only be a matter of speculation which, in any case, adds nothing to the explanatory power of the operant and respondent paradigms. Bandura disagrees. He believes some speculations have a sound basis and that to ignore them is to oversimplify matters.

Acting as a mediator between the environment and a person's behaviour is the mind. What a person does is determined in part by what he intends, what he hopes and what he expects to achieve. In turn, the effect of the environment on his behaviour will in part depend on his perceptions and values. Such mental activities are known as *intervening variables*. These are hypothetical in that they can't be linked to any physiological process operating within the nervous system: their usefulness depends on their ability to account for the data i.e. the observable effects of the interaction between a person's behaviour and his environment. Bandura, and a growing number of behaviourists, think these variables are necessary to the adequate understanding of behaviour:

> Humans do not respond simply to stimuli; they interpret them. Stimuli influence the likelihood of particular behaviours through their predictive function, not because they are automatically linked to responses occurring together. In the social learning view, contingent experiences create expectations rather than stimulus-response connections.   (Bandura, 1977, p.59)

For Bandura the antecedents and consequences of behaviour function in similar ways, via the mediating role of cognition. Specifically, people's experience of their environment (their own and that of others) leads them to *expect* certain outcomes from certain courses of action in certain circumstances:

> The likelihood of particular actions is increased by anticipated reward and reduced by anticipated punishment. ... People do not respond to each momentary item of feedback as an isolated experience. Rather, they process and synthesise feedback information from sequences of events over long periods of time regarding the conditions necessary for reinforcement, and the pattern and rate with which actions produce the outcomes. (Bandura, 1977, pp.96–7)

Certainly in both respondent and operant experiments researchers have found that learning is speeded up if subjects are informed of the contingencies at work, suggesting that a person's mental processes play an important part in both types of learning.

Awareness of the relationship between behaviour and its consequences is only one amongst many 'mental processes' involved in learning. Attention, memory and imagery are others which Bandura uses to explain how modelled behaviour is acquired. It is, he claims, this process of observational learning – or *modelling* – that accounts for the acquisition of most behaviour.

Modelling

Modelled behaviour is learned in the following way:

(1) A sees B performing a behaviour and attends to his actions.
(2) A forms an idea of how that behaviour is done: its constituent parts and the order in which they occur.
(3) He notes that the situation in which the behaviour occurred and the consequences for B.
(4) When next in a situation in which that particular response would be useful (to achieve a desired consequence) A re-produces it according to his mental image.

Bandura argues that we know this process is occurring (or something very like it) because:
(a) behaviours learned in this way are often not used until some considerable time has passed since the modelled behaviour was observed
(b) if you ask someone how to do something before thay have had the opportunity to perform they can often tell you how to. They can 'talk you through' the behaviour in question, be it following a map or putting together the parts of a garden shed.

As indicated earlier (cf. (2) and (3) above) modelling is essentially a means of giving information about the nature of certain responses (new to the observer) and the usefulness in terms of likely consequences. Modelled behaviour can be learned deliberately or casually. An example of the latter is the quite often unconscious copying by children of their parents. In addition to the modelling that occurs when people perform behaviours modelling can also occur via symbolic processes such as verbal or written accounts or instructions. In conclusion then, modelling appears to be the process best able to account for the acquisition of most behaviours. The ability of an individual to profit from the various forms of modelling depends, amongst other things, upon his previous learning history, physical capabilities and, particularly, his ability to use language.

Observers whose conceptual and verbal skills are underdeveloped are likely to benefit more from behavioral demonstrations than from verbal modelling.   (Bandura, 1977, p.40)

Reinforcement of behaviour will subsequently determine whether or not behaviour thus learned will be performed.

The importance of modelling

The process of modelling suggests why certain behaviours come to be adopted rather than others, both on an individual and a group (societal) level. Take aggression as an example. Western culture is dominated by the use and threat of punishment as means of control (Skinner 1953). Given the powerful influence of modelling as a means of learning is it any wonder that many abusing parents had similar experiences themselves at the hands of their parents? By contrast, a culture that neither models nor rewards aggressive behaviour (the Hutterites would be one example) is singular in the near absence of aggressive behaviour shown by its children (Bandura and Walters 1959).

In 1965 Bandura randomly allocated a number of nursery children to three groups. Each group was shown a film of a child (the 'model') beating up a life-size Bobo doll. The incident was identical in each, but in the first film the model was rewarded for his behaviour with sweets, soft drinks and praise ('reinforcement condition') in the second film his behaviour was punished by spanking and a telling off ('punishment condition'); whilst in the third film nothing happened to the model following his behaviour ('no consequence condition'). After viewing the film each child was placed in a room with lots of toys, including a replica of the Bobo doll. Children who had watched the 'reinforcement' film or the 'no consequence' film imitated the aggressive behaviour of the model much more than children who had seen the model being punished. Interestingly, when all children were offered incentives for imitating the aggressive behaviour ('decals' and fruit juice) all differences disappeared.

As Bandura himself has pointed out, the origins of behaviour (modelling) and the conditions that maintain it do not necessarily derive from the same learning paradigm. Therefore, unlike respondent and operant learning theories, there is no direct link between the explanation and treatment of behaviour. Changing a child's aggressive behaviour may involve exposure to non-aggressive models (peers playing co-operatively); but not necessarily, and probably not as the only intervention.

Modelling can also be used to facilitate the performance of behaviours in situations of anxiety. Seeing a model perform a feared activity without coming to any harm has been shown to bring about a reduction in anxiety and to persuade hitherto reluctant clients to 'have a go'.

Modelling can encourage the performance of behaviours already within the repertoire of a subject who has not deployed them, perhaps because of the absence or loss of reinforcement. Seeing a model being reinforced for doing something can have a similar effect to arranging direct reinforcement for the behaviour (as witness the children who exhibited aggressive behaviour after seeing the model rewarded for beating up the doll, and the same level of aggressive behaviour exhibited by all the children when offered direct incentives). Finally, modelling forms an important part of the many strategies that involve behavioural rehearsal.

Effective modelling

The effectiveness of modelling has been shown to be enhanced by a number of factors (Bandura, 1977). These are:

(a) A model who, in the eyes of the subject, has some standing (e.g. the status and power that come with popularity) is most likely to attract his attention to and influence his behaviour. (But see (c)).

(b) A model seen to be reinforced for performing a behaviour is more likely to be imitated.

(c) Some point of comparison or similarity between the model and the subject is essential. If the subject perceives the model as utterly unlike himself he may well think that he has no chance of *acquiring* the behaviour being modelled, or, more importantly, of being *reinforced* for performing the behaviour. (See next section.)

(d) Giving the subject the opportunity to practise the behaviour soon after seeing it being modelled facilitates its establishment in the subject's repertoire.

(e) Reinforcing the subject (arranging reinforcement) for performing the new behaviour also helps to establish it – a strategy not peculiar to modelling.

Bandura's theory of self-efficacy

As suggested in (c) above, there is a difference between whether or not a person thinks he will be able to do something and whether or not he thinks that doing it will achieve what he wants e.g. obtain for him the same consequences as for the model. Bandura describes this as the difference between a person's *efficacy expectations* and *outcome expectations* respectively. More often than not people are less certain about their ability to do something than whether or not doing it would get them what they want. From this Bandura has developed a theory of behaviour change which attempts to explain the success of the treatment strategies derived from all the theories outlined in this chapter as due to the mediating effect of one intervening variable, namely efficacy expectations. According to Bandura, treatment success depends on the degree to which it creates or strengthens a subject's expectations of personal efficacy ('I *can* do it') and the most potent means of increasing a person's expectations of personal efficacy is via 'performance accomplishment'. This, he says, is why behaviour rehearsal is so important and so often effective.

Unfortunately the usefulness of self-efficacy as an intervening variable seems extremely limited. At first glance it appears to be at least possible to assess its importance by comparing the measure of people's efficacy expectations with what they then go on to do (such amenability to experimental procedure being a necessary prerequisite of any variable we wish to include in an empirical model of learning). But on closer inspection it is difficult to define what a person's performance expectations are without recourse to the performance itself, in which case we are adding nothing. For example, I may ask X whether or not he thinks he could approach and handle a snake and get a Yes and No answer respectively. In a subsequent experiment I observe that X does make an approach to the snake but in fact fails to handle it. What am I to conclude? That X failed to handle the snake because of a low self-percept of efficacy? I can only really know that X is right to say he could handle the snake by recourse to whether or not he did in fact. Certainly one could argue that what people believe is not the same as what they do (there could in principle be a discrepancy) but Bandura's point is that there is a very high correlation between performance and self-efficacy expectations.

When the assessment of one variable (self-efficacy) is so closely related to another (performance) the predictive value of the first is of little value. Even though Bandura claims people's performance can be improved merely by enhancing their self-efficacy expectations i.e. that the two variables can be manipulated independently, it remains the case that the methods used to do this can all be interpreted as altering people's level of skill (e.g. behavioural rehearsal) or, minimally, giving them extra skill-related information (e.g. watching others perform) and it is this which accounts for improved performance.

Consider an empirical study cited by Bandura himself in support of the theory's usefulness (1984). Collins (1982) selected children of differing mathematical abilities on the basis of standardised arithmetic tests. Within each level (low, average and high mathematical ability) she found that some children scored high on perceived mathematical self-efficacy and others low. Regardless of their ability level, the children with high self-efficacy scores solved more arithmetic problems, chose to rework more of the problems they had failed, and did so more accurately. Bandura claims that perceived self-efficacy is causally responsible for these differences. It is this final claim which is problematic.

Collins' study, along with a number of others discussed by Bandura (1984) provides support for the claim that self-efficacy is a good *predictor* of performance. However this leaves unresolved its status in the *causal* sequence. Collins' results demonstrate that children with high perceived mathematical self-efficacy perform well at such things as solving arithmetic problems, persisting with attempts to solve problems and getting more problems right. However, it could be argued that their high levels of self-perceived efficacy are the result of these other abilities (e.g. arithmetic ability, persistence) and that these (having been previously reinforced), and not self-efficacy, account for the better results eventually obtained by these children.

We have sketched some basic criticisms; against these counter-moves can be made, but we would hold (this is not the place to elaborate) that those made to date are inadequate. These criticisms indicate why seductive variables such as self-efficacy and self-esteem should be treated with caution. They appear to carry more meaning that they do.

COGNITIVE THEORY

Traditional learning theory is and was anchored firmly in Watson's (1913) claim that psychology is the study of overt behaviour and not of the mind, and until recently behaviour theorists have eschewed any attempts to include the mind (as such) in the analysis of behaviour. The 'mind' refers not to the brain but to the numerous ways in which people try to organise and structure their experience (compare the 'intervening variables' discussed above). For instance, regarding someone as a friend will determine, to some extent, how you interpret their actions. If he or she walks past you without speaking you will probably rationalise that they did not see you. An acquaintance or someone you dislike will probably get labelled rude or stand-offish for exactly the same behaviour. Often we continue to 'fit' our experiences into our perceptual framework until something occurs (or there is an accumulation of somethings) which forces us to rethink that framework e.g. a friend who spreads unpleasant rumours about one is likely to be reclassified rather than his behaviour rationalised. Values and prejudices, expectations and beliefs all function to filter and classify our experiences of life. But the simple fact that we get things wrong, and that often there are several equally plausible alternative hypotheses, indicates that the business of ordering and interpreting is not unproblematic. Even the area of describing one's own emotion is fraught. One social work text-book put it like this.

> . . . we believe that clients often require help in the identification of their emotions. This requirement has been well described and its relative importance assessed by a character (Bradley) in Iris Murdoch's novel *The Black Prince*. Bradley at one point asks 'What emotion has so invaded me? Fear? It is sometimes curiously difficult to name the emotion from which one suffers. The naming of it is sometimes unimportant, sometimes crucial. Hatred?'
>
> (Timms and Timms, 1977, p. 139)

Indeed, since the point of the Iris Murdoch quote is precisely that the cognitive act of naming an emotion can *determine* the nature of that emotion, to say 'clients require help in the identification of their emotions' fails to capture the complexity.

Heider (1958) coined the phrase 'naïve psychologist' to describe the man in the street in his endeavours to make sense of his own behaviour and that of others. At the other extreme is the (social) psychologist. He is nowadays preoccupied with explorations of how people's thoughts (variously categorised) mediate between behaviour and the environment. For the learning theorist the interest lies in whether, and in what ways, certain sorts of cognitions connect with certain sorts of behaviour and behavioural disorders, such as depression. Do thoughts and mental narratives precipitate certain moods and/or behaviours or are they a consequence of them? If such connections were to be identified our understanding of behaviour might be improved so as to enable us to make more accurate assessments of behavioural problems, and construct more effective forms of intervention.

But the inclusion of cognitive variables in the analysis of behaviour has been fiercely resisted for a number of reasons, some more sound than others. After listing the case against we shall present the case for, together with some words of caution. The discussion is more complex than in the preceding sections, because the academic debate is still very active and it is still too early to have a clear view of the outcome; we do however try to extract its implications for current social work practice.

The case against

The first objection is that cognitive variables are difficult to operationalise – that is, it is difficult to say when someone is engaged in a particular mental activity. One has to rely on self-report data which are notoriously unreliable (e.g. Curran, 1979) and the usual misgivings about this kind of data are exacerbated by the sheer impossibility of external validation. For instance, one often has to rely on self-report data regarding sexual problems but it is in principle possible to say what an observer would see if he were present. Exposing the subject of cognitive research to the scrutiny of an observer would add nothing however, and would not provide a means of checking the reliability of the subject's statements about her thoughts or feelings (except possibly for grossly incompatible behaviour).

The second objection is that when one sets out to define 'mental processes' and to identify their occurrences one invariably has to resort to a description of 'what people do when' . . . they are sad, or angry or lonely. So, the argument goes, why burden ourselves with an extra variable when two (behaviour and environment) will do?

Third (and all three objections are inter-related), such concepts are redundant as they do not, in fact, improve our predictive powers or make more sense of behaviour than the respondent and operant paradigms of learning (compare our earlier discussion of Bandura's theory of self-efficacy).

Finally, whereas observable events and behaviour can be manipulated to assess how changing the one will affect the other, subjective events such as what people think cannot be systematically varied to examine their impact or demonstrate their relationship. Although arguments can be made that particular mental processes are plausible associates for particular behaviours it is also the case that any behaviour that is explicable in terms of one such process can readily be redescribed by recourse to another. Depression may be the result of negative thoughts about oneself; it may be the result of loss of self-esteem; or it may be connected to an unrealistic assessment of ability and situation.

The concern is that the new 'cognitive variables' are little better than their Freudian counterparts – the id, ego and super-ego – and are as much in danger of being regarded as real entities central to the explanation of behaviour as these became, rather than as 'useful' organising concepts. This then is the thin end of an explanatory wedge (mentalism) that behaviourists have fought long and hard to exclude in their endeavours to place the analysis of behaviour on a more scientific and, for the practitioner a more accountable, footing.

The case for

But it is also true that the hard-line behaviourist is a species under threat. Consider a case study:

Mrs P was in her forties. She had suffered from schizophrenia for many years and lived alone in her own home. Social Services had been involved for a number of years because of Mrs P's low level of self-care, and the problems she presented in the community. Never self-sufficient, Mrs P one day took to her bed and nothing seemed able to move her. Neither social worker, home help, nor meals-on-wheels were able to lure her out of bed. Until, one day, a relief home-help said something to Mrs P that indicated that she, the home-help, saw Mrs P as an old age pensioner. Consequently Mrs P got up, dressed, resumed the management of some of her affairs, made an appointment with her hairdresser. . . .

Two explanations, which highlight the problems of cognitive theory, present themselves. First, the home-help's comments implied that Mrs P must be an old age pensioner as she was in receipt of services typically, in her experience, provided for the elderly. Mrs P did not wish to be regarded as an old age pensioner. She did not mind others seeing her as ill and needy, but not old and needy. Her perception of the desirability of these domiciliary services had been altered and this effected a change in her behaviour. This would be one cognitive hypothesis. Secondly, some operant theorists might respond to this in the following vein. First they would point out that it is not unreasonable to hypothesise that the services being provided to Mrs P reinforced her 'staying in bed behaviour'. Following this, the situation could be changed by removing some or all of these reinforcing contingencies and/or providing punitive consequences. The home-help's remarks were clearly punitive, and to such an extent that they outweighed the reinforcing effects of the other contingencies (domiciliary services etc.). Whilst it was indeed the home-help's remarks that effected a change, one does not need to introduce Mrs P's interpretive thoughts into the narrative. One does not actually know what she thought. All one knows is that following the relief home-help's visit, her behaviour changed; and the description of what happened is sufficient. But is it? It is important that it was the relief home-help who made this remark, and not someone Mrs P knew well. In the latter case, Mrs P, an intelligent woman, might have seen the remark as yet another ploy to get her 'up and moving'. It is difficult, and some would say unreasonable if not perverse, to resist the notion that what one thinks affects what one does.

The interpretation of events is one area of cognitive functioning to which we shall return. Another reason Bandura presses for the inclusion of cognition in the understanding of behaviour, and which forms an important part of social learning theory, is the demonstrable ability of people to regulate their own behaviour 'from within'. That is to say we determine some of the consequences of our own behaviour. For instance we can deny ourselves the pleasure of a coffee break until we have finished the task we are engaged on or we can reward ourselves for a job well done either with something tangible (the purchase of a record) or with a mental 'pat on the back'. Similarly we can perform certain behaviours, sometimes for long periods, that are not intrinsically rewarding (or extrinsically reinforced) by dint of long term goals towards which we strive. All these things, and others, point to the need to acknowledge that cognitions play a nontrivial role in the process of learning.

Further, people think; they make judgements; they have preferences; and they solve problems. The latter they often do by talking or thinking through the feasibility and implications of the various courses of action open to them. This provides a means of dealing with the environment other than by trial and error. This mental tackling of problems is both efficient and effective and is made possible by the symbolic thought processes (words, imaginal representation and so on) unique to man. It has an observable and communal counterpart in shared problem solving. It allows the individual to 'borrow' the problem-solving skills of others, or to collect information outside her personal experience. At their best, case conferences are largely cognitive exercises in this sense. One might argue that problem solving and creative thinking are the least 'hypothetical' examples of actual cognitive processes, in that whilst unobservable (an individual thinking) it takes little prompting to 'externalise' this kind of cognitive activity; ask someone how they reached a decision and they can usually tell you. Thinking and problem solving are skills that can be learned. Such skills are an important part of the social work task, and also provide the social worker with intervention strategies for disorganised clients. The cognitive processes that cause the headaches (one might say) and with which the literature is more often exercised are such categorisations of thought and other mental activities as 'cognitive bias'; 'expectancy'; 'self-esteem'; 'self-blame' and the ways in which these affect behaviour. For instance, if certain cognitions are clearly 'depression related', are they causal, symptomatic or consequential? Let us consider the phenomenon of depression.

The cognitive analysis of depression

The study of depression has in effect provided the backcloth for the proliferation of cognitive concepts. As Coyne and Gotlib remark:

the plausibility of cognitive explanations for the development and persistence of depression has been a major factor in spreading the 'cognitive revolution' to the study of psychopathology.

(1983, p. 472)

Because of this, and because depression is such a common problem, we shall develop our discussion of cognitive theory through a consideration of the work of Seligman and Beck, two of the foremost proponents of a cognitive approach to depression. We shall give more attention to Beck's work, since his approach is the more developed in regard to intervention strategies. But we begin with Seligman's 'learned helplessness' theory which seems to fit well with social workers' experience of disadvantaged people, with our profession's concern with social issues and individual misfortune.

Learned helplessness

Seligman's learned helplessness model of depression was developed through a series of experiments in the animal laboratory (Seligman 1975). These experiments, in which animals were subjected to uncontrollable pain (that is, pain they could not escape or avoid), suggested that animals can learn that there is *no* connection between their own behaviour and the events that follow it, just as they can learn other kinds of connection between behaviour and consequences. Following the experience of uncontrollable trauma, they develop a syndrome – learned helplessness – whose chief characteristics are apathy and difficulty in learning, from new experiences, that one *can* avoid or escape and obtain positive reinforcement. Later experiments, still in the laboratory setting, confirmed that an apparently similar sequence of events can take place in the case of human subjects. However, some key questions remained unanswered. In particular, who becomes helpless (not everyone does) and what determines how far – to what new situations – learned helplessness spreads?

To deal with these questions, a reformulation of learned helplessness theory has been proposed (Abramson, Garber and Seligman, 1980) which sets the theory firmly in the cognitive camp. The authors suggest that these questions can be answered by examination of the person's beliefs about the uncontrollable experience along three dimensions:

(1). The *personal-universal* dimension. Does the person think their

inability to control outcome is due to their own special inadequacy or
do they regard the situation as one whose outcome nobody could
have controlled?

(2). The *specific-global* dimension. Does the person view the experience (e.g. of failure) as specific to this particular task or set of
circumstances or as 'yet another' piece of evidence of their general
inadequacy?

(3). The *chronic-acute* dimension. Do they regard their experience as
evidence of permanent inadequacy or just a temporary weakness?

A number of rather vague intervention guidelines are drawn from
Seligman's theory: it is important to attend to peoples' beliefs about
failure and misfortune and to adopt a task-oriented approach with an
emphasis on persuading people to undertake actions which confirm
that they can in fact affect outcomes.

Seligman comments on broader policy issues, suggesting that the
sense of helplessness so commonly encountered in groups such as the
elderly, ethnic minorities and the poor, can in large part be attributed
to social policies which severely limit their ability to effect changes in
their circumstances. Other writers have interpreted their own and
others' research findings in the light of learned helplessness theory: on
the elderly in institutional care; the victims of rape; the severely ill; the
bereaved and those who experience academic failure (Garber and
Seligman, 1980).

An appealing theory, but how much empirical support does it
enjoy? We can only say that research and controversy continue, with
some findings appearing to confirm the key ideas and others being
flatly contradictory. This is also the case with the ideas of Beck (1967;
1976) whose work we now consider.

Beck proposes a threefold conceptualisation of the psychological
aspects of depression. The concepts he uses are: *cognitive triad*,
schemata and *faulty information processing*, and they are operational-
ised as follows:

Cognitive triad denotes the very negative way in which depressed
persons typically regard themselves, their current situations and their
prospects.

Schemata denotes the very rigid ways depressed persons have of
looking at the world based on their interpretation of previous
experience. These are, in essence, the converse of the 'rose-tinted
spectacles' of the optimist.

Faulty information processing The operation of the above schemata can be seen in the errors depressed people make in interpreting their environment and the things that happen to them. Thus the depressed woman whose boyfriend terminates their relationship will probably conclude that *no-one* wants her (negative generalisation). Depressed people typically home in on the negative aspects of situations, to the exclusion of positive and equally valid ones. Thus I may ignore the ten compliments paid to me about my new haircut in favour of the one more reserved comment, which I will probably construe as one of downright dislike.

Is Beck correct in claiming that the cognitions of depressed people are distinguished by these three 'tendencies'? If so, are they as Beck would claim, causal, or do they develop as a consequence of depression? Would attention to these processes improve our understanding and treatment of depression, and would it enable us to identify who is likely to become depressed and in what circumstances?

One would be delighted, albeit a little surprised, if the answer to these last two questions was an unqualified Yes. And of course it isn't. But what is more disappointing is that in a review of research into Beck's model of depression Coyne and Gotlib (1983) concluded there is scant evidence to support his claims. The most that can be said with reasonable certainty is that depressed persons 'present themselves negatively on a variety of questionnaire measures in a variety of situations' (1983, p. 500). Grounds for these negative conclusions range from the poor methodology of some of the studies to the existence of competing explanations for results that at first blush seem to favour Beck's claims. For example, the tendency of depressed patients to evaluate their actions more negatively than non-depressed persons could be attributed to other variables such as non-assertiveness or high levels of social anxiety (1983, pp. 479–80; relevant studies are Alden and Cappi, 1981, and Clark and Arkowitz, 1975). In a longitudinal study examining the relationship between cognition and depression, Lewinsohn *et al.* (1981) concluded that the thinking patterns that were correlated with depression had no predictive value:

To wit: prior to becoming depressed, these future depressives did not subscribe to irrational beliefs, they did not have lower expectancies for positive outcomes, or higher expectations for negative outcomes, they did not attribute success experiences to external causes and failure experiences to internal causes, nor did they perceive themselves as having less control over the events in their lives.   (1981, p.218)

Because Beck attributes a primary role to cognitive factors in depression, viewing affective (mood) and behavioural factors as secondary, his therapy focuses on changing the ways in which the depressed person thinks about himself and the world. Although the theoretical basis for Beck's therapy is questionable the therapy itself has enjoyed greater success and, along with other cognitive therapies, is fast becoming the therapy of choice for many working with depressed people. But these successes must be regarded cautiously. There are a number of reasons but the most important consideration is that the majority of studies of the use of cognitive therapies include in the therapeutic package unadulterated behavioural components of demonstrated effectiveness (e.g. behavioural rehearsal, homework, modelling). In a recent review of a range of cognitive therapies Miller and Berman (1983) claim that a quantitative analysis of 48 studies demonstrated that whilst cognitive therapies are superior to no-treatment or to placebo controls, there is no evidence to support the claim that they are more effective than other therapies (particularly, than well established ones such as systematic desensitisation). This finding holds across different types of problem and different groups of people. So cognitive behaviour therapy does not seem to be more suited to particular sorts of people or particular sorts of problem (such as depression). Miller and Berman (1983, p.45) also speculate that the failure to find any difference in effectiveness between primarily cognitive approaches and those emphasising behavioural techniques may arise from similarities in the practice of theoretically divergent practitioners.

The question is therefore, at best, an open one. Even the proponents of cognitive therapy urge caution:

the efficacy of stress-inoculation is encouraging but not yet proven. the data on the full usefulness of [this] procedure have yet to be obtained.   (Meichenbaum, 1977, p.181)

And one of the staunchest advocates of the inclusion of cognitive mechanisms in the analysis of behaviour has said:

On the one hand, explanations of change processes are becoming more cognitive. On the other hand, it is performance based treatments that are proving most powerful in effecting psychological changes. . . . Symbolic procedures have much to contribute as components of a multiform performance-oriented approach, but they are usually insufficient by themselves.

(Bandura, 1977, p.78)

To the question whether to choose overt behavioural techniques or cognitive treatments the answer, eight years on, remains the same.

Conclusion

Overall the evidence suggests that overt methods of behaviour change should be the starting point for intervention. Often the way people think and feel does in fact change following changes in their behaviour. This may be because when behaviour changes the person's experience of the world changes for the better (if therapy has been successful) and she experiences more control over her life, enjoys more positive reinforcement and positive social interaction than hitherto. But clearly this is not always the case. Sometimes treatment simply fails and it is possible that particularly strong or dysfunctional cognitions could account for some instances of failure of treatment proven successful in otherwise identical situations (though this is not by any means the most common cause of failure identified to date – see Foa and Emmelkamp, 1983). Even when treatment 'succeeds' a person's thoughts can render such success meaningless and even undesirable. For instance, writing about the problems of child abuse Gambrill (1983a) quotes one mother whose behaviour had changed in the course of treatment (unspecified) but whose feelings about her child remained of a kind that seemed certain to colour even non-abusing behaviour to the child's detriment:

I don't beat Johnny any more, but I hate the son-of-a-bitch like I always did. (Kempe and Kempe, 1978)

A locution, incidentally, which displays a nice disattention to the literal meanings of words!

Cognitive techniques are outlined in Chapter 6. What follows are guidelines for the inclusion of cognitive techniques, based on their present empirical status and on the present status of the theories underpinning them.

(1) Always begin with an assessment of the problem in traditional behavioural terms, and work out an intervention strategy based on behavioural techniques of demonstrated efficacy.

(2) Include one of the cognitive techniques if a person's thoughts and mood seem of central concern (e.g. depression). Even so, use only with other behavioural techniques.

(3) Accord to people's thoughts and feelings the same importance as to such factors as stage of development, intelligence, and previous learning history. How people think about their problems should colour the way you describe them and the treatment you are proposing. If it does not, you may fail to engage the client.

(4) Be particularly alert to 'faulty thinking' and 'self-blame'. You may be able to counter these in the course of ordinary assessment and intervention using corrective feedback and modelling.

(5) If your intervention strategy does not seem to be working, and, after a careful look at the situation, you decide that your assessment of the 'ABC' of the problem was accurate and your intervention was appropriate, take another look at the way the client is thinking and talking about the problem and the treatment. Like Mrs M (p.38) what someone thinks about rewards and punishment may well be at such odds with your judgement that the client is actually sabotaging an otherwise good intervention plan.

(6) Attend to your own world view and biases, as these can predetermine what you look for and what advice you give with no other, sounder basis.   (Gambrill, 1983b)

At the moment then, the debate within learning theory points to the need to maintain the three models of learning set out earlier as distinct processes i.e. respondent and operant conditioning, and modelling. This is not to deny their inter-relatedness but simply reflects the absence of an adequate way of conceptualising the phenomena they describe within one conceptual framework. The growing evidence of the importance of cognitive factors places especial strain on the adequacy of the respondent and operant paradigms of learning, but it is important to stress that, whatever the intrinsic appeal of cognitive factors, this research is still in its infancy and generally lacks the empirical support enjoyed by these paradigms. As yet endeavours to integrate cognitive factors into these paradigms have not greatly enhanced their value. Further it is misleading to talk of a cognitive theory of learning *per se*. The endeavour can at best be described as one of ascertaining the role or roles of certain mental processes in the acquisition and performance of behaviour. There is little enough agreement as yet about what these processes are, what are the most important ones and how they should be described, apart from the important question of the theoretical and empirical evidence for associating which factors with what behaviours or moods, and in what ways. But perhaps most important, the separation of these processes into the categories we have used seems to offer the easiest way of grasping the issues involved and of approaching the problems of assessment and intervention to which we shall now turn.

3

How to Begin a Behavioural Programme: I

The principles that guide behavioural work are few and simple, and the key to good behavioural work is to keep these to the forefront of your mind and to think behaviourally about every task and problem. In the present chapter and in Chapter 4 we give an account of the process from first meeting to drawing up an agreement between worker and client.

When to use the behavioural approach

If the person's problem is lack of money, the social work intervention should focus on money. Material problems do indeed cause psychological distress, but it does not follow that the solution should consist of a psychological procedure. Yet even with a clearcut material problem, it is sometimes appropriate to consider a circumscribed piece of behavioural work. An example from behavioural social work practice may help to explain.

> Mrs Giles came to social services on several occasions requesting help with her finances. Usually the problem was no fault of hers, and required a letter or phone call to sort it out. The intake social workers decided that it would be more satisfactory for Mrs Giles herself to learn the skills the workers had been using on her behalf. With modelling, practice and positive reinforcement, the skills of asking at the Social Security Office and phoning and writing to them was gradually shaped up.

Where a psychological focus is appropriate, behavioural help should not be restricted to whatever your agency considers to be

'typical' behavioural cases. (Some child guidance clinics refer only
enuresis or encopresis to their resident behavioural practitioner; and
many psychiatric units will offer behavioural treatment only to
patients with phobias and those who lack social skills.) The answer to
the question 'could a behavioural approach help with this kind of
problem?' is quite likely to be 'yes'. A more difficult question is
whether it is worth a try in the individual case: will it be feasible and
will it work – for *this* client?

Perhaps your assessment of the client's motivation is discouraging.
Perhaps you cannot get the resources that you are sure you will need.
Or perhaps the client carries a thoroughly depressing label, such as
'personality disorder' or 'persistent recidivist'. McAuley and
McAuley (1980) are pessimistic about helping with child behaviour
problems in disorganised and isolated families.

It would certainly be preferable if you could have plenty of
opportunities to develop your skills as a behavioural social worker
before you test them out on the more difficult types of case. In this
context it is worth reminding ourselves of the research by Goldberg
and her colleagues which led its authors to conclude that social
workers' efforts ought to be directed towards helping families
showing early signs of difficulty rather than devoting years to severely
disrupted families whom they were unable to help in any measurable
way (Goldberg and Warburton, 1979). Nevertheless, we believe that
with tact and skill and modest goals one can try to help even in quite
unpromising circumstances. You should keep a close check on
progress for a reasonable amount of time (weeks rather than months)
and if you find you are getting nowhere, then is the time to record the
fact and go back to simply monitoring the situation or close the case.

Now to begin our overview of the assessment process. Not every
assessment, of course, leads to intervention. Your task may be to
prepare a report for others; or you may decide that intervention is not
appropriate, that the help required is not behaviour modification
and/or you should refer elsewhere. Even in these circumstances, the
assessment approach we shall describe will often be of value. You will
need a general assessment with a clear description of the central
problems from the client's and the agency's viewpoint; and a
formulation of the present position that both explains and suggests a
way ahead. For behavioural intervention you will have to take the
assessment further, selecting an initial focus, describing the problem
even more thoroughly, and obtaining a baseline against which to

judge progress. Your behavioural analysis, along with consideration of the resources available, leads logically to a programme of intervention.

Our account may make it seem as though there is one set order for doing things – in fact, this is very far from the truth: the processes we shall describe constitute components of the work rather than phases. There is sure to be some to-ing and fro-ing and a few false trails followed by returns to base. Even when you hope you have left assessment and planning behind and are pressing ahead with intervention proper, you may be stymied by crises, re-routed because more important problems come to light, or forced to think again because the programme you have so laboriously put together is not producing the hoped-for changes.

GENERAL SOCIAL WORK ASSESSMENT

Beginnings

Contrary to the impressions of some critics of our orientation, behavioural social workers begin by listening carefully to the client and establishing a good relationship. (See Fischer 1978, or Sutton 1979 concerning non-psychodynamic social workers' emphasis on empathy, warmth and genuineness.) The basic skills and attitudes required need not be spelled out here; suffice it to say that they are as important in this approach as in any other. So you listen, you explain your role, and only after the client has had her say do you begin to guide the interview.

The presenting problem is taken as the starting point, and the client should be encouraged to give as much detail about it as she is able right away.

The social history

A general social history and assessment is important for several reasons: as a way of getting to know your client as an individual; because agencies may want various types of information – medical, probation and social services departments all have particular requirements; and because you need to find out about the client's strengths and skills and the things that are going well in his life, and to note the resources that could be drawn on, particularly the presence of other people who are concerned.

The social history or social enquiry report will vary according to the purpose it is to serve, and we would not suggest radical departure from normal practices. In child care, for example, typical headings might include marriage and family relationships, landmarks from birth onwards, parental management methods, information about separations, reunions, and childhood illness.

How, then, does the behavioural worker's social assessment differ from a report by someone with a different orientation? Firstly, it will usually contain more about the person's present circumstances and less about his past.

Relevance of the Past

How much attention is paid to past history depends on who the client is, and what the problem is. For example, a worker in child psychiatry would want to know about the child's developmental history; in dealing with a psychiatric problem, information about its onset and about previous episodes will help both in assessment and in deciding the form of intervention required; a person's work history is clearly important in considering job prospects.

An historical line of enquiry provides clues as to whether a difficulty is of long duration, whether it resembles previous problems, or whether its development suggests the influence of a medical condition. Such information may contribute to an understanding of the problem even though it does not provide all the answers about how to help now. For example, a woman with a strong aversion to sex told of being raped by friends of her ex-husband: this information did not materially affect the procedures used to improve her current sexual relationship, but it helped the social worker to empathise with her client and ensure that the sex therapy programme was carried out slowly and cautiously.

Details of the client's past may also assist in formulating a hypothesis about the present problem and how it might be resolved. For example, a young woman felt anxious about a variety of situations. Considering these, the worker thought they might have something in common: testing of her abilities. The client recounted how her parents used to deal out threats and punishments with regard to her performance at school. This information helped to confirm the worker's hypothesis that this woman's anxiety involved fear of being evaluated. A person who is depressed after the death of a relative may describe an earlier loss, how it affected him and how he gradually took up the threads of normal life again; this may provide clues as to how to help him to recover on this occasion.

There is something to be said for helping people to see how problems develop: placing difficulties in context often reduces feelings of guilt, confusion or anxiety. For example, a depressed mother, who had a very difficult pregnancy and birth, has a temperamentally hard-to-handle child, and has experienced a whole series of losses, including her husband's desertion, will find it helpful if you can get her to see that anyone in her position would have problems in coping. It is also the case that some clients may demand an explanation in terms of their past life; and until they get one, they may not be willing to work to change the present.

But it is the present that is the main focus for the behavioural worker: current setting, triggers and consequences of behaviour. You can't alter the past, whereas you have a fair chance of changing events that are going on now.

Other distinctive features of social assessment by a behaviourally-orientated worker are:–

—Clear descriptions of problems that are kept separate from inferences about events or inner states that cannot be verified directly

—Inferences or hypotheses labelled clearly as such.

These features will be explained in detail later in this chapter.

Assets and resources

A crucial part of assessment is to look for factors that will be helpful when you come to devise your intervention programme. Focusing on these has an additional spin-off: in attending to such items you will be helping the client to see both himself and his situation in a more positive light.

Qualities of the client that are relevant from this point of view include his abilities, his motivation to work for change, and his capacity for self-management. Key aspects of his environment include both material resources, and people who care and might be willing to help. (Resources that the social worker may be able to marshall will be discussed when we come to programme planning (pp.106–7).

Abilities

Notice what skills the person already possesses. Could these be used or built upon?

When working with children key questions include: can he talk and understand what people say to him? Does he follow instructions from his parents or anyone else? Can he wash, dress himself and so on? What games is he good at? Whom does he get on well with? The child's parents may have skills that show themselves in areas of their lives other than in their interaction with the 'problem' child: they may get on beautifully with his siblings or with other people's children; they may be able to exercise authority at their work; they may have warm, happy relationships with each other. (Good parental partnerships are associated with success in child management programmes.) Perhaps they are particularly good at drawing or woodwork or games or arithmetic, or have taken responsibility in a union, a church committee or a parent-teacher association.

Adult clients may be well able to make and keep friends even though at present they do not treat close relatives with similar kindness and courtesy. They may have talents they do not currently use: letter-writing, accounting, hobbies, sport. Community workers may be especially interested in such skills as driving, typing, public speaking and experience of committees. Job-finding groups emphasise the presence of job-related abilities that may not be immediately obvious to the members: budgeting and handling money, handyman-type skills, being used to dealing with the public.

Finally, consider the person's previous attempts to cope with problems. What has she tried? Unsuccessful attempts may need 'reframing' ('You don't give up easily', 'It's obvious that you really care') rather than being seen merely as evidence of failure.

Motivation

The term 'unmotivated client' is heavily overused by members of the helping professions. Motivation is situation-specific: the person who cannot 'even' get her children to a weekly playgroup may be the same person who works long hours and endures all kinds of hardship in order to keep her family together. Motivation is also a function of past history: experience of powerlessness can engender apathy, inability to learn new things and a fatalistic attitude. So rather than slapping on the label 'unmotivated' (and thus excusing ourselves from further efforts), we should both consider the client's learning history and also look for factors in the current situation that might make it seem worth her while to expend effort towards possible but not guaranteed changes.

It is important to analyse and discuss both long-term and short-term consequences of co-operation with a behavioural programme, and to look for ways to strengthen the incentives and minimise any disincentives.

Long-term consequences of co-operation. No client is going to work hard in focused interviews, carry out behavioural rehearsals, do homework assignments, or spend time on record-keeping unless he believes that the outcome of the behavioural programme will be of genuine benefit. This highlights the need to attend to the person's own stated goals, and any possible spin-offs we can predict. There may be other consequences we can draw to the client's attention: more free time when the child's disruptiveness has been modified; better relationships after the family contract programme; reduction of feelings of depression after the marital problem has been resolved. But there can also be consequences that the client might not view so positively: extra 'free time' may be seen as 'empty time'; the school refuser's return to school may mean many lonely hours for his house-bound mother; a resumption of sexual intercourse could lead to an unwanted pregnancy; increased social skills and independence for the handicapped teenager could spell trouble to caring parents. If the client has such concerns, then possible solutions must be discussed.

The long term consequences of *not* tackling the problem may also have to be spelled out in order to increase motivation: the legal consequences of non-attendance at school; a bleak future for the handicapped person when parents are no longer available to provide care; family breakdown if relationships continue to deteriorate. But these consequences, and the positive ones too, may be – or may seem – far away in an uncertain future. Many of us are unaffected by such distant negative or positive reinforcers, and while it is useful to have discussed them and to refer back to them during intervention, you need to consider short-term consequences as well.

Short-term consequences of co-operation. The client's motivation must also be examined in terms of the immediate consequences of taking part in the programme. Are there any positive reinforcers for the first steps of the work (that is, before there is any obvious progress towards the ultimate goals)? Can you enhance motivation by making use of what reinforcers are available?

Some clients will be influenced by approval from the social worker, others hardly at all. Some will have other people to reinforce their efforts: a husband who praises his wife's persistence in doing assignments, a favourite teacher who notices a child's improved school behaviour, a neighbour who applauds parents' attempts to cope with a difficult son or daughter. Certainly most people need a bridge between long-term consequences and present effort. A key part of assessment is identifying the right bridge and seeing if it is available.

If there is no sign of potential reinforcers in the client's own environment, the worker needs to create some. The principles and procedures required to enhance 'motivation' are the same as those that feature in any positive reinforcement programme. To illustrate what we mean, a couple of case examples:

> In a behavioural social work case reported by Oliver (1981) a woman who had a long history of minimal co-operation with various professional helpers was given the chance to talk about whatever she liked contingent upon undertaking assignments and keeping to the topic during interviews.
>
> Another client whose motivation was in question was Jean, mildly mentally handicapped and extremely disorganised – to the extent that she was unrepresented at court because of failure to keep appointments with her solicitor. Jean's probation officer began by working on appointment keeping, gradually raising his demands for punctuality (shaping) and giving praise and cups of coffee as reinforcers.

Both of these 'unmotivated' clients turned out to be as 'motivated' as anyone else, once the social workers had taken steps to deal with the difficulty.

A closely related theme is the client's capacity for self-management. We shall consider this in the next section.

Self-management skills

The kind of difficulties that are often described as 'self-control' problems are easier to overcome if the person is able to monitor and reinforce his own behaviour without need of an outsider to pat him on the back, or follow him around with a clipboard.

It seems that some people are more 'self-directed' than others. However, for most of us, there is considerable variation as to which particular behaviours are governed 'from within': for example, you may be able to carry out a slimming plan without anyone to encourage you, but quite unable to keep your case records up-to-date without occasional reinforcement from a colleague; while your friend keeps perfect records but is grossly overweight and smokes like a chimney. As a part of your assessment you should try to discover in what areas of her life the client displays self-management skills.

Self-monitoring. Is the person good at noticing what she feels, thinks and does? To some people, the very idea is quite foreign. Others may monitor some behaviours willingly and accurately, but not other behaviours: for example, children will often keep a record of bed-wetting but not of obedience. For covert behaviour, the differences between people are even more striking: recognising rising tension before an explosion of anger; tracking the effects of alcohol; distinguishing feelings of craving for a drink as against feelings of boredom or anxiety. Asking people to describe their problems may provide clues.

Self-talk. What does the person say to herself when faced with a problem to be solved? Does she make unrealistically pessimistic or optimistic statements to herself, or does she pause, assess, and make coping self-statements: 'What should I do next?'; 'If I do it slowly, I can do it OK.'

Self-reinforcement and self-punishment. What sort of reinforcers, positive or negative, and what sort of punishments does the person administer to herself – is she generous, harsh or sparing with such consequences? Or does she depend entirely on other people for these?

Goals. Lastly, is the person realistic in the sorts of goals she sets for herself? Some people demand far too much of themselves: they tell themselves they should be loved by everyone, be omni-competent, top of every class.

The relevance of all of these factors is especially clear in relation to anxiety and depression and problems of impulse control; but every behavioural programme should be planned with some awareness of them, because self-management is best built where it can be, and needs to be compensated for where it is lacking.

Features of the environment

People. At an early stage it is crucial to find out whether there are people in the client's environment who can lend a hand with behavioural monitoring and with the programme itself. In work with children one is thinking particularly of parents, but there may be other people in regular contact with the child who are willing to assist. Grandparents, older children, teachers and family friends are obvious examples. In the case of a little boy who often absconded from his ESN school, the milkman gave invaluable assistance by enquiring regularly about the child's whereabouts and giving him a weekly ride on his float if he had stayed in class for a full week. A child with enuresis earned a weekend at the home of a much-liked member of the school domestic staff as a back-up reinforcer with a star-chart system (Chelfham Mill School, 1976).

In work with adults, friends, flat mates and colleagues may prove to be willing and reliable helpers, as well as relatives. Indeed, assessment of a person's network of friends and acquaintances is usually vital, and unhappily, those who turn out to be quite isolated are often those who do least well.

The client's relatives or friends are especially important when you are planning a programme that requires a 'mediator' – someone to observe and record behaviour and deliver reinforcers or alter antecedents, administer relaxation instructions or accompany the person into situations that make him anxious. The person who lives alone will pose a particular challenge; but so will the person who lives with people who do not seem able to help, perhaps because of pressing problems of their own, or lack of skill. People who say they do not approve of giving reinforcers ('Why should I reward him for what he ought to be doing anyway?'; 'I won't use bribery') may be persuaded to try your approach as an experiment; but those who do not wish to relinquish current punitive or indifferent ways of interacting with your client pose a very difficult problem. Techniques such as modelling, rational problem-solving, persuasion or negotiation may help gain their co-operation. Once the behavioural programme has got off the ground, there is a good chance that monitoring of progress will produce some encouraging results to reinforce their efforts and change their minds. Mediators have carried out successful interventions with the mentally ill (Hudson, 1978) and with children with a wide variety of problems (Tharp and Wetzel, 1969; Patterson *et al.*, 1973; McAuley and McAuley, 1977; Herbert, 1981) and have assisted in the treatment of alcoholics (Azrin, 1976), agoraphobics (Gelder, 1979) and many others. Most of these authors refer to difficulties faced and ways in which they can be overcome. Considering the kinds of clients and problems tackled in these projects, it is hard to see how much headway could have been made without mediators.

Clubs, churches, and community groups are another source of help. Even if it is not possible or appropriate to draw them in on a formal basis, they may well act as models or reinforce changed behaviour patterns – for example, parents may win compliments for their child's improved behaviour, alcoholics will be encouraged to remain sober once they have made some new friends, ex-psychiatric patients may be welcomed when they attend social gatherings run by their local church, and previously depressed and apathetic residents will be received gratefully when they offer their skills to a community action group. One unemployed, depressed young man seemed to 'take off' after achieving a few simple tasks which led him to join a local residents' association – he developed his skills in organising and leadership, made many friends and only reappeared at the psychiatric unit to present local demands for better hospital services! The relevance of all this to arguments for locally-based ('patch') social work will be apparent.

Material resources. Only a brief note on this aspect of the client's assets. Most clients of social workers are poor, and it may well be that their lack of material resources will be the main focus of social work help. Poverty brings with it a number of obstacles to behavioural work. The key obstacle, of course, is the fact that physical needs and living from hand to mouth both drain energy away from efforts to deal with non-material problems, and also throw up crises which have to take priority over any carefully planned and measured progress towards behavioural changes. Furthermore, long-term poverty, or the sudden experience of redundancy or disablement or marital breakdown and their financial aftermath, all tend to produce feelings of helplessness, thus affecting motivation to try and make changes. It is therefore extremely important to understand and acknowledge – by words and by actions – the financial problems that many of our clients endure.

On the positive side, some clients may have material resources that can play a part in a behavioural programme. For example, if the clients have a telephone you can ring regularly to check on how assignments are going, to collect data, and to prompt and give social reinforcement. A client's tape recorder is useful for getting samples of family discussions to study, and for playing tapes of relaxation or other instructions. If the family have spare cash, then it (and the things it will buy!) will increase the range of potential reinforcers for both adults and children.

We shall consider material resources available to the social worker when we discuss intervention planning. We continue with more on assessment.

Listing of problems/goals and selection of an initial focus

After obtaining general information, you will need to narrow the focus again to get a comprehensive picture of the difficulties the client is facing. A list is drawn up with the client's help; in some instances this can be done during the interview via a series of questions; or else the client may be asked to write a list herself either on the spot or as a homework assignment.

Here is a boy's own list of things that get him into trouble at home:

Late for a bath
Standing on the dog
Coming in late
Not coming in straight from school
Not changing school clothes
Answering back
Fighting with my sister
Getting the blame for things you have not done
Fighting with the pillows on the bed
Walking out when your mum is talking to you

(Source: Hutchings *et al.*, 1981)

This is a list of school problems prepared by a group of boys:

> Shouting in the classroom when the teacher has gone out
> Talking when there is an examination on
> Getting up when he tells you not to
> Talking to someone behind you and he does not like it
> Disrupting the class
> Distracting attention
> Pulling faces when he is out of the door
> Not listening when he is speaking to you
> Messing about
> Throwing things about
> Making a noise on the table
> Writing on the table
> Taking some stuff from ripped chairs
> Making a mess on the floor
>
> (Source: Hutchings *et al.*, 1981)

Here is a list written by a woman who was suffering from depression and considered to be a possible child abuser:

> Both kids quarrelling and in and out of our room all night.
> Andy (three) – screaming, throwing things, destroying plants, my makeup, anything he can lay his hands on, hitting me, telling me to go away.
> Jane (five) – cheek, doing opposite of what she's told, crying when she doesn't get what she wants, breaking toys.
> Jim (husband) – giving children chocolate and sweets when I say not to, especially right before meals, laughing when the kids disobey me, for example pulling up plants, no interest in my family, refuses to eat until the kids and I have finished, spends too much time with his family, no time together alone.
> Home – not being able to get work done on time, especially tidying up and ironing. I always seem to be short of cash at the end of the week. We get people dropping in when everything looks a mess:

With the social worker's help such a list can also be written as a set of goals:

> Children to play together without quarrelling, stay in own room all night.

Andy to leave other people's things alone, talk to me nicely, and talk quietly.

Jane to talk to me nicely, do what she's told, keep her cool when frustrated and play nicely with her toys.

Jim to give sweets only when I agree, to back me up with regard to rules, to eat with me, to spend more time with me and to ask about and see my family more.

Plan a work programme and stick to it, put budget into effect, find a way of dealing with visitors.

(Note: it is desirable to turn problems-to-be-eliminated into positive behaviour changes wherever possible.)

It will not usually be necessary to tackle every problem on the list and it is best to select just one or two to begin with. Priorities have to be established. This is a matter for negotiation between the parties, and what follows is a series of suggestions about key factors to be taken into consideration.

The client's viewpoint

What is causing the client most distress? What change would bring him the most satisfaction?

The worker's (and agency's) viewpoint

Is the behaviour dangerous? Causing grave concern to others?

External constraints

External factors may make some matters more urgent than others. For example, a court summons may be threatened unless a child returns to school; perhaps a committee is soon to take a crucial decision, and the members want to be able to argue their case persuasively; a job interview may be on the horizon, so that job interview skills need shaping up right away.

Likelihood of early improvement

This judgement of how long it will take for change to occur should if possible be based on the literature. For example, there are many reports of quite early success with simple phobias, with children's disobedience and with circumscribed assertiveness problems; but depression, complex anxiety problems, stealing, and problem drinking are more difficult to modify and usually take a long time. Low-rate (very infrequent) behaviours and behaviours that are hard to observe and therefore hard to follow with new kinds of consequences are not promising targets: delinquent behaviour is often in this category.

The prospect of rapid improvement might well override other considerations because success may powerfully reinforce the client's efforts to carry out the behavioural programme, and in addition give him a sense of control or mastery, which will begin to erode any feelings of helplessness he may be experiencing. Summing up in less behavioural language: the client's motivation will be enhanced.

These considerations must be balanced against the possibility that a more complicated problem – such as serious marital discord – may prevent work on simpler, quicker-to-modify problems.

The cost to the client

Here again the worker needs to draw on the literature (as well as experience). Some programmes require more effort (including emotional effort) than do others. Even though the programme details have yet to be worked out, it may be possible to predict, for example, that relaxation sessions would take hours with Mr A; that Mrs B would find it very hard to persuade her husband to take part in sex therapy; that to stop spoon feeding her child would cause Mrs C great discomfort. Where such demanding items can be postponed it is better that they should be.

Probable timing and sequence of different changes

For example, it is sensible to focus on obedience before going on to teach a child to use the toilet because obedience is needed if the child is to follow the instructions that will form part of the toilet programme. Staying out late may be strongly associated with delinquency, so that reducing the number of late nights ought to be addressed first.

Difficult behaviour when it's time to get ready for school might be easier to change after the bed-time problems of the night before have been successfully overcome.

Wahler and Fox (1978, cited in McAuley and McAuley, 1980) have drawn attention to 'co-variation of behaviours' – a little understood concept that can have very cheering implications. It is suggested that certain classes of behaviour co-vary, that is, if one class decreases or increases in frequency the other class changes in tandem. Wahler and Fox found this to be the case with independent play and opposition to parents. Another example is delinquent acts outside the home and obedience to parents, so that stealing might decrease as obedience to parents increases. (This might be because parents become more rewarding and better models as a result of the home programme.) Since it is notoriously difficult to change behaviour like stealing (where one cannot get into the immediate situation to alter the antecedents and consequences), the prospect of dealing with it indirectly by working on other goals in the home would be good news indeed. Sadly, this remains speculative, but the positive results of family work with delinquents (see Chapter 9) might be explained in this way.

Snowballing of positive effects

The notion of co-variation ties in with another frequently reported and heartening aspect of behavioural work: the 'snowballing' of positive effects. For example, a mother with child management problems learns the skills to improve these and finds that her feelings of depression lift and her husband enjoys her company more; a child whose enuresis is successfully treated becomes more popular and confident. A boy of twelve preferred to hide in the coal shed all day rather than go to school. Sensitive interviewing led to the hypothesis (confirmed by the boy himself) that he was mercilessly teased at school because he was overweight. The social worker and the boy agreed to concentrate on slimming as their first goal and, after losing weight, the boy returned to school of his own accord. In selecting an initial focus for intervention it is not unreasonable to expect that we may not have to deal with all the problems on the list, and we certainly need not feel obligated to take everything on board right away.

Overview of problem selection

Consider the following case example:

> A mother's presenting complaints are her younger child's bad behaviour at nursery school and encopresis at home. The problem overview adds to the list: marital problems, husband's occasional heavy drinking, this child's messy eating, disobedience and tantrums, an older child's cheek, mother-in-law's constant criticising, desire for a housing transfer and a query about state benefits.
>
> The client rates the encopresis as the worst problem. You feel that it would help most if the marital situation could be improved – but her husband is not interested. You do not want to focus first on encopresis because it would be hard to deal with before the child can co-operate in a programme that involves doing what he is told. Also, you'd like a medical check.
>
> You feel the mother is under considerable stress and you do not want to place more demands on her until you have done what you can to relieve at least some of it. You therefore decide to tackle housing and money problems as quickly as you can. After that, you will focus on the child's disobedience and tantrums. These are often linked and may well respond to a fairly brief programme of positive reinforcement and time-out which you can teach the mother to administer.

When you have some evidence of having achieved your goals with regard to the chosen target problem, you will consider whether to intervene in the remaining problems. If on the other hand, you do not get the progress you had hoped for, you will re-evaluate your aims and choice of initial target. For example, the husband or the mother-in-law may be sabotaging the programme, or the client may turn out to be too preoccupied with other problems to be able to give her full attention to the tasks you have set.

To sum up, the ordering of problems takes into account:
(1) the client's wishes.
(2) external constraints.
(3) the worker's educated guess as to what can be achieved at an early stage.
(4) the need to avoid too heavy demands on the client.
(5) the likely time sequence of behaviour changes.

(6) prospects of snowballing of positive effects.

Theory, knowledge of other people's work, experience and clear thinking all play their part in assisting the worker and client to weigh the pros and cons of alternative starting points.

A target problem having been selected (if it is a behaviour to be modified) it must be described and analysed in considerable detail. In Chapter 4 we consider the kind of information needed and the various methods by which it can be gathered.

4
How to Begin a Behavioural Programme: II

Describing the Problem

The behavioural problem should – if at all possible – be described in such a way that client, worker, and anyone else involved would agree on whether the behaviour had occurred or not; in other words, one is seeking a *specific* and *reliable* description. Some of the ideas in this section have a great deal to offer to the writer of a report that will be acted upon by other people, such as a social enquiry report for the court: Tutt and Giller (1983) comment that recent criminal justice legislation in the UK points report writers towards consideration of concrete issues and away from the nebulous and subjective material which has so often been the hallmark of social enquiry reports in the past.

Deficit or surplus

The first issue is a relatively simple one: is the problem an absence of some behaviour (doesn't get up before noon, never attends meetings)? Or is it a question of behaviour that happens too often (tantrums, stealing) too intensely (stares fixedly at people) or at the wrong times or places (talks about depression at parties, social chat at committee meetings)? In other words, is the problem a behavioural surplus or a behavioural deficit?

Specificity

Avoid woolly language, and describe the behaviour in concrete terms if at all possible (what would you see or hear when the problem occurs?) Overt actions, such as hitting a brother, attending meetings, obeying mother or talking about suicide are comparatively unproblematic in this respect; but even with these you might be able to improve on the description: how hard are the blows and is a weapon used? What constitutes 'attending a meeting' (as against dropping in, leaving early, not paying attention)? How soon after mother's request does the child obey? What exactly does the person say about suicide?

Vague terms to do with feelings, and which summarise a range of behaviours (often attached to the word 'personality'), such as 'aggressive', 'depressed', 'cheeky', 'uncaring', or 'anxious' can usually be translated into their behavioural indicators. For example, 'anxiety' can mean any or all of the following: avoiding certain situations; talking about feeling anxious; showing non-verbal signs such as nervous mannerisms, shaking, tense posture, breathlessness; rating oneself as anxious on a checklist; reporting feelings like butterflies in the stomach and more. In the case of a child described as schoolphobic, you would want to know whether he is afraid of the lessons, particular teachers, other children, the journey to school, or being parted from mother. 'Aggression' can mean aggressive feelings, aggressive verbal or aggressive motor behaviour. Words like 'anxiety' or 'aggression' can be useful summary terms, but a report that does not explain them in behavioural terms as well is less helpful than it could be, and might even be misleading.

Even less acceptable are theory-based terms that indicate the writer's inferences about behaviour and its causes but do not tell us what the behaviour is. 'Acting out', 'heavily defended', 'weak superego' are examples from the psychodynamic schools. But behavioural workers can fall into the same trap, using words like 'attention-seeking', or 'unassertive' without specifying further.

Current causes or maintaining factors

The core of behavioural analysis is the 'ABC' of behaviour: Antecedents – Behaviour – Consequences. We have emphasised the need to specify the behaviour. We now turn to the 'A' and 'C'.

Antecedents

The setting in which the behaviour occurs or does not occur is often important. This usually means the place and the people who are present: pub, playground, supermarket or cinema; other children, grandmother or girlfriend. Setting also refers to time of day and whether school day or holiday, workday or weekend.

If the behaviour of interest is a respondent behaviour, then we are concerned to identify the eliciting stimulus (conditioned or unconditioned). For example: criticism from husband precedes angry outbursts, sight of a long queue precedes anxiety attacks at the supermarket check-out. With operant behaviours, we are looking for signs that a particular behaviour will be reinforced or punished. Other boys shouting 'Go on, don't be a coward!' might precede throwing a brick; mother saying 'Don't you feel sick?' might precede vomiting.

All of these are examples of overt antecedents, but covert events may be crucial: thinking you will make a fool of yourself, feeling angry or feeling tired may be more important antecedents than what is happening in the outside world.

Missing the antecedent in your behavioural analysis can lead to serious mistakes in behavioural work. For example, a child who is disturbing her parents at night and who is afraid of the dark requires different handling from a child who is not afraid, just awake and bored.

Consequences

What happens after the behaviour? For example, it may be that solicitous questions follow when a psychiatric patient recounts his delusional beliefs whereas sensible comments are met with indifference; parent coming to the bedroom follows a child's yelling; getting a lolly follows a tantrum in the shop. In family and marital situations it can happen that friendly advances to another person are repulsed (punishment), or that compliance with requests is followed by removal of something unpleasant like nagging or taunting (negative reinforcement).

Again, it may be necessary to look to covert events as well: is the behaviour followed by some self-approving thought ('that impressed them!', 'that's got me out of trouble') or by a reduction in a painful feeling, as when avoidance or escape from a frightening situation leads to a reduction in feelings of anxiety?

How far back and how far forward?

Of course there are endless chains of antecedents, behaviours and consequences, and these grow longer when you include covert events as well. For example, Patterson (1976), studying family interaction, has shown how an aggressive outburst from one child can be traced back to something another member of the family did quite some time before. A row over breakfast on Tuesday can be traced to one partner's experiences at work on Monday and indeed to the boss' own breakfast with his wife on Monday morning. And so on ... One person's antecedents and consequences are often someone else's problem behaviours.

But in fact the beginnings and the endings of the 'ABC' of behavioural analysis are often clear and 'natural'. In the example above we obviously cannot investigate the private life of the employer, nor do we need to in order to formulate the difficulties our clients are facing and devise a useful programme to deal with them. Just as most behavioural workers subscribe to the rule of the least intervention necessary, so they prefer to operate with the least analysis sufficient to produce a workable hypothesis. If the evidence eventually shows that we did not get it right we have to go back to the drawing board, seeking more information, perhaps paying more attention to covert events or taking in a longer chain of behaviour, possibly including more people.

Measuring the problem

An important part of the behavioural description of a problem is a measurement or, preferably, a series of measurements. Once a behaviour has been clearly described, it is necessary to decide what sorts of measurement are appropriate.

Frequency

Behaviours that have a clear-cut beginning and end can be counted; number of times Mrs L got up before noon, Jimmy came home after ten o'clock, Mary went to school. Calculating averages over time periods we get: Mrs L got up before noon on average once a week over three months, Jimmy came home after ten o'clock on average twice a week over three weeks, Mary went to school on average once a week during two terms. With many behaviours it is necessary to produce a percentage, that is, number of times behaviour occurred out of number of 'opportunities': Jimmy obeyed 30% of mother's requests, Mary went to school on 40% of the school days between January and

July, 65% of Mrs J's utterances during the family discussion were criticisms or interruptions.

Intensity

This can be a useful feature of description of moods, wishes or beliefs (in addition to counting the occasions when these are experienced). How bad did the person feel on a scale of 1–10? How strongly did he believe that he was likely to be a failure on a scale from 1–100? Overt behaviours too can sometimes be assessed in this way: loudness of yelling, violence of temper tantrums. (For details of rating scales see pp.97–102).

Duration

This is often relevant. How long did the tantrum last? How many minutes did Ann play quietly by herself? And we might add distance here: how many stops did Mrs A travel on the bus? How far did Mrs T go with her new walking frame?

Other examples of useful measurements are numbers of people attending meetings, quantity of drinks or cigarettes consumed, amounts of money saved.

Measurements should be taken as soon as possible after selecting the target problem. Sometimes they will provide a valuable check as to whether the problem is as serious as the preliminary discussion has suggested. Parents may say a child is 'always' stealing, disobedient, hitting her brother. In some such cases, careful measuring over a week or so may show that things are not so bad. If this happens, it may be the parents' beliefs about this child in comparison to other children that need modifying.

GATHERING THE BEHAVIOURAL DATA

We have outlined several types of information to be obtained before a behavioural formulation can be achieved: a specific and reliable description of the behaviour; a specific account of its antecedents and consequences; and a measure or series of measures. There is a wide variety of methods and instruments for obtaining all this information. Indeed, two behavioural journals are devoted to this topic (*Journal of Behavioural Assessment* and *Behavioural Assessment*) and there are numerous books on the subject. We would like to make some general suggestions, taking into consideration the constraints upon most social workers, including lack of training in this field, and lack of measuring instruments both printed and mechanical.

The interview

A description of the problem and its possible causes can be obtained by careful questioning. The client is asked for blow-by-blow accounts of recent occurrences. 'What' (not 'why') questions are the key: what would I see if I saw you doing it? What would you be doing if you were feeling cheerful again? Tell me exactly what happened, what she did, who said what to whom.

It is essential to ask for two or three *examples* of problems the client complains of: this will help you move from a general, abstract description to a more concrete one. Another useful device is the '*typical day*' account: the client takes you through all the events of a typical day or part of a day, giving a detailed narrative of everything that happened.

Here are some extracts from a 'typical day' interview with a single woman who has been complaining of feeling depressed.

Social Worker: ... I would like you to give me an idea of how you spend a typical day. Take yesterday, was that fairly typical?

Client: Yes, it was. I did absolutely nothing. I just felt I couldn't cope at all ...

Social Worker: You felt really low. All the same, I really want to know exactly what you did ... I want you to sort of talk me through your day. What time was it when you woke up in the morning?

Client: A bit before six, I think ...

Social Worker: Right. Did you get up right away?

Client: No, I didn't get up till eight.

Social Worker: Did you fall asleep again, can you remember?

Client: I didn't. No. I just lay there tossing and turning and going over things.

Social Worker: What sort of things?

Client: Oh, things like not wanting to have another day like the one before, how I got nothing done, how I haven't any friends ...

(*Later*)

Social Worker: When you were out getting cigarettes did you talk to anybody?

Client: No.

Social Worker: So you came back at about three. What did you do next?

Client: Nothing much.

Social Worker: What's 'nothing much'?

Client: I sat and watched TV but didn't concentrate on it. I had some bread and jam. Then I fell asleep for about two hours.

(*Later*)

Social Worker: Good. Now could you tell me how you would compare yesterday with other days? Was it better than usual for you, or pretty average, or was it a very bad day?

Client: Middling to bad, I think ...

Besides giving some helpful structure, a focused interview along these lines will provide much of the information needed to move from a general complaint ('I'm fed up'; 'I can't cope'; 'The children are getting me down') to a concrete description of problems (crying at certain times, sitting doing nothing, seeing no one, sleeping all afternoon), and the beginnings of the 'ABC' type of analysis ('I get up late, drag Mary out of bed, have to dress her, she says she has a headache, I let her miss school'). Antecedents in particular may not be recalled without a lot of probing, but the 'typical day' interview is likely to help.

Questions of frequency, intensity and duration can sometimes be answered in a focused interview. But these features are usually difficult to recall reliably. There are exceptions: some events are easy to remember because they are vivid or because they happen extremely rarely. This might apply to such events as quarrels involving violence, episodes of stealing, the water being turned off by the landlord, or the one occasion a teenager got up in time for breakfast in the previous month. Times can be clearly recalled because the client has been concentrating on this aspect: for example, a mother knew exactly when her daughter got home each night over the past week because she had waited up for her. But generally speaking is is very difficult for clients to answer questions about frequency, duration or intensity without having previously made a deliberate plan to track, count and measure.

Nevertheless, careful interviewing does produce a great deal of the data the behavioural worker requires. Your interview style has to be focused, and you have to 'shape' the client's skills in behavioural description, giving examples of what is wanted and reinforcing useful replies. Asking the client to track events between your meetings will help you to obtain a more detailed account next time.

Direct observation, however, will usually add a great deal to the information obtained via interviews, and we discuss this in the following section.

Planned observation

In the course of an interview, you can observe certain behaviours: how people communicate, aspects of social skills, non-verbal indicators of anxiety or depression. On a home visit you will see the state of the house, the children's behaviour, perhaps an interchange with a neighbour or a phone call. The chief disadvantage with this informal type of observation is that people's behaviour may be far from typical: after all, being interviewed by a social worker is quite unlike the situations in which their problems normally come to the fore.

More formal observation – where the worker does not interact with people at all, but encourages them to go about their business – is subject to disadvantages of a similar kind: there is plentiful evidence of the effects that knowledge of being observed has on people (even when they are observing themselves). Nevertheless, where it can be arranged, we would recommend planned observation because it does help you to obtain a more representative sample of people's 'natural' behaviour.

A period of observation can be tacked on to an interview: for example, a couple with marital problems could be asked to discuss a controversial topic; a mother whose interaction with her child is said to be 'distant' or 'inappropriate' could be asked to have a game with the child or to give the child instructions; a client with agoraphobia could be invited to accompany the worker for a walk as far as she is able. Asking the client to re-enact an event or to role-play a future or hypothetical scene are further from reality but are nevertheless useful ways of obtaining a sample of key behaviours. For instance, a client might demonstrate what he said to his friend (and how he said it) before a quarrel broke out, or 'act' how he plans to ask his employer for more time off. Setting up role-plays of this kind, whether of actual happenings or future occasions, can take a lot of planning, and is best taken 'clip by clip', for example, 'Do the first bit, when you go to Jim's bed and tell him to get up . . . Now the bit where you ask him to get dressed'.

Alternatively – and this makes for greater formality and probably for greater embarrassment – one or two full sessions of observation can be arranged. This approach is particularly useful in cases where a child's behaviour is the central concern. McAuley and McAuley (1977) give the following advice: limit the observation period to one and a half hours and choose a time when most of the family are present and when problems are most likely to show up. Restrict people's movements to one or two rooms, and ban TV and visitors. If people feel anxious, give them set tasks to do in order to provide some structure. McAuley and McAuley suggest that children over the age of about eight are unlikely to behave naturally in this situation. However, it is our impression that observation visits are in fact useful with a range of clients, not just children. We have found that after about twenty minutes people become fairly used to the worker's presence. Similarly, a community worker might observe a meeting of an association or a committee and expect to get a representative picture of how the members carry out their tasks.

The use of audio- and video-tapes is becoming more acceptable to social workers, and in our experience clients are not averse to these if the purpose of recording is explained and confidentiality is guaranteed. The amount of information that can be obtained from a fairly short sample of people's behaviour is greatly increased if a recording is made: pinpointing of 'ABC's, and various kinds of measurement are made possible that could not all be achieved during a single 'live' observation.

Another bonus with tapes is that while going over them with the clients you can stop the tape to ask questions, such as 'Is that typical?', 'Is he usually like that when you ask him to explain something?' Some workers find it useful to ask questions of this kind during 'live' observations of children and parents (R. McAuley, *personal communication*, 17 December, 1984).

Clients too can be taught to observe, or may be willing to make tape recordings for the worker to study, for example, of family discussions.

Behavioural Records

Having found a way of 'getting at' the information it remains to choose a method of noting it down on paper.

Narrative recording

Simplest of all – and well within the capacities of many clients, including children – is straightforward narrative recording, which is just a written equivalent of the kind of blow-by-blow account of events that we discussed in the section on the interview. Such records can be made by the social worker during observation sessions, but we have chosen some narrative recordings written by clients in order to demonstrate their utility:

(1) A record made by a member of a boys' group (Hutchings *et al.*, 1981):

. . . I went to my tutorial and I started messing around in the class e.g. going up to my tutor and singing in his face and not doing what I was told to do. Anyway he told me to sit down and I never so he told me to stay behind after the rest of the class leave, so when the class left he slammed the door and came up to me and grabbed my coat and shaked me. I said 'get off you B— and C— and he said 'mind your language' and I said 'I will if you leave go of me', but he did not and I said 'if you don't get off I will get my father on you and he will put you six feet under' and he said 'I don't care who you get on me' but I said 'I know because you won't know what will hit you.' He said 'put your chair up' and I said 'no', but in the end I did and he said 'you can go' and when he was locking the door I called him by his nickname Stinkie. He behaved in a cruel way by grabbing me and shaking me.

(2)   Records by a husband and wife with marital problems:

. . . J home late and no apology. P called for water and I ran
upstairs. Then I came into kitchen. J asked for supper 'Where's my
supper?', tapped on table. I said sorry and asked how was his day.
Got his meal out. J said it's all dried up . . .'   (*Wife*)

'Home at 7.00. A didn't say hullo, and ran upstairs to P. Then stuck
my meal in front of me and started washing up. I said meal dried up
and she said sorry and asked about my day. I told her about the
hold-up over deliveries that had set us back, but she clattered dishes
and I don't think she was listening . . .' (*Husband*)

It may be useful to use a prepared format. Here are two examples
from Hutchings *et al.* (1981). (Note that these records were made after
the initial assessment phase of the boys' group):

(3)   *Day*: Monday
      Time: 4 o'clock
      Which shop: Barener
      Who you went with: Nobody
      What you bought: Cigarettes and a polo tube
      How did you behave: I behaved reasonably well and I have
      done all the things that come into my head and I behaved well.
      When I asked for some polo tubes I said 'please, thank you'
      and I smiled, and when I went out of the shop I said 'goodbye'.
      How did the shopkeeper behave: Reasonably well. Not as good
      as I expected.

(4)   *How I behaved with a teacher I don't like*
      I behaved for one lesson and I used my manners because
      usually I just go and say something without my manners. Mr
      Smith was pleased and said 'Where have you learnt those
      manners from?' and I said 'I don't know sir'. I done
      everything good and he said 'no wonder you hate me because
      I keep getting cross with you. If you behave like that every
      lesson you will get on fine and you will get to like me a lot
      better.'
      How the teacher behaved
      The teacher behaved as well as I should think so and was

speaking in a pleasant voice and he used his manners but not as better than me and behaved well for the next lesson.'

Where a particular problem behaviour has been clearly identified, it is helpful to provide a format with spaces for antecedents, behaviour and consequences. Thus:

(5) *What happened before*
   Husband back from pub 11.00pm. T had come down and was sat in front of TV and turned it up loud. Husband switched TV off.
   Behaviour
   T kicked his dad and put TV on again.
   What happened after
   Husband slapped T. I said 'leave him'.
   What happened before
   As above
   Behaviour
   T started yelling.
   What happened after
   I gave T a cuddle and his dad gave him some crisps.

As these examples show, deciding what to call an antecedent and what to call a consequence is not easy in problems of complex interaction: the couple in example (2) might need to work on both *his* lateness without warning, lack of apology, and criticism, and *her* lack of attention to him. In example (5), the tantrum is the presenting problem but the coming downstairs late at night is another, which may have to be addressed first, even though it might not have seemed crucial to the parents.

Charts and checklists

A detailed diary can yield a frequency, intensity or duration measure, but simple charts or checklists do this job better. We offer some examples, but would urge that each chart is constructed with the particular problem and client in mind, so as to make it as easy and attractive as possible: for example, one client liked to have different coloured paper for each day; children appreciate pictures and 'themes'. Some clients can fill in a few words of explanation along with the ticks. Getting the client's assistance in preparing the chart can help encourage recording – and probably lessens the likelihood (in the case of children) that it will come to harm!

Swear Words (Record by mother with difficult child)

		Total
Monday ~~////~~ /		6
Tuesday ////		4
Wednesday		0

Figure 4.1

Obedience and Requests (Record by mother of disobedient child)
(R – request or R + – request obeyed)

Monday	7.30–8.30	R R R R R	% requests obeyed 0%
	4.00–6.00	R R R R	% requests obeyed 0%
	6.00–8.00	R + R + R + R +	% requests obeyed 100%
Tuesday	7.30–8.30	R + R R R +	% requests obeyed 50%
	4.00–6.00	R + R R R	% request obeyed 25%
	6.00–8.00	R R R R	% requests obeyed 0%

Figure 4.2

No. of times I wanted to hit Jimmy (/) hit him (X) (Record by mother who has difficulty controlling her anger)

9.15–10.15	/X////X	Total 7 urges 2 smackings
10.15–11.15	//X/	4 urges 1 smacking

Figure 4.3

Minutes till quiet after put to bed (record by parents of child with 'bedtime problem')

Monday	30
Tuesday	35

Figure 4.4

In by 11.00 (✓) or minutes late (Record by parents of teenager)

Monday	✓
Tuesday	5 minutes late
Wednesday	✓

Figure 4.5

Times I said something in the meeting (Record by new member of committee)

	Total
12 January	0
19 January ////	5
23 January ////	5

Figure 4.6

Number of people at the meeting (Record by playgroup committee)

13 February	12
20 March	15
28 March	20

Figure 4.7

A chart recording 3 kinds of behaviour in code (Record by parents)

Time	Monday	Tuesday
9.30–10.00	H H H S	H H H S
10.00–10.30	P H P P P	H H H P P

KEY H = hit person or object; S = spoke nicely to me; P = played appropriately for five minutes.

Figure 4.8

Next some examples of a *combined chart/diary format* (i.e. leaving space for details in addition to frequency count).

Social Contacts (Record by woman suffering from depression)

	Number	Details
Monday 2 January	1	Next door neighbour – just a few words
Tuesday 3 January	4	Neighbour – as yesterday Neighbour – had her in to coffee Rang daughter for chat Spoke to lady in park with dog
Wednesday 4 January	3	Man in park Spoke to six people at lunch club Asked neighbour to tea tomorrow
Thursday 5 January	2	Neighbour to tea Phoned niece
Friday 6 January	0	

Figure 4.9

Record by mother of difficult child

Time	Number of tantrums	What happened before/situation	What happened after
7.30–8.00	0		
8.00–8.30	3	1 When asked to eat some egg 2 When asked to put on gloves and boots 3 When told he must go to nursery school	Ignored Said I'd tell father. He put on gloves and boots Took him there, still yelling

Figure 4.10

Record by parents of young woman suffering from mental disorder

Time	No of times mentioned delusions	What happened before/situation	What happened after
7.30–8.00	None	Eating, talked about the news	
8.00–8.30	3	1 Mary (sister) asked about 'voices' 2 Dad said hoped she'd be better today 3 Nothing much – cleaning up	1 Mary argued with her 2 Mary argued with her 3 Dad argued with her
8.30–9.00	2	I said I was going to the shops	I ignored it and went out

Figure 4.11

Record kept by chronic schizophrenic patient and her brother

Day	Up by Noon/ Time	Dressed/ Time	Cooking	Made Tea	Washing- up	Anything Else
Monday	√10	√11.30	Peeled potatoes Heated soup Cooked potatoes	//// 5	/// 3	Swept floor Dusted
Tuesday	No	√ 3	Peeled potatoes Cooked potatoes	// 2	/// 4	Tidied room
Wednesday	√11.45	√ 3	Boiled egg Peeled Potatoes	√ 1	/ 1	Vacuumed Dusted

Figure 4.12

Contracts, star charts, points systems

Under 'Procedures' we will be discussing contracts and star charts and points systems (pp.126–7, 150–5). These serve a dual purpose: as a framework for an operant programme and as a measure of its effects. In children's programmes especially, the charts ought to be as attractive and imaginative as you and the clients can make them. Indeed, the production of these items has become a fine art in behavioural establishments for children. For the less artistic, what about, for example, a glass jar that is gradually filled with coloured marbles, each marble representing the completion of a task or the absence for half a day of some problem behaviour?

Rating scales

For intensity, and for levels of behaviours that are hard to count or measure objectively, a rating scale is useful.

Here is a simple 3-point rating scale for certain aspects of social skills:

Scoring: 3 = good; 2 = fair; 1 = poor.

	Role-Play 1 (3 Jan)	Role-Play 2 (20 Jan)	Role-Play 3 (1 Feb)
Gaze	3	2	3
Voice	1	2	3
Posture	1	2	2

Figure 4.13

This is a combined frequency count and 3-point rating scale:
Times I felt angry with the kids
Scoring: + = angry; + + = very angry; + + + = so angry I felt like hitting them

Monday am	+ + +
Monday pm	–
Tuesday am	+ + + + +
Tuesday pm	+ + + +

Figure 4.14

This is a diary and 3-point rating scale (excellent–moderate–terrible):

Episodes when I was criticised or told 'no'

Day	What happened/situation	My reaction	My reaction
Monday	(1) Pub. J said I was getting fat	I ignored it.	Excellent
	(2) Pub. J said I should go out with a better class of girl.	Went hot. Asked what he meant	Moderate
	He said Jean was nicer than Mary (Jean's my ex).	Said 'none of your business' and changed the subject.	Excellent
	(3) Landlord said 'hurry up'.	Said 'F— off' in a loud voice.	Terrible
	Landlord said 'what did you say?'	'sorry'	Excellent
	(4) J refused lift.	Thumped his car.	Terrible

Figure 4.15

'Ready-made' questionnaires and rating scales

These can obtain an overview of the client's problems and may get at items the client might not report spontaneously. They are especially interesting and useful if you want to compare your own work with that of other practitioners who have published their results in the professional journals. Some are suited for repeated use throughout the programme, as we shall discuss in the section on evaluation.

When considering a ready-made measure there are one or two precautions you ought to take: find out whether it has been tested for validity and reliability (does it measure what it says it measures? and does it do so each time it is used and no matter who uses it?) and whether it is suitable for your particular client group. Usually, an established measure will have been well-tested, and at some stage in its history it will have been discussed in a professional journal. Busy social workers who have little chance of hunting through the literature could check the position in one of the following ways: ask a friendly expert (clinical psychologists are often willing to advise) or consult a textbook that deals with assessment (e.g. Cone and Hawkins, 1977).

Some instruments are filled in by the client himself and others by people who are in a good position to observe him. For example, Spence (1980) has devised a pair of questionnaires on children's social skills. One is for teachers and includes such items as:

Has he got friends among his classmates?
No close friends/one close friend/several/at least one close/many/at least two friends
Does he become angry when criticised by staff?
Always/usually/sometimes/rarely/never
Are the child's verbal responses very brief and/or infrequent?
Yes/No

The other is a self-report questionnaire for children, with such questions as:

Do you . . . feel worried using the telephone? Yes/No
Do you . . . often get into fights with other people your own age? Yes/No

There are a number of other social skills questionnaires often used in research and easy to use in practice, for example the Rathus Assertiveness Schedule (Rathus, 1973), the Gambrill-Richey Assertion Inventory (Gambrill and Richey, 1975) and scales for assessing 'social-evaluative anxiety' (Watson and Friend, 1969).

The Beck Depression Inventory (reproduced in Lewinsohn *et al.*, 1978) is another well-tested questionnaire of the self-report variety. It can be used to assess level of depression and to pinpoint particular aspects such as sense of failure or indecisiveness.

Rutter's checklist of child behaviour problems (Rutter *et al.*, 1970) is a useful instrument to help pinpoint problems, and to decide how serious the concern is, as is Eyeberg's Child Behavior Inventory (1980).

Lastly, we commend a set of questionnaires devised by Walter Hudson. They are reproduced in full in Fischer (1978) and Bloom and Fischer (1982) and cover marital satisfaction, contentment, self-image, sexual relationships, relationships with children, relationships with mother or father and peer relationships. The client is presented with a series of statements, for example, 'My children get on my nerves', and rates them on a 5-point scale.

Our selection is very far indeed from being comprehensive but we hope you will consider these instruments as a start.

Universal rating scales

Target complaints procedure

If you are not successful in your search for an easy-to-use measure that seems to fit your client and target problem, a useful alternative is the Target Complaints Procedure. It is certainly subjective, but has been shown to correlate with a variety of other ratings in a variety of client problems. The client ranks his problems in order of priority and then rates each one on a 13-point severity scale.

No Problem |__|__|__|__|__|__|__|__|__|__|__|__| Very Severe
(Orme and Gillespie, 1981).

SUDS

Another individualised subjective measure that is very easy to use is the SUDS (Subjective Units of Discomfort scale). The client rates his discomfort in a particular situation on a scale from 0 (no discomfort at all) to 100 (extreme discomfort).

Here is an example of a frequency count/diary/SUDS format.

| *Times I Went Out* | | | Anxiety level |
Date	*No of times*	*How far?*	*(SUDS)*
May 6	2	1 corner shop	30
		2 park with dog	20
May 7	1	1 park with dog	15
May 8	2	1 park with dog	10
		2 bus stop with J	10
May 9	2	1 park with dog	0
		2 school gate	20

Figure 4.16

To sum up: interviews and summaries of interviews have always been central to social work, and without wanting to denigrate them, we feel that a broader approach to assessment and recording is appropriate in view of the many technical advances in this field. In particular, we suggest that you use repeatable measures to collect hard data if at all possible. This will pay dividends – for your client, for your own job satisfaction, for your agency, and (a longer shot, this) for the increase in our knowledge of what works. In our section on evaluation we shall return to this matter of repeatable measures and hard data.

FORMULATING THE PROBLEM

By the end of assessment, you should have assembled the following: an overview of a client's difficulties and assets; a general picture of lifestyle and social background; and a more detailed description of the problem that is to be your main focus. You now require a formulation of the problem. In formulation, you are summarising key points from the data you have obtained, and placing them in a framework that suggests future action. Thus, a typical formulation would include: a brief description of the presenting problem; your view as to whether it or some other problem should be addressed; some comment on what may have caused and what might be maintaining the problem; and a proposal about intervention with reference to resources available.

Beginning with the less formal, here is an example of a case formulation as part of the information given to foster parents.

Moira has not learned to ask nicely – she just grabs, and if the grab is unsuccessful she yells and throws herself about. Probably people have not been consistent in their handling of Moira: sometimes they have punished or ignored this behaviour but at other times they have let it get her what she wanted. This means that she is unlikely to give up easily. It will probably help a lot if you make a big effort to show her that asking nicely is well worth her while, and to praise the other children in front of Moira for asking nicely.

Next, formulations of two cases that were taken on for behavioural intervention. To save space, we have omitted a lot of detail, concentrating on the specifically behavioural part of the formulation, showing the use made of learning principles and of the behavioural analysis that has formed part of the assessment process.

Mrs White's family are particularly upset about her delusional accounts of rats and snakes, her refusal to go out of doors, and the effects all this has on their own social life. It appears that she has long since lost the habit of asking other people about themselves and has ceased shopping and travelling on buses. An additional problem that came to light is that she does not eat all day, and constantly complains of feeling 'weak'. My observations indicate that she gets much positive attention for her delusional talk and her complaints, even though they drive visitors away. The family do not enquire about her eating habits, nor do they try to 'make it worth her while' to re-develop the skills she has lost. They do show affection for her, however, and said they would welcome help, even if this required quite a lot of time and effort on their part. Mrs White herself said she would like more visits from me, and that she misses 'the old days' when she was on top of the housework and not such a burden on everyone.

Mr and Mrs Kent have two or three rows a week, sometimes resulting in their not talking to each other for several days at a time. The most frequent cause is their disagreement over how to handle their teenage son, Andy. Andy is unemployed, and often fails to organise his supplementary benefit. He demands or else just takes money from his mother. His father sometimes hits him, and shouts at Mrs Kent for giving in to him. Andy refuses to meet with me, but Mr and Mrs Kent have already shown that they are able to analyse Andy's behaviour: no real incentives for claiming his benefit or indeed taking responsibility for getting the means to do the things he likes (going out to rock concerts in town, visiting friends, darts). And their own behaviour: Mrs Kent finds it easier to be 'soft' with Andy, though she always regrets it when the row with Mr Kent begins. Mr Kent agrees that he is not around when Andy gets money from his mother; all he does is lose his temper after the event. The couple are willing to begin to think of ways of altering the contingencies for Andy, such as rewarding him for appropriate behaviour and ensuring that inappropriate behaviour does not pay off. Mr Kent is prepared to try to carry out some alternative behaviour to shouting and physical violence, such as leaving the scene for a set time.

We conclude with an excerpt from a case formulation included in a court report on a family where child abuse was suspected. The report recommended that surveillance and support to the family would be appropriate, but considered that the accusations against the parents were not proven. Regarding the mother of a child who was thought to be 'at risk':

Observations indicate that her general management methods are effective and non-punitive. As to the suggestion that her emotional attitude to the child is abnormal, our observation of the two of them in the day centre suggests that:
(1) J is not an emotionally demonstrative child and

(2) Recognising this, his mother does not push a great deal of physical affection on him.

(Contrast this with comments by another worker: 'While there is no evidence of physical abuse, the emotional deprivation that J is experiencing is hard to assess'.)
Regarding the father:

> Observations of the children's interaction with their father indicate a willingness to approach him, sit on his knee etc . . . There is no doubt that he has been verbally abusive to his wife and to professionals, the former in the context of stress and heavy drinking, the latter after he was accused of child abuse. I have not however seen any evidence to suggest that he has a generally 'aggressive' personality.

SETTING GOALS AND SELECTING A METHOD OF INTERVENTION

Goals

In many cases, the assessment and the formulation indicate both the goals to be aimed for and the methods that should be employed to achieve them. Goals will emerge from the problem specification: more of something that is lacking or less of something that is not wanted. If Mary does not go out and do her shopping then the goal will be framed in terms of going out shopping. If Jude drinks too much, then the goal will be reduction or elimination of drinking alcohol. But it may be equally effective to seek an increase in an alternative and incompatible behaviour: for instance, instead of focusing on less sobbing and less depressive talk, it would usually be better to aim for an increase in enjoyable activities and cheerful, interesting talk.

A further refinement in setting goals is to specify sub-goals, or way-stages towards the desired state of affairs: for Mary, just going out a couple of times a week would constitute some improvement; for Jude, drinking only at certain times of the day; for our depressed client, just one evening spent doing something pleasant per week. In working with children's behaviour problems, a small decrease in, say, disturbing parents at night, or an increase in dry nights would be a suitable initial goal. The point of this is to build in some reinforcement for initial efforts and a possible increase in feelings of mastery – for worker and client alike.

Selecting a method of intervention

Selecting a method follows from the review of goals. Our first and most useful piece of advice is that you consult the literature – not just the remaining chapters of this book, but the many other, and fatter, books, and the behavioural journals – looking in their indexes for items on the type of problem, the type of client, and the possible complications that might attach to any particular method of work. Advice from more experienced workers will make the task easier. You should remember, however, that there are no straightforward 'recipes': you have to adapt whatever methods you are considering to the specific characteristics of each case according to the individual behavioural analysis and the assets, resources and wishes of the individual client. A further set of constraints and opportunities lies in the skills you yourself can bring to the work, and the resources that you are able to muster. Having selected a method, be sure you are going to be able to carry it through!

Resources available to the social worker

Material resources. We have already considered the client's own resources. A lot of ingenuity and ability to communicate your confidence in what you are planning (plus some skills in arm-twisting) should help you to obtain more resources from elsewhere. For example, has your agency got funds for the general purpose of preventing reception into care? A few pounds will go a long way if used to supply small tangible rewards, buy stars for a star chart, contribute towards some outings or buy an alarm clock for a family with difficulties in getting up on time. After all, such expenses are as nothing compared to the cost of many Intermediate Treatment projects with their expensive equipment and travel. Are there some toys stashed away somewhere in an office cupboard? (Incidentally, tact should be exercised in working with parents who might, quite appropriately, prefer to be the providers of reinforcers.)

Some behavioural workers have managed to tap resources in the wider community. For example, the Shape Project for young offenders has negotiated the opportunity to use university sports facilities. Community centres, schools or colleges may be willing to lend their premises and equipment.

Video machines and tape recorders – as methods of recording, for feedback, and simply as reinforcement (e.g. making and showing a film of the mothers' and toddlers' group or the street party) can be borrowed if not already part of the agency's regular tools of trade.

Time is another crucial consideration. Although total worker time is unlikely to be greater than for other kinds of intensive social work intervention, behavioural programmes do often require many hours' work concentrated into a short time-span. Some behavioural practitioners take several hours over the first assessment session. An operant extinction programme can cause a temporary worsening of the problem and will be extremely stressful for parents trying to operate it: it is wise to visit daily for the first few days. Home observations are very time-consuming, and may have to take place when you are not normally working, e.g. evenings or early morning. In some circumstances telephone calls can substitute: this is a good way of collecting daily data or simply encouraging the client with his tasks.

People. A family aide or a volunteer can be most helpful in sharing the work. A secretary helped one of us with many cases: phoning to ask for progress reports, giving positive reinforcement over the phone – and sometimes mild punishment ('Mrs Hudson will be disappointed').

Some workers in the USA have brought in popular and successful people to act as models: and volunteers can help in innumerable ways – as models, as providers of reinforcement, and as 'partners' for social skills practice. For example, one of us acted as a 'date' for a young man receiving social skills training (social work students may be particularly suitable for this kind of helping, since they are likely to give the client an easier time). Failure hurts people (both clients and social workers!) so we strongly recommend that you check, in advance of coming to an agreement with your client, whether you have sufficient resources to offer the kind of help your client needs.

WORKER- CLIENT AGREEMENTS

After you have completed your assessment and formulation, and selected procedures to tackle your clients' problems, you will want to consider whether to set down a formal agreement or contract. Such agreements are quite usual in behavioural work, and are a 'piece of behaviourism' that has been taken up by social workers who would not call themselves 'behavioural'.

A formal agreement has several advantages. It will clarify what is expected of both the professional and the client; and it will prepare the client for what lies ahead – both of these features are examples of what is sometimes called 'pre-therapy training', a factor shown to enhance the effectiveness of intervention. It will provide a structure to the work to be done together – yet another aspect of effective helping. The agreement will also serve to motivate both parties: this is because our learning history usually causes us to stick to our word, particularly if it is written down, even if there is no legal sanction. Lastly, the written agreement serves as a reminder of what is intended and hoped for, and as a basis for later evaluation of what has been achieved.

Nevertheless, some workers are doubtful about the appropriateness of formal agreements, and certainly they are not suitable in all cases. Some clients are likely to feel intimidated or suspicious, thinking that they are being coerced into signing. Certainly, it is as well to bear in mind the unequal power relationship that usually exists between worker and client, and to consider the possibility of a somewhat less formal agreement, perhaps simply a letter stating what is being offered and what will be asked of the client.

The key features of the typical behavioural worker–client agreement are that it should be written, and that it should spell out goals, intervention method, and the behaviours of both worker and client. Common additional items are number and duration of meetings, length of contact, confidentiality (particularly important in groupwork), homework assignments and record-keeping.

Although there are some similarities with the contracts described under 'Procedures' (pp.150–5) the worker–client agreement differs from the family contract in that it does not aim for 'reciprocity' of efforts in quite the same way, since the goal is to improve some problem of the client's rather than a shared relationship problem. And of course, there are very few sanctions or bonuses to be built into it: the client is rarely in a position either to reward or to punish the worker; and the consequences for the client of keeping to the agreement or not are mainly to do with the success or failure of the programme. (Sheldon, 1980, refers to the 'on your head be it' variety).

There follow some examples of agreements ranging from the informal and simple to the formal and complicated.
First a letter:

Dear Mr and Mrs Poole
This is the letter I said I'd send summing up what we decided last week. Please tell me if you think I have got any of it wrong or left anything out.

We agreed to meet every Thursday at 2.15 (Mr Poole will be there whenever he can get time off work). I will be with you for at least one and a half hours. I will help you to learn and practise techniques to help you cope with feelings of anxiety: ways of relaxing and changing what you say to yourself. We will spend some time out of the house, so that I can help you in a real-life situation.

You will also practise at home and out of the house with Mr Poole at least once every day for 1 hour. You will keep a diary of what you do and how you feel for us to examine together each time I visit.

I am confident that if we keep to this arrangement we can expect you to be going out on your own several times a week, and feeling little or no anxiety about it (not more than 15 on your scale) by the time our weekly sessions cease, at the end of July.

Signed ....

Next, a very simple agreement:

I agree to come to all 9 weekly sessions of our Social Skills Group. I will co-operate in practising skills and role-playing and will do the preparation assigned between meetings. I will try to support the other members of the group and not take up more than my fair share of the group's time. I will avoid criticism or joking that might not be helpful to any fellow member. I understand that ....
[names of workers] will attend each meeting punctually, prepare

for meetings, and contribute all they can to the working of the group.

Signature .... Date ....

(Source: Burgess *et al.*, 1980)

Lastly, an example of a family contract and worker–client agreement combined:

AGREEMENT between   Mrs L Crowe
                     Marie Crowe
                     Joan Rees, Probation Officer

This AGREEMENT is effective from January 10, 1980 and will run until March 8 (10 weeks). The overall aim is to help Mrs Crowe and Marie to get along better together.

Mrs Crowe agrees to
—be at home to see Miss Rees each week at the pre-arranged time
—remind Marie to stay in
—keep to the programme agreed weekly with Marie and Miss Rees
—if Marie keeps to the weekly programme Mrs Crowe will take her to London and buy her a dress (cost up to £20) on Saturday March 6 [Bonus Clause]

Marie Crowe agrees to
—be at home to see Miss Rees each week at the pre-arranged time
—remind her mother to stay in
—keep to the programme agreed weekly with her mother and Miss Rees

Joan Rees agrees to
—visit Marie and Mrs Crowe each week at the pre-arranged time
—offer help with any problem that we all three agree is relevant to the overall aims of this AGREEMENT
—if Mrs Crowe keeps to the weekly programme Miss Rees will provide transport to Oxford Station on Saturday March 6 [Bonus Clause] If any party breaks the AGREEMENT on two occasions, the AGREEMENT will be reconsidered. If any party wishes to re-negotiate the AGREEMENT this must be done at the weekly meeting.

[The weekly programmes are mini-contracts which include commitments concerning regular pocket money, swearing by Marie
and nagging and criticism by Mrs Crowe.]
Signed ....
....
....

No account of worker–client agreements would be complete
without reference to the study by Stein, Gambrill and Wiltse (1978) of
decision-making in cases of child abuse or neglect. Contracts between
the social workers and the natural parents formed the basis of the
work of the experimental team. These spelled out what was expected
of the parents, and the workers agreed to advise the court to return
the children to their care if the parents fulfilled their part. The
contracts specified outcome goals (return of the child), sub-goals that
would have to be achieved in order to attain this outcome, time-limits
and the responsibilities of workers and clients. Attached to these
basic contracts were a series of 'schedules' which specified the
behaviour-change plans, covering such behaviours as excessive use of
drugs or alcohol, housekeeping, and parent–child interaction. The
children in the behavioural contracts group were significantly more
likely than those in the control group to be taken out of temporary
placements and either returned home or placed in permanent care.
We have heard the Alameda Project described as 'coercive' – to that
we would simply reply that the position of these parents should be
contrasted with that of others who, generally speaking, get no clear
answer to the question, 'What do I have to do to get my child back?'.
   In summary, we believe that there is sufficient evidence, direct and
indirect, to warrant the use of a written agreement with your client if it
is ethical and practicable to produce one. And – drawing on
experience – we add some rather basic advice: make sure that each
person has a copy and refer to it frequently!
   This concludes our overview of the early stages of behavioural
social work. We have looked at assessment, recording, selection of
procedures and worker–client agreements. We have skimmed over a
number of issues that are as crucial to behavioural as to other forms
of social work: forming a relationship, indicating concern and
empathy, offering hope, and preparing the client for the work to be
done together. Implicit in the approach is a particular kind of role
relationship between the worker and the client: that of teacher and

trainee. This means that insofar as the client is interested in and able to absorb the theory, the empirical rationale and the techniques of behavioural work, he should be provided with the opportunity to do so. In practical terms, this means explaining every step, and enlisting the client's help in analysing behaviour and planning the programme. Handouts and the loan of books or tapes will be appropriate for some people. The relationship between worker and client is characterised by openness: many behavioural practitioners make a point of sharing the record-keeping and showing the client whatever is written down. In these ways it should be possible, first, to avoid the problem of clients being kept in the dark, and, secondly, to give clients not just help with a current difficulty but also a means of dealing with future difficulties without having to become a client again.

EVALUATION

The baseline

The initial measurement of the target problem (or problems) is called the baseline. This serves a very central purpose in behavioural work – indeed, some would claim that the baseline is the hallmark of good behavioural practice. The baseline provides a criterion against which one can later judge the effectiveness of the intervention. We measure the initial state of affairs, begin intervention, and go on measuring at intervals throughout the programme. If the problem starts to improve after the programme begins and goes on improving, then we have reason to believe that this programme is worth continuing with. When the goals agreed at the start have been achieved, then we can make plans for ensuring that the improvement will hold, and then we can close the case. If, on the other hand, our measurements tell us that things are remaining the same or getting worse, then we must try something different, or acknowledge this failure and stop wasting the client's and the agency's time on this particular intervention.

We reproduce below some graphs that begin with a baseline. The graphs demonstrate the value of a baseline followed by repeated measurements during intervention in determining whether a problem is getting better (or worse).

Notice that our first example has a stable baseline – that is, the behaviour rate does not vary much before the intervention begins.

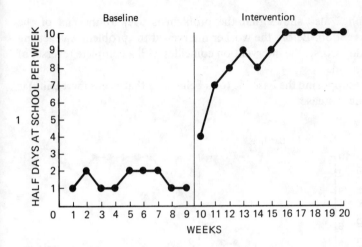

Figure 4.17

Graph 1 gives some encouraging information: a problem exists and is not showing any signs of getting better; soon after intervention begins, there is a rapid change in the desired direction.

Now suppose that the baseline (for a behaviour that needs increasing) is on the decrease before intervention begins:

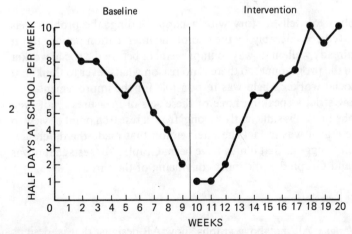

Figure 4.18

Graph 2 also shows that the problem is over at the end of the intervention. Before the worker intervened the problem was getting steadily worse; the intervention coincides with a complete reversal of this trend.

Or supposing the baseline (of a behaviour that needs increasing) is on the increase:

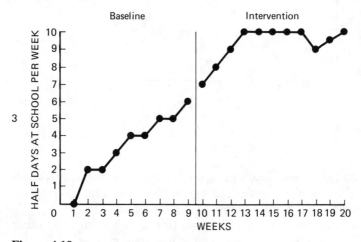

Figure 4.19

Graph 3 too tells a story with a happy ending: the problem has improved considerably by the end of the intervention period. But it was already well on its way to improvement before the social worker began the programme, so there is no reason whatsoever to think that the social worker's help was responsible for the improvement.

Now strictly speaking none of these sets of measures – not even Graphs 1 or 2 – is sufficiently 'strong' from a research point of view to prove that it was in fact the intervention that made the difference. Graph 1 suggests that it may have been, Graph 3 suggests that it was not, and Graph 2 is the most convincing of the three.

Single case designs

AB designs All the above graphs show AB designs, that is, designs that require only measurements of a single behaviour before and after intervention begins. We may be pleased with what they show, but it is not scientifically respectable to credit ourselves with having brought it about. Nevertheless, an AB design is a vast improvement on the more subjective 'evaluation' which lacks a baseline (or, indeed, any kind of progress measure).

Multiple Baseline designs There are many more complex single case research designs. We recommend particularly the Multiple-Baseline design. This is actually a series of AB designs used together. One kind of Multiple Baseline design involves intervening with different behaviours, one after another (i.e. at different times); and looking at the repeated measures during baseline and intervention to see whether improvement coincides in time with the start of intervention. This is called a Multiple-Baseline-Across-Behaviours Design, and the following three graphs show this particular design (Figure 4.20).

Instead of looking at separate behaviours of a single client or family, you could look at a single behaviour in separate settings – such as school, home, with father and with grandmother (Multiple-Baseline-across-Settings Design). Or at a single behaviour in a series of clients – first intervening with Jim, then Mary, then Alphonsine (Multiple-Baseline-across-Clients design).

A problem with the Multiple-Baseline design is that if the clients influence each other's behaviour (e.g. children in the same family), if the behaviours are interconnected (e.g. aggressive talk and physical aggression), or if behaviour in one setting generalises to another setting (e.g. being disobedient at home and in the shops), then you will find that the behaviour that is being baselined is changing before you come to intervene – out of turn, as it were.

If this had happened in our example of a Multiple-Baseline-across-Behaviours design, 'tasks per day' would have begun to increase *after* 'times up by noon' had begun to increase but *before* intervention with tasks had started. If this occurs, you will not be able to say with certainty that your intervention method is responsible for the improvement. Look at the baselines to check this out: if they remain stable until you intervene with the behaviours they are measuring, then the Multiple-Baseline design is doing its job. Changes related closely in time to each sequential intervention do suggest that the improvement is not merely coincidence or caused by some other unknown influence: they strongly suggest that social work intervention is having an impact.

We do not consider the further variations on this theme to be

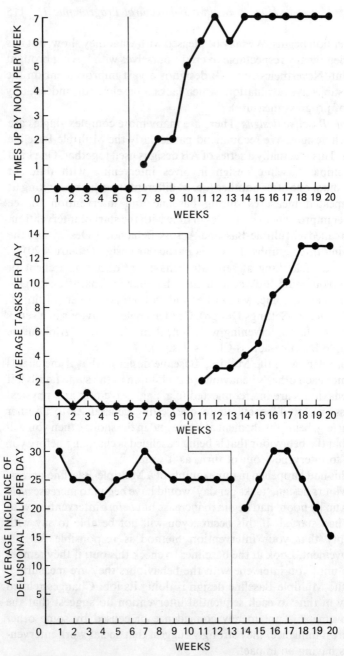

Figure 4.20 *Multiple-Baseline-across-Behaviours Design*

appropriate for an introductory text, and it is willingness to try out these ideas that we want to encourage, not avoidance of them because they seem to demand too much of the hard-pressed social worker. We do suggest, though, that after some experience with AB and Multiple Baseline designs, you consult some of the literature suggested in the Appendix and try to develop this aspect of your behavioural work. More social work examples of single case experiments would help to build up the store of knowledge of behavioural workers in all professions: the bulk of the literature has tended to reflect the fact that single case researchers have mainly worked in structured settings and with less complex problems than social workers typically have to deal with.

Footnote on follow-up

Many behavioural programmes can both help with present difficulties and also impart skills that might help your client avoid the need for further contact. Nevertheless, you should not just close the case: you should arrange to see the client again (or at least write or phone him) after a minimum period of three months. Ideally, the client should continue to collect information about the problem in the same way as during assessment and intervention; failing that, a brief re-assessment is needed. This will tell you whether the improvement you achieved was durable, whether there have been even more improvements, or whether things are getting worse again. If the latter, then 'booster' sessions or an entirely new programme might have to be considered.

Follow-up, then, is another matter to agree with your client either at the time of the original working agreement or when the programme ends. Follow-up is another aspect of behavioural work with professional–ethical implications.

5

Behavioural Intervention Procedures I: Respondent and Operant Procedures

In Chapter 2 we introduced the learning theory principles from which the behavioural intervention procedures have been derived. The behaviour that is influenced may be visible, or it may be covert (feelings and thoughts). And it need not be our clients' behaviour, it can just as well be our own or our associates' or the behaviour of other people in our clients' lives. In unitary approach language: the target system need not be the same as the client system.

Behavioural procedures are used deliberately by professionals, but they are often seen in action (not used deliberately and not always appropriately) in families and other groups. This aspect of the person's current situation is an important part of assessment information: we have referred to it under assessment, and will do so repeatedly in this chapter.

We give descriptions of the most common procedures under the following headings:

(in this chapter)
—procedures based on respondent (classical) learning principles
—procedures based on operant learning principles
(in the next chapter)
—modelling, based on social learning theory
—self-management, covert and cognitive approaches
—combinations of procedures.

These divisions are of necessity arbitrary and do not by any means reflect the realities of behavioural work; procedures are very rarely used singly – they are put together in programmes according to individual requirements. In particular, we must emphasise that *procedures that include positive reinforcement should be used in every case*. Even when the central problem is 'too much of something – something to be got rid of', alternatives to the unwanted behaviour must be built up so that the person gains from the intervention and obtains more, not less, positive reinforcement than he did beforehand. The infuriating child, the old person who makes life a misery for his family, the committee member who wastes everyone's time, and the community group member who makes racist remarks are all candidates for this: one of behaviour modification's best slogans is 'Catch the customer doing something right'.

RESPONDENT PROCEDURES

These procedures are derived from research into behaviour over which we normally feel we have no control, such as feelings of anxiety or anger or sexual arousal; and into the way these feelings become associated with particular stimuli or 'triggers', for example, you feel upset at the sight of a person who has ill-treated you or a person who resembles him or her. The key principle is to break the connection between stimulus and unwanted or maladaptive response, and institute a new, desirable response.

Relaxation training

Relaxation sets the scene for methods that require the client to produce mental images, for example traditional desensitisation and covert sensitisation (see below). But relaxation training can be a treatment technique in its own right. Many people find it a pleasant procedure; and it can be helpful for such problems as tension headaches and insomnia, and a useful component of self-management programmes for coping with anxiety or anger. The method may be familiar to female social workers and their clients from antenatal classes.

Here is an excerpt from a typical set of relaxation instructions: 'Make yourself comfortable . . . Now make a tight fist with your right hand and tense the muscles of your lower forearm . . . Hold it

. . . and let the tension go . . . Relax . . . Notice the difference between tension and relaxation . . .'

This process continues with the upper arm, the other arm, the forehead, face, neck, chest, shoulders and back, stomach, legs and feet and buttocks. The client is asked to concentrate on slowish, fairly deep and regular breathing. It is helpful to provide written relaxation instructions to be delivered by someone else, or a tape to use at home.

Once the client has mastered this rather long-drawn-out relaxation method, the instructions about tensing the muscles are dropped, and gradually the whole process is shortened. When the training is successful, the person eventually learns to relax very quickly, perhaps just focusing on one set of muscles that are particularly tense.

People vary considerably as to how long it takes them to learn the skill of relaxation: some require weeks of practice. (For more detailed advice on how to conduct relaxation training, see Stern, 1978; Gambrill, 1977; Cormier and Cormier, 1979.)

Exposure methods

The number of variations of exposure treatment makes the literature extremely confusing, and this is compounded by the fact that there is lively disagreement about why these methods work. Happily, there is convincing evidence that they *do* work (at least for the treatment of fears and phobias). They are also coming into use in dealing with sexual problems and problems of anger-control.

Systematic desensitisation

This is the oldest respondent method. It entails repeatedly pairing a new, unproblematic response with a stimulus that has previously aroused unpleasant feelings until the problem response has been ousted by the new one. Thus, you might seek to establish a feeling of calm in place of anxiety, or amusement instead of anger, to the extent that when the person meets with the stimulus that once triggered a feeling of upset, she now reacts with the alternative feeling.

Systematic desensitisation involves four steps.

Step 1 – The hierarchy The worker and client together work out a list of situations from one that is easy to cope with (1) to one that is most upsetting (9). For example:

(1) Baby spits out food.
(2) Baby dribbles and has a dirty face.
(3) You feel tired and baby needs changing.
(4) Baby vomits on your best blouse.
(5) Dirty nappy – and you have just changed her.
(6) Baby doesn't stop crying when you pick her up.
(7) Baby red-faced and has been yelling for 30 minutes.
(8) Baby red-faced and has been yelling for 30 minutes. Clean nappy has been dirtied immediately.
(9) Baby red-faced and has been yelling for 30 minutes. Clean nappy dirtied immediately. You want to look nice and feel alert for an important appointment tomorrow. It is 4.00 am.

To complete such a list the client needs to describe a sample of problem situations clearly and rank them. You also have to check that the client is able to *imagine* them. All of this takes time – perhaps several hours – and even so, you may have to make changes later.

Step 2 – Relaxation The next step is teaching the client to relax, using the method described above.

Step 3 – Imaginal exposure In Step 3 the client imagines the situations in her hierarchy while relaxing. She starts with the easiest, signalling to the worker (for example, raising a finger) when she has a clear picture in her mind. The worker then asks her to imagine the next situation. If the client loses her feeling of relaxation, she signals that this has happened, and the worker tells her to drop the disturbing image and relax again (perhaps facilitating this by imagining herself lying on a beach, for example). They then return to the situation that is one step easier.

One very important point about the use of hierarchy: do not allow the session to end with the client failing on an item. The danger here is that her anxiety or anger will be exacerbated and will get worse during the interval between appointments; so make sure that when you part, she has achieved something and is still feeling calm.

Step 4 – Practice in the real situation The central issue is that somehow or other *you must get the client back into the upsetting situation.*

There are several ways of achieving this. One way is to follow each item covered successfully in imagination with real-life (*in vivo*) practice in the same situation; and for this you need a hierarchy that can be produced to order in real life. A hierarchy allowing for item-by-item real-life practice after exposure in imagination might look like this:

(1) Rocking baby in pram.
(2) Sitting close to baby, and touching her face and hands.
(3) Holding baby with helper nearby.
(4) Holding baby with helper outside room.
(5) Changing baby with assistance.
(6) Changing baby, with helper some way off.

Sometimes the client will defy all efforts to teach her relaxation skills or home circumstances may make practice impossible. If this is the case, some alternative is needed: possibilities include simply being with a person you trust, sucking sweets, even whistling or singing. When using some of these alternatives, you will have to abandon the use of the hierarchy in imagination. This is no cause for concern; though relaxation and imagining may help some clients, making the programme easier to cope with, traditional desensitisation has, to a large extent, been superceded by *in vivo* exposure.

Graduated in vivo *exposure without exposure in imagination*

Most experts nowadays consider that for almost every anxiety problem you can dispense with the imagining (and relaxation) altogether and just work on a short real-life hierarchy (see, for example, Marks, 1978). Here is an example:

(1) Walking past school (with social worker, then alone).
(2) Standing outside school at weekend (with social worker, then alone).
(3) In school with social worker at weekend.
(4) In classroom with teacher at weekend.
(5) In playground with social worker on schoolday.
(6) In school building on schoolday but not in class.
(7) In school, in class with other children.

The approach most favoured nowadays is graduated exposure *in vivo*. A short hierarchy is produced, and the client starts with the most difficult item she can manage. For example, in a case of agoraphobia, much effort is put into a fairly rapid programme, usually with the worker as escort initially, keeping further and further away until the client can cope entirely alone. Sessions should last at least an hour, preferably two, and should always end on a note of success, never at a point of high anxiety. Given that there has been detailed assessment and the client's own self-assessment is carefully listened to, this approach can be used very readily by social workers in the community.

Aversion therapy

Social workers are extremely unlikely to become involved in aversion therapy but we include a brief comment for the sake of completeness. Opponents of behavioural approaches tend, mistakenly, to view it (along with punishment, an operant procedure) as a typical behaviour therapy procedure.

Aversion therapy is falling into disuse. It was developed for the treatment of such conditions as alcoholism and has in fact done rather badly from the effectiveness point of view. It is still used for certain clients whose problem has not responded to other methods, and who are willing to participate – some sex offenders fall into this category.

The client is given either drugs to make him sick or a mild electric shock when on the point of performing the undesired behaviour (in reality or in imagination). When the procedure is effective, it is assumed to be because the behaviour becomes associated with the unpleasant feeling by a process of classical conditioning.

Bell and pad (treatment of bedwetting)

The equipment usually consists of a pad which detects moisture, and a bell or buzzer that wakes the child when he begins to urinate; personally-worn equipment working on the same principle is also available. Besides arousing the child, the noise causes him to contract his muscles and stop the flow of urine. He then gets up and goes to the toilet. After repeated association of full bladder, waking up and contracting the muscles, these three events become permanently linked and the bell can be phased out. (Further details concerning the use of this procedure are given in Chapter 8.)

Altering the antecedents of respondent behaviour

Often it is appropriate to try to change the antecedents of respondent behaviour, as well as or instead of the behaviour itself. Talking soothingly to a child before he enters a frightening situation, avoiding confrontation with a man who may become aggressive, helping a couple receiving sex therapy to identify 'turn-ons' and 'turn-offs' are fairly straightforward examples.

In these cases, it would be desirable also to consider other ways of modifying the child's anxiety, the man's bad temper and the couple's sexual problems. But consider the teenager who gets angry when he is unfairly criticised by his father, or the mother who feels at the end of her tether when her child disobeys her for the umpteenth time. In these cases desensitisation to the upsetting situation is not appropriate: the main focus of intervention must be the behaviour of the other people who trigger the client's anger. With anxiety, the trigger may be threats or unrealistically high demands: for example, a child may develop a terror of examinations because of his parents' insistence that he should always get 'A's. One client, who had had apparently successful treatment for agoraphobia carried out from the clinic, was still terrified of leaving her flat; and considering the high crime rate in her district and the fact that she was frail and elderly, it was a necessary part of the social work task to help her find another place to live.

These examples point to a key distinction: is the anxiety realistic? Is the anger appropriate? (We are, of course, referring to the *feeling*, and not to overt aggressive behaviour which may sometimes be effective and acceptable but is more often self-defeating and antisocial.)

OPERANT PROCEDURES TO INCREASE OR TEACH BEHAVIOURS

Most of the following procedures involve a rearrangement of the consequences of behaviour (also known as 'contingency management').

Positive reinforcement

The most important of all the behavioural procedures, this has many variations, only the most common of which are described here. It means arranging for some carefully chosen positive consequence (the reinforcer) to follow a specific behaviour. The consequence must be a thing or event that has the effect of causing a subsequent increase in the behaviour in question. After William has cleared his toys away, his mother reads him a story – if toy-clearing increases, then story-reading is a reinforcer. Mrs Green's social worker says 'Uh-huh . . . now that's very valuable information' after Mrs Green talks about her childhood – if talking about childhood increases, then the worker's comment is a reinforcer. A consequence is only a *potential* reinforcer until it is proved to be effective.

Types of reinforcer

Each person is different in regard to what will serve as a reinforcer for his behaviour. One way of classifying reinforcers is to divide them into three groups: social reinforcers, tangible and activity reinforcers, and generalised reinforcers.

(1) *Social reinforcers* – for example smiles, praise, attention. These work for most of us, but this depends on one's learning history and on who delivers the social reinforcer. Some children do not respond to praise from a grown-up, though they are much influenced by praise from their friends; and most of us could name people whose praise matters to us a great deal, and others whose praise is the last thing we want. But, overall, social reinforcers are immensely powerful. Very often, an effective programme can be devised relying on these reinforcers alone. For instance, Jim thanks Mary each time she helps him with repair jobs; Pete's mother praises him for tolerating his little sister's pestering and for letting her share his toys; the chairperson acknowledges each member's contribution; the team leader comments favourably on the social workers' willingness to take on 'unpromising cases'.

(2) *Tangible and activity reinforcers* – for example, sweets, crisps and cigarettes; swimming and trips to the cinema. Although it would be a mistake to make confident generalisations about this, it is likely that tangible reinforcers will play a major role in work with younger children and with some severely mentally handicapped people. For example, young children may be toilet trained using small treats such as crisps for sitting on the potty. Activity reinforcers have a wider

appeal: ten-year-old Jack gets a game of football with his father after doing his Saturday jobs; Mrs Brown gets an afternoon down-town with a friend after following her child management programme meticulously.

(3) *Generalised reinforcers.* These include money, stars, points and tokens. They can be exchanged for a wide range of 'back-up' reinforcers, and are often to be preferred because of the choice they permit and because there is no risk of satiation. Generalised reinforcers have the great advantage of being easy to deliver immediately after behaviour occurs, whereas it is often not possible or desirable to provide exactly the reinforcer that is wanted at that precise moment.

The familiar star chart is an example of a positive reinforcement programme using generalised reinforcers: The younger the child, the more value there is in making the chart attractive and amusing, so that the child will want to show it to other people and take pride and pleasure in his progress. If possible, the design should reflect some interest of his, or illustrate the behaviour or the reinforcers involved. For instance, Peter is saving up for a football, and will earn outings to the local game with his father. His chart could look like this:

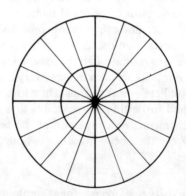

Each section represents 100 points, to be coloured in as he earns them. A quarter of the ball (8 sections) earns him a game, and the whole thing (32 sections) earns the actual football.

Mary wants a pair of fluorescent socks. They will cost her 20 stars.

$*$	$*$	$*$							

You get one star for every night you get to bed by eight, washed, in pyjamas, with no arguing.

Timing of reinforcement

In order to get the behaviour established in the first place, you should ensure that the reinforcer is given *immediately* after the behaviour, and *consistently*, that is, every time the behaviour happens. A system with points or tokens makes these criteria easier to meet, since it would be awkward to offer some kinds of reinforcer immediately and consistently – for example, activity reinforcers like trips to the cinema or even certain tangible reinforcers like baked potatoes. However, in many situations, 'immediacy' is a counsel of perfection, and except for very young children and severely handicapped people some delay will not seriously detract from the programme's effectiveness. What is needed here is a 'gap-bridging' word of praise or promise: 'Well done. That will go towards earning you a choice of pudding on Sunday.'

Once the behaviour is occurring at a satisfactory frequency, the reinforcers need to be thinned out gradually: this is because of the particular potency of intermittent reinforcement in maintaining behaviour (making it very hard to extinguish), and also, of course, because it is essential that the behaviour pattern should hold in the real world where intermittent reinforcement is common and consistent reinforcement is unusual, to say the least. The gradual change in the frequency of reinforcement could be introduced to a child like this; 'Now you are doing so well and being so grown-up about getting ready for bed, we'll give you surprises instead of rewards every single night . . .' An adult could be told that reinforcement will gradually become more 'natural'. You must go on monitoring the changed behaviour very closely while the reinforcers are being thinned out; if there is a drop in frequency the thinning out has probably not been gradual enough, and it will be necessary to return to the previous rate of reinforcement.

Pairing of reinforcers

If tangible or token reinforcers have been used, it is important to try to ensure that these are superseded by social reinforcers, if at all possible. This is done by pairing the tangible with the intangible: saying 'well done' or giving a child a hug, along with the token or sweet. The aim is to get the person to associate the two sorts of reinforcer until social reinforcement becomes effective by itself. If this is achieved, you have brought the client into a more natural relationship with his environment, which will support the new behaviour pattern without the aid of a contrived programme.

Positive reinforcement is the procedure most often used with a vast range of problems, where there is a shortage or absence of any desirable behaviour of the type we usually classify as 'voluntary'. But it plays a part in every behavioural intervention of every description, if only to maintain or increase the client's participation in the work.

To repeat some of what we said about 'motivation' (p.65–9) we should note that incentives – that is, *future rewards* – are another way of influencing the behaviour of 'future-orientated' human beings. As Bandura (1977) points out, people can and often do work for potential rewards that they have not yet experienced. However, in the cases we have to help with, some reinforcement that 'bridges the gap' is usually essential. Yet another variation – very commonly found in everyday life – is the giving of a *reward for future behaviour*: 'You can go out to play now if you will do your homework later.' Usually this will be effective only with people who feel guilty if they do not keep to the bargain. These two variations are not generally included in lists of behavioural procedures. Our view is that they may be effective in some cases – but more often than not your assessment will indicate that they have already been tried and have failed.

We turn now to some variations of the basic positive reinforcement programme. Both *chaining* and *shaping* are methods of teaching new behaviours (as against increasing the frequency of a behaviour the person already sometimes performs).

Chaining and backward chaining

Usually when we say that some new behaviour needs to be learned, we do not mean a single response but rather a whole chain of behaviours. Chaining involves reinforcing completion of the first link in a chain, then the first and second, then the first, second and third, and so on until the whole chain is complete. A mentally handicapped young man learns how to count his money; then how to buy something from a shop; then how to check his change. Learning how to use a shower might cover: first, how to turn on the water; and then get wet; then soap oneself; and so on. Some books (e.g. Carr, 1980; Mori and Masters, 1980) have helpfully listed the components, step by step, of many self-care tasks and we give some more examples in our chapters on mental handicap (pp.218–19) and the elderly (p.247). If you have to do your own task analysis, the only solution is to perform the task yourself or watch someone else do it, noting every separate action. It can be quite a complicated operation to divide up the familiar tasks that we carry out automatically.

Some chains of behaviour have endings that are naturally reinforcing: feeding oneself is an obvious example; others include dressing, preparing a meal and laying the table – sometimes it is just the feeling of 'a job well done'. In such circumstances *backward chaining*, is preferable. The helper carries out the early parts of the chain, and the learner gets reinforced by the helper and also 'naturally' for the last link, then the last two links, and so on backwards. For example, putting a spoonful of food into your mouth, raising spoon to mouth, lifting spoon to elbow height; or pulling down the bottom of a sweater, pulling sweater over chest and back, pulling arms of sweater to wrists; or putting on some talcum powder, drying between your toes, drying your feet, rubbing your back.

Chaining is not always necessary: people can learn a task without having it broken up if they are quick learners and the task components are already in their repertoire; then modelling (see pp.140–2) and positive reinforcement for the whole sequence are generally all that is needed. The client groups most likely to benefit are mentally handicapped children and adults and old people suffering from dementia.

Shaping (successive approximation)

When someone cannot perform a behaviour or link in a behaviour chain right away, the solution is shaping. The person is reinforced for behaviours that are progressively more and more similar to the desired behaviour. In shaping, as in chaining, you are setting increasingly demanding criteria for the level of achievement that will be reinforced. Once the person is succeeding at one level, the standard is raised, and this process continues until the hardest level is attained.

Just as chaining requires a list of behaviours making up the chain, so shaping requires a list (or hierarchy) starting with what the person can manage now, and on up, step by step, to the desired form of the behaviour.

In a famous shaping experiment, Isaacs *et al.* (1960) began by reinforcing just eye movements of a mute psychiatric patient, then mumbling, and so on until the patient was asking clearly for chewing gum.

Here are some examples of shaping hierarchies: (1) Mother to watch child playing; (2) Mother to watch and make comments on what the child is doing; (3) Mother to show interest by asking questions, laughing, praising the child. Or (1) Group member to look at other members while they are talking; (2) Group member to make non-verbal signs to show she is listening, such as nodding, smiling or saying 'uh-huh' at least once during each person's utterances; (3) Group member is to ask at least one question during the discussion or else make a comment on someone else's statement, for example, 'You're right', 'I feel the same'; (4) Group member to make at least one statement of her own.

Shaping happens naturally in parent–child relationships, but sometimes things can go wrong. A not uncommon problem is that a parent 'starts well', for example reinforces babbling and then 'baby talk', but thereafter fails to raise the criteria for reinforcement, so that we find the five-year-old child still talking like a two-year-old.

Note that shaping can lead to progressively less desirable as well as to improved behaviour. A parent gives in to (reinforces) whining, then decides to hold out – but gives in when the whining changes to yelling. After a time, the parent again tries to hold out – but gives in when the yelling turns into a full blown tantrum. This parent has shaped up tantrums. Thus it is that half-hearted efforts to modify behaviour can make a bad situation worse.

Prompting and fading

In teaching new skills, *prompting* is a key component. Prompts can be physical (raising a person's head while teaching him to look at his companion during social skills training); gestural (finger to lips during a role-play to remind the client to speak more quietly); or verbal (saying 'Mike, now pull your sweater down' while teaching a handicapped child to dress himself). *Fading* comes in when the person has mastered the skill but still needs prompting. It involves gradually dispensing with the prompts, beginning with the physical, then the verbal or the gestural, depending on the situation. Thus, in our social skills training example, the physical prompt would be replaced by just a quiet hint ('Head up, Bill') and later by a gesture (tapping your chin). With the handicapped child, the process could take longer, first just touching the client's hands instead of guiding them through the action, while still saying 'Mike, pull your sweater down', then fading the latter to 'down', before dropping the prompt altogether.

Prompting and fading are invariably used in combination with chaining and are most often associated with teaching skills to children and the mentally handicapped, but they should not be overlooked as valuable components in a wide variety of programmes for the rest of our clients.

Removal of punishment

The analysis of behaviour in its setting may suggest that the behaviour that people say they want to see more of has in fact been receiving punishment – perhaps not intended as such. The simple expedient of stopping the punishment may be sufficient to allow the behaviour to reappear. Thus, John has been teased for his efforts to dress himself or Jane has been handed more and more work as a result of offering suggestions at team meetings. If people stop teasing John and Jane's workload is kept down to average size, John will perhaps resume his attempts and Jane her contributions. It is sensible to tell the people concerned that they will no longer be treated as before but will in future receive positive reinforcement for their efforts!

Negative reinforcement

Hitting your brother has the effect of terminating your brother's teasing, so you are more likely to hit him again next time he teases you. In other words, something disagreeable is *removed* following the behaviour and this causes a subsequent increase in the probability of that behaviour. Negative reinforcement is one of the 'negative' or 'aversive' behavioural procedures. It is another way of reinforcing (strengthening or increasing) behaviour.

Negative reinforcement is an extremely common mechanism of control in everyday life. But it is hardly ever used in professional intervention programmes. A rare example is given by Ayllon and Michael (1959) describing the case of a psychiatric patient who insisted on being spoon fed. The nurse allowed food to drop on to the patient's clothes while feeding her, and the patient, who cared a lot about her appearance, soon began to feed herself again.

A variation is where an unpleasant consequence is avoided altogether if a particular behaviour is performed (that is, avoidance as opposed to escape). Threats of unpleasant consequences *may* make Johnny do his homework, turn off the TV or eat his rice pudding, particularly if such threats have been carried out in the past. The threat of examination failure does indeed make most students work. And it is often in order to avoid family breakdown, eviction, or imprisonment that people agree to contact with social workers.

The system adopted by Leeds magistrates for dealing with persistent truancy appears to be an example of negative reinforcement: they tell the children that the proceedings will be adjourned and that they will be expected to have attended school regularly during the interval if they want to avoid residential care or a more punitive decision by the court; this procedure is repeated for periods of increasing length over several months (Lamb 1984). (There appear to be worrying 'side effects', indicative of the need for a broader set of goals and interventions with children in trouble.)

But negative reinforcement is not an approach to be recommended. In many cases that come to our attention, such as child behaviour problems and marital discord, it has, like punishment, been tried already and has failed. However, we should stress its importance as a mechanism in family situations especially. Behavioural writers have described a bad marriage as one where coercion – the use of negative reinforcement and punishment – is the main means by which the partners seek to influence each other's behaviour (Patterson and Hops, 1972). For example, Mrs Peters would like her husband to help her with the children. She nags him, 'Jim, you never help. What sort of a father do you think you are?' etc, etc. And if he turns on the TV when she would like him to read the children a story she says, 'All you do is sit in front of the box, you fat slob.' The usual result is a great deal of unhappiness and resentment, until the person on the receiving end discovers a more effective way to escape or avoid unpleasantness: withdrawal or departure. For these reasons, where a system of negative reinforcement is noted, you should try to dismantle it and instead help the people concerned to find more positive methods of mutual influence. And this applies to groups of all kinds – neighbourhoods, work places, and social work departments.

OPERANT PROCEDURES TO REMOVE OR DECREASE UNWANTED BEHAVIOUR

Operant extinction

This is the least problematic of the several operant procedures that may be useful for removing unwanted behaviour. It is appropriate only if careful observation and analysis suggest that a particular consequence is maintaining the problem behaviour. Very often that consequence is attention in some form – not intended as a reinforcer, of course: relatives listening and asking solicitous questions when you complain (even though your complaints are trying their patience); parents fussing over a toddler having a tantrum; anyone giving in to nagging or other forms of coercion.

The procedure is to stop this reinforcement – *completely*. This is not always easy to achieve, and you need a clear plan as to what will constitute 'ignoring' or 'not giving in'. The person who announces, 'What filthy language! It's shocking, and I'm going to ignore it', is not in fact ignoring it! Ignoring something can be quite stressful – the difficulty will be eased if people are given an alternative, incompatible task e.g. mother to leave the room, do some housework, look at a magazine; family to ask questions about a different topic. The problems are compounded if some kind of physical intervention is called for, as when a child is likely to hurt himself or others, or a parent fears that the wails from the bedroom may be due to real pain. In such circumstances an agreed routine will have to be devised: moving the child elsewhere or making a quick check without fuss.

If extinction is working there will usually be a rise in the problem behaviour's frequency and/or intensity first of all (the 'extinction burst'). You need to warn clients of this, because if they give up in despair the behaviour will not merely return to its earlier level, it may remain at the higher level, and it will most certainly be more resistant to change when another attempt is made. So key aspects of this kind of programme include giving full information if the worker is relying on parents or others to change the contingencies, plus much support – frequent visits, phone calls, careful monitoring. It is also helpful to 're-label' the situation when the problem gets worse: for instance, suggest that the exacerbation is evidence that the extinction programme is being carried out properly and that the chances of success look excellent.

Later on, there may be another brief and temporary return of the problem behaviour. Again, people must be forewarned and reassured.

Another obstacle to the use of extinction is the objection that it will be very distressing to lose reinforcement all at once. For example, a woman who had reinforced her child for every little sniffle, every health-related complaint (of which there were large numbers daily) said 'Won't it be a shock to her?'. The answer is 'Yes, but we'll work out a programme of rewards for good behaviour so that she doesn't lose out overall'.

Time-out

Conceptually, time-out seems to occupy a position mid-way between operant extinction and punishment. It is likely to be useful when one cannot specify what particular consequences may be reinforcing a problem behaviour. Time-out means depriving the person of *all* the reinforcers present when the behaviour has occurred. The full name for it is Time-out from Positive Reinforcement. As will become clear, this procedure is not usually suitable for clients over the age of about six, though it is sometimes used in residential settings with older clients. It is not suitable where parents have used long periods of isolation as punishment (McAuley and McAuley, 1977).

Like extinction, and like all other techniques designed to remove problem behaviour, time-out should only be used in combination with other procedures that build up or increase desirable and preferably also incompatible behaviours.

Usually, time-out involves placing the child in an uninteresting room, or in a corner, or excluding him from some activity *for a brief period only*, for example, two minutes. The place should not be his own room, nor anywhere that offers opportunities for pleasurable activities, but it should certainly not be a place that is unpleasant or frightening. A typical time-out sequence might go like this:

> Johnny starts teasing the cat – parent says, 'Johnny, stop teasing the cat'. . . Johnny continues . . . 'Johnny, stop teasing the cat or you go to the corner.' Johnny continues – parent (calmly) either takes him or tells him to go to the corner, and says he must stay there till he has been quiet for two minutes. After two minutes' silence, Johnny is calmly taken out (no fuss, comforting or discussion).

Typically, the child is required to remain quiet for a set amount of time before being released from time-out. With small children who yell for several minutes, McAuley and McAuley (1977) suggest removing the child during a quiet moment, rather than requiring a two minutes' silence. Some workers using time-out with children too big to be moved bodily advise exacting penalties for each minute the child refuses to go to time-out (reduction of pocket money or points).

The same amount of support and rehearsal and careful monitoring are needed with time-out as with extinction programmes (see McAuley and McAuley, 1977 and Herbert, 1981). Indeed, because it can be misused by parents being overly harsh as well as by those who are not firm enough, it needs to be used with great caution. This said, feelings of distaste for this type of procedure need to be balanced by the fact that time-out is often the quickest way of helping a despairing parent to gain some control over both child and self.

Punishment

Here we are using the word 'punishment' not in the everyday but in the learning theory sense. Not everything that people intend as a punisher actually works that way – indeed, it may turn out to be a reinforcer. For example, for some children, being criticised by an adult, being smacked even, may serve to increase rather than decrease the behaviour that precedes it. Even some adults get a kick out of riling a person who is intending to punish them for something they have done.

Like time-out, its close relative, punishment is not to be embarked on unless other, positive procedures are really not appropriate or have proved to be ineffective by themselves. This is especially important to bear in mind with regard to physical punishment. Our reasons for this advice are both ethical and practical. Punishment can have several adverse effects: (1) it can cause depression, anxiety or aggression; (2) the person may withdraw or develop strategies such as lying in order to avoid or terminate punishment; (3) it can make the person who is punished fear and dislike the person who administers the punishment and this may lessen the importance of that person as a model and the value of any positive reinforcement that person delivers; (4) the person who uses punishment may act as a model for aggressive behaviour; (5) fear and dislike may generalise to other people who resemble the person in some way; (6) the effects of punishment may generalise beyond the target behaviour to a range of similar but desirable behaviours, for example, a child who is punished for being cheeky may cease even to assert himself appropriately; (7) punishment, like other procedures for decreasing behaviour, does nothing to encourage new, effective behaviour.

In addition to all this, physical punishment often fails to achieve the results aimed for, and if it does, the results may only last for a short while.

In spite of all these reasons against using physical punishment, it has to be said that there are exceptional circumstances when it would be right to use it: if a person's behaviour is dangerous to himself or other people and alternative kinds of intervention are likely to prove impracticable, or slow, or are unlikely to work. Thus, if a child keeps running on to a busy road a slap as he steps off the pavement is probably better than positive reinforcement for staying on it: the latter would be awkward to arrange and would take too long. Operant extinction by withdrawing attention from severe head-banging would lead to an increase in this dangerous behaviour before it eventually began to decline.

We should add that non-physical punishment may be equally destructive (yelling, sarcasm, etc.) and that calm, firm use of physical punishment, such as a slap, may be less harmful to a child than an uncontrolled though non-physical aggressive outburst on the part of the parent.

Other kinds of punishment do not have the adverse effects we have detailed to such a serious degree. Even these, however, should be avoided if at all possible, and should always be combined with positive reinforcement procedures.

Response cost

The most commonly used form of punishment, particularly with children and adolescents, is response cost (also called 'negative punishment' or 'punishment by withdrawal'). It involves taking something away after an undesirable behaviour: docking pocket-money, deducting points or tokens, stopping some enjoyable activity. Such expedients may form part of a family contract, where penalties for not fulfilling specified obligations are written into the contract; or of child management programmes where parents fine each other for not carrying out the procedures correctly.

Deciding on type of punishment

If a punishment procedure is deemed to be essential, consideration of the type to employ needs as much care as did choice of reinforcement procedure. Most often, the type you use will be response cost. It is crucial to devise a form of punishment that really works from the very start of the programme so that there can be no argument for intensifying it later. This is because people's tolerance tends to rise if gradually increasing levels of punishment are administered: they become habituated. If tokens are taken away, it must be a sufficient number to make a noticeable difference; if some activity is stopped, it must be something the person actually enjoys.

Timing of punishment

As is the case with positive reinforcement, punishment is most effective if it comes immediately after the behaviour to be modified. It is no wonder that fines or imprisonment months after an offence do not seem to reduce further offending! Also, it is important to consider what we mean by 'after the behaviour': after reaching for the biscuit tin or after the biscuits have been eaten? Some research (Walters and Demkov, 1963) suggests that this timing decision will affect the outcome: 'reaching for the tin' punishment would improve 'self-control' whereas 'after the biscuits have been eaten' punishment would increase distress after a misdemeanour (guilt). Whether such distinctions apply to most humans is unclear.

Again like positive reinforcement, consistency is important. But there can be no 'thinning out' of punishment; if a behaviour recurs it must again be punished. Otherwise there is a danger that the unwanted behaviour will be placed on a schedule of intermittent reinforcement. The hope is, of course, that the problem behaviour will not recur, but will have been superseded by some more desirable pattern of behaviour, aided by a lot of positive reinforcement within the overall behaviour change programme.

In our society, punishment – or attempts to punish – is frequent, but often ineffectual. Punishment is used inconsistently, or delayed till long after the behaviour in question, or else a mild punishment is tried first, and built up to greater intensity later. The same is true of families and other small groups. We therefore conclude this discussion of punishment with a reminder about assessment. As with negative reinforcement, you need to look for punishment as a mechanism in the client's current situation even if you have no intention of using it in a planned behaviour change effort. Punishment plays a major role in unhappy families, and an important objective is to do away with it and try to replace it with a more effective and satisfying pattern of interaction.

Altering the setting and the antecedents of operant behaviours

The basic operant procedures all involve altering the consequences of behaviours in order to reduce some and build up others. Perhaps not enough attention is paid to another aspect of operant behaviour: the settings in which behaviours occur or do not occur, and the antecedents of the behaviour.

If your behavioural analysis indicates that particular settings are important, it may be feasible and desirable to ensure that the settings themselves are changed. The presence or absence of key people may be significant. If a child behaves disruptively with one particular adult only then your main focus should be on that adult's behaviour rather than on the child's. Absconding from a children's home might suggest something about the home rather than the absconder. Noise and distractions might be affecting a child's homework performance. Chilly bedrooms, tiredness and lack of privacy or time can all influence marital relationships.

Signals, as well as settings, are important. It is sometimes enough to inform people that a certain behaviour will be reinforced, or just that it will not be punished, for that behaviour to appear. Written prompts, words of encouragement, clear instructions are examples. A simple enough notion, but sadly lacking in some settings.

In this chapter we have given an overview of the many – and notably effective – procedures stemming from the two major learning theories: Pavlov's classical conditioning and Skinner's operant conditioning. In Chapter 6 we will dip a toe in the rather murky waters of some modern styles of intervention, and then return to firm ground with a look at some relatively well-established packages which draw on the procedures we have described already with (sometimes) a judicious admixture of newer techniques.

6

Behavioural Intervention Procedures II: Cognitive – Behavioural, Self-Management Procedures and Combinations of Procedures

THE USE OF SOCIAL LEARNING THEORY

Bandura's social learning theory (see Chapter 2) has influenced the way the procedures discussed in the previous chapter are used. Bandura argues that they work for reasons that their originators did not recognise: they work because of what they do to people's *thinking*. Thus, reinforcement, punishment, and desensitisation teach or remind people about what they can achieve and about the effects of their behaviour: according to Bandura, their value is informational. Using Bandura's ideas, the worker will make a special point of attending to the client's thinking throughout the behavioural programme. Bandura's influence is important in relation to the cognitive–behavioural approaches described later in this chapter. We begin with a brief account of modelling, the procedure most closely associated with his name.

Modelling

Modelling (teaching by demonstration) is both a key behavioural procedure in its own right and an important ingredient in many different kinds of programme. Behavioural workers have been known to model an amazing range of behaviours from holding a snake to chatting up a woman in a pub to handling the contents of a rubbish bin. There is also the modelling of beliefs or attitudes: indicating one's conviction that it is all right to enjoy sex, that it is appropriate to mention one's achievements in a job interview, that black people have a right to council housing.

Modelling works better if the model is liked and respected and seen to be successful, and is specifically rewarded for the behaviour being demonstrated. These facts have influenced workers to co-opt people who might be more effective models that the workers themselves: a football star, a popular child, the secretary of a successful residents' association. Another point to bear in mind is that the model should be similar to the observer. 'Similarity' covers fairly obvious features like age, sex and race, and also current or recent problems. Parents who have difficulty in dealing with their children's behaviour may be helped by other parents who have managed to overcome such difficulties; in groups, the relatives of psychiatric patients or of elderly people with dementia can act as models for others in the same situation. The similarity concept also suggests the value of not having too wide a gap between the capabilities of model and observer. This ties with the notion of the 'coping model': a shy person who has managed to overcome shyness; someone who has to control feelings of annoyance at a child's naughtiness rather than someone who has no such feelings; the person who still experiences urges to over-eat or to resort to drugs or alcohol. There are obvious advantages in 'peer' rather than 'professional' help. An additional bonus here – as anyone who has tried to model social skills for adolescents will confirm – is that these models know what the appropriate behaviour is like: if you are over thirty you may not be aware of how to invite a girl to dance at a disco.

Formal modelling can be divided into clear-cut steps:
(1) Specify the behaviour to be demonstrated and ask the observer to attend to it
(2) Arrange demonstration
(3) Ask the observer to imitate the behaviour immediately after the demonstration
(4) Give feedback and reinforcement, and if necessary provide repeat demonstrations
(5) Give further practice, and so on.

Formal modelling plays a major role in social skills training. But it is used in teaching any kind of new behaviour, for example, in the treatment of phobias, and in helping parents develop child-management skills.

Even if a formal piece of modelling is not part of your programme it is useful to be aware of the mechanism occurring naturally within the worker–client relationship and in all the interactions that make up people's social experience, in families and friendship groups, in classrooms and on street corners.

SELF-MANAGEMENT, COVERT CONDITIONING AND COGNITIVE PROCEDURES

Over recent years, a number of techniques have been developed that rely on the client's own management of the antecedents and consequences of his behaviour. Many of these techniques focus to a great extent on covert behaviours, especially thoughts. As we have noted, Bandura (1977) and Beck (Beck *et al.*, 1979) are leading proponents of cognitive approaches within the behavioural tradition. Other influential figures in this field are Meichenbaum (1977), Ellis (Ellis and Grieger, 1977), and Cautela (1972).

The effectiveness of the covert conditioning and cognitive–behavioural techniques is not well established, and we recommend that the simpler, operant and respondent approaches and modelling should always be considered first – there's a lot of mileage to be had from them. Nevertheless, the advent of these techniques does mean that there may be a way forward with some problems for which, previously, there seemed to be little that the behavioural worker could sensibly offer.

We give here a brief overview of the best established of the self-management and cognitive procedures: some of them are quite complicated, and you would need further special training in order to use them confidently; others can readily be introduced by the worker who is already using the non-cognitive procedures with a reasonable degree of competence.

Self-management

We begin with a short account of 'overt' self-management. This is really no different from rearranging antecedents and consequences in programmes where a worker or a mediator organises matters, except in requiring greater involvement of the person whose behaviour is being modified: we might call this do-it-yourself behavioural intervention. (See Cormier and Cormier, 1979 for a thorough description). Self-management programmes include the following components:

(1) *Self-monitoring.* Self-management programmes emphasise the self-monitoring of behaviour. The client himself observes and measures (see Chapter 4).

(2) *Stimulus control.* The client introduces new stimuli into her environment or removes others that elicit unwanted behaviours. For example, placing an encouraging notice about slimming on the refrigerator, putting a note beside the kettle with a reminder to ask Jimmy how he got on at school, arranging a special place to do homework, or keeping the alcohol out of sight.

(3) *Self-reinforcement.* This simply means providing one's own positive reinforcement. Ordinary everyday items can be used: a treat after completing a piece of work, such as a phone call to a friend after doing one's daily assignment, or reading a magazine after working out the housekeeping budget.

Alternatively the client could use covert self-reinforcement, silently praising himself. Some people are very unskilled at this (though they may be expert at covert self-punishment!) and need to practise out loud and encouragement to recognise when they deserve to be rewarded. Building in some sort of self-reinforcement can form a useful ingredient in many kinds of programme, and indeed most of the covert and cognitive procedures include it, as we shall see.

Covert conditioning procedures

This group of procedures were introduced by Cautela (1972), and have been reviewed by Kazdin and Smith (1979) with the general conclusion that considerably more evidence is needed for all of them, and some, indeed, have yet to be supported by well-designed outcome research.

Covert sensitisation is the best-established of the covert conditioning procedures, and has some research backing. This is a form of self-imposed punishment or escape training or aversion therapy. (It is unclear exactly what mechanism is operating!) The term 'sensitisation' was employed in order to indicate that the procedure is intended to sensitise (as against 'desensitise') the client to certain stimuli. This technique has been used with some success by clients who have a strong impulse to engage in behaviour which they themselves wish to stop: people with alcohol or drug problems, compulsive shop-lifters, and sexual offenders. The client imagines himself on the point of performing the unwanted behaviour and then imagines something that causes him to feel sick or distressed. Later, he goes on to visualise himself refraining from the behaviour and feeling relieved and pleased.

One of us supervised a case in which a persistent 'flasher' (indecent exposer) visualised himself going through his customary chain of behaviours, beginning with getting into his car to drive to the park, then getting out and waiting for a woman to come by, and so on. Having specified the chain of behaviours, he and his probation officer selected the point at which he would learn to interrupt it. He then learned to associate feelings of horror – induced by imagining himself before the court in the presence of his mother – with taking out his car for these expeditions. Eventually, he imagined himself staying at home and watching TV, thus avoiding the horrific consequences. Note that it does not seem to be necessary for the imagined unpleasantness to have any logical connection with the undesired behaviour; though in this case the client decided that the court scene was more powerful and easier to conjure up in imagination than scenes that would make him feel sick. Encouraged by the success of this case, the same author tried covert sensitisation on herself: imagining a diseased lung in a dish in front of her, and associating it with taking out a cigarette. The image did pop up whenever she took out a cigarette (for several weeks at least) but she found herself pushing it away again (the image, not the cigarette!) – and so the programme was a failure.

Covert modelling is an imagined version of overt modelling used mainly for problems of anxiety or temper control. The person 'runs a film' of someone else carrying out a behaviour he wishes to be able to perform himself. For example, a boy with difficulty controlling his temper visualises his admired older brother coping effectively with being criticised by a classmate; a shy woman imagines a more confident friend entering a group of strangers. There is a small amount of research showing that covert modelling is more effective with the use of models who are like the client, who are 'coping' models, and who are reinforced for the modelled behaviour, and that imagining several models is preferable to imagining just one; but perhaps the most interesting part of the story is that the method has sometimes been found to work as well as real-life modelling – though not as well as 'participant' modelling, that is, modelling combined with practice (Kazdin and Smith, 1979).

Covert reinforcement, covert extinction, covert negative reinforcement and *covert punishment* have not even this limited research backing, and we mention them here as techniques with *may* prove their worth in the future or may be dropped altogether from the behavioural repertoire. All of the covert conditioning approaches require a highly motivated client who is willing to practise often, and who has a considerable gift for producing vivid imagery.

Thought stopping

The aim is to teach the client to halt the progress of recurrent troublesome thoughts. The procedure was developed for the treatment of obsessional disorder, but has been used for other kinds of problem, for example the depressed person thinking, 'I'm stupid and ugly' or the anxious person, 'I'll never cope with that'.

The client relaxes, thinks the thoughts, signals that she is doing so, and then the worker calls out 'Stop!' Later the client practises doing it herself, first aloud and then more quietly until she can do it subvocally. It is not clear whether this is a covert punishment or negative reinforcement procedure, or whether it works by simply distracting the client's attention. It does not work with everyone, but it can provide some people with a strategy for controlling a behaviour that feels as though it cannot be controlled (Wolpe, 1973). Some authors suggest that it should be combined with teaching the person to produce alternative, more constructive thoughts after the 'Stop' (Bellack and Hersen, 1977). How this latter might be achieved is described by several workers who provide more comprehensive cognitive therapy models (see next section).

You will have noticed that all the covert conditioning procedures are based on operant or respondent principles, treating thoughts much like any other behaviours. The cognitive procedures that we turn to next are far more of a departure from traditional behavioural practice.

Beck's cognitive therapy

Mainly used in the treatment of depression, this approach aims to identify and modify 'negative automatic thoughts' relating to the person's current and future situations and to the person's view of herself. For example: 'I'm stupid'; 'Nobody likes me'; 'I'll never make any friends'. With the worker's help, the client begins to learn to recognise such thoughts and to assemble contradictory evidence. For example: 'I am good at my job'; 'My workmates invite me to go to the club with them'; 'I have made a number of good friends in my life'.

Homework assignments require the person to record the unconstructive thoughts as they occur, and rate how strongly each one is believed at the time (usually on a 1–100 scale). Later she must not only track and rate the unconstructive thoughts, but also dispute them – writing down the arguments and evidence against – and then re-rate them, noting down a more constructive alternative for each.

The rationale for this approach relies particularly on the view that thoughts are the key antecedents to depressive mood and behaviour. However, the homework assignments include behavioural tasks to test out whether the beliefs are valid: for example, will the person's friends accept an invitation or do they really reject her? The client also plans and records activities that give pleasure and experience of 'mastery' or personal achievement. Other behavioural procedures are introduced as required.

Evidence in favour of this approach is accumulating (e.g. Rush *et al.*, 1977; Blackburn *et al.*, 1981) but is still not sufficient to justify its use with seriously depressed people in preference to drugs without very careful monitoring of results. Its use for anxiety conditions has even less research backing, though interest in this area of application is growing.

Ellis' rational-emotive therapy

This approach has some similarity with Beck's. One main difference is that rather than gently leading the client to identify and reconsider his beliefs, the worker confronts and argues more vigorously. Ellis has produced a list of beliefs or attitudes which, he says, may not be held explicitly but are certainly acted upon. For example, 'Everyone must love me'; 'I must always do everything perfectly'; 'It will be terrible if I make a mistake'. The worker tries to persuade the client that he is more competent than he believes, challenges him to think again. Ellis' A-B-C method involves teaching the client to analyse situations as follows: A is the Activating event (I don't get the job I apply for) and C is the emotional Consequence (I feel very upset and despairing). But it is incorrect to say that event A causes feeling C. In fact, feeling C is caused by belief B, what I say to myself about event A (I am a total failure and nobody wants to employ me). If you want to change feeling C, the unhappy reaction to event A, then you must dispute belief B. For example, 'I would have liked the job, and I am disappointed' is more rational than 'I am a total failure' because 'I know I can do the work, and I can do lots of other things well'. (A useful account of the mechanics of carrying out rational-emotive therapy is to be found in Lewinsohn *et al.*, 1978). Ellis does not focus particularly on depression. Like Beck, he includes behavioural as well as cognitive components: for example, using desensitisation for anxiety problems.

We would stress, as Ellis does, that behavioural approaches should always be combined with this method of working. An appealing approach, which we have found helpful personally, but not necessarily appropriate for clients who have a hard time wrestling with words and logical arguments. And, sadly, it has only modest backing from outcome research.

Meichenbaum's self-instructional method

Meichenbaum's emphasis is on 'private speech' and on helping clients 'talk to themselves' in ways that help them to act confidently and competently. He notes that young children often do this out loud, and so do adults in some situations, for example when learning to drive or following a new recipe. Meichenbaum (1977, p.20) gives an example of his own, while skiing, 'What am I doing on this hill? Now, slowly, line-up the skis; good. Bend; lean back'; and another from work with an impulsive child 'What is it I have to do?' (problem definition), 'carefully draw the line' (focusing attention and guidance), 'I'm doing fine' (self-reinforcement), 'That's OK even if I make an error, I can go on slowly' (self-evaluative coping skills and error-correcting options). The client (often a child) is trained in these self-instructional procedures, saying them aloud at first and gradually learning to do it silently. Modelling and shaping are used to teach the new coping skills. Meichenbaum and others have presented evidence for this method's effectiveness in helping 'hyperactive' and impulsive children; aggressive or 'disruptive' children; psychiatric patients who need to learn to behave more 'normally' in social interactions; and patients with phobias. Often the procedure is used in combination with other behavioural methods. The evidence so far is promising, particularly with children, but not overwhelming (Meichenbaum, 1977).

Anxiety management and stress-inoculation (anger-control)

WASP: Wait, Absorb, Slowly Proceed. This mnemonic is a useful example of the kind of self-talk taught to clients receiving these forms of training.

What is being attempted is to teach the client a coping strategy that can be brought into use in a variety of situations. These methods are used mostly with anxiety in cases where there is not one but many different occasions for the client to feel upset and either act inappropriately or else try to escape or avoid. There are several versions of this kind of coping skills training, for example systematic rational restructuring (Goldfried *et al.*, 1974), anxiety management (Suinn and Richardson, 1971). The key components are teaching about the role of cognitions, self-monitoring of self-talk and problem behaviour, problem-solving training (defining the problem, selecting a solution, evaluating feedback), modelling and rehearsal of positive and coping self-talk, plus behavioural procedures such as relaxation, and behavioural homework assignments.

Novaco (1975) has developed a stress-inoculation approach to the control of anger. First the client receives a detailed explanation of the conceptual framework of the approach: the role of emotional arousal and of particular thought patterns in producing the client's reaction to the anger-provoking event. A key point is that there are several stages in dealing with anger: preparing for the stress, recognising and coping with the feelings, and reinforcing oneself for having coped successfully. Next, cognitive and behavioural coping strategies are rehearsed, such as relaxation, assertive behaviour, or coping self-talk such as 'This is going to upset me, but I know how to deal with it' (Preparing for provocation); There is no point in getting mad' (Impact and confrontation); 'My muscles are starting to feel tight. Time to relax and slow things down' (Coping with arousal); 'I handled that one pretty well' (Reflecting on the provocation).

Novaco has worked with people who had serious anger-control difficulties (1975) and later, as a prevention measure, with police officers (1977). Other workers have used the method with some success to help in the modification of marital violence (Saunders 1984), and of child maltreatment (Barth *et al.*, 1983).

Once again, it must be said that the research backing is not yet wholly convincing, but these methods do seem to fill a gap in the professional's repertoire when seeking to help with some difficult and important problems.

COMBINATIONS OF PROCEDURES

As we have already said, it would be odd indeed to find just one behavioural procedure used 'neat'. But there are several major lines of approach which are well-developed 'packages'.

We begin with a couple of simple two-procedure packages.

Differential reinforcement

This is a combination of reinforcement of an alternative behaviour that is incompatible with the problem behaviour, and operant extinction for the problem behaviour itself. For example, whilst withdrawing reinforcement for John's fooling around and baby talk, his parents reinforce him when he helps look after his sister and plays nicely with her. Mrs Black's social worker pays no attention to her gossip about the neighbours, but shows a lot of interest in Mrs Black's account of how the week's assignment went and her plans for the next part of the programme. The committee chairman ignores irrelevant chatter but pays close attention and makes notes of relevant contributions from the members.

This is one of the most commonly used of all the operant methods, especially in work with parents who are learning to modify their children's behaviour. As a combination of two procedures, it has the properties of each, including the risk of a temporary increase in the unwanted behaviour (see our account of operant extinction pp. 133–4), and the advantages of building up new behaviour rather than just removing unwanted behaviour. It is always important to see if there is an incompatible alternative that can be increased when faced with something that needs to be decreased.

Praise and time-out

This is another very useful combination of operant procedures, frequently used to increase a child's obedience and decrease disobedience. We present the package in the form of a flow chart from McAuley and McAuley (1977). (See pp. 124–8, 134–5 for our description of the components.)

Points systems including response cost

Some points systems encompass response cost as well as positive reinforcement. As we noted in the section on positive reinforcement, such systems have the advantage of providing consistent consequences to follow after specified behaviours. Points can be awarded or taken away immediately after the behaviour or at regular intervals (say at the end of the morning, the end of the afternoon and bedtime) where this is more convenient and the recipient is an adult or older child.

Points systems are suitable for children between the ages of about seven to about twelve. The systems can get very complicated, so it is wise to consider the possibility that the meticulous and fair system that you laboriously constructed may be less effective than a cruder version that is easier to operate. The basic steps are as follows:

(1) Choose and specify the behaviours to be rewarded or punished by response cost.
(2) Make a list or 'menu' of back-up reinforcers – the activities or items the person would like to earn.
(3) Make a 'price list' for the reinforcers, in points or tokens. Decide which behaviours will lose how many points.
(4) Decide when the points can be spent, and whether they can be saved up for long-term (distant) reinforcers.

Praise and time-out

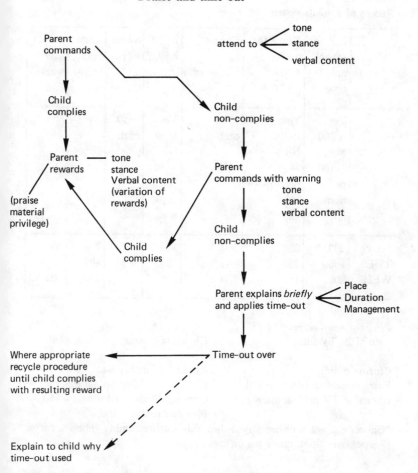

N.B. When teaching this procedure often verbal instruction is not
enough. The worker should always attempt to role-play time-
out and supervise the first time-outs.

Here is an example of a points system, and three days of recording:

Record of a points system

	Left for school on time	Home for tea by 4.30	Chores* as requested	In by 8.30	Swear words	Total points earnings	Points saved weekend
	Yes +200 No −100 per 5 mins late	Yes +200 No −50 per 15 mins late	100 each	Yes +200 No −50 per 5 mins late	−50 each		
MON	200	200	300	150	−100	750	50
TUES	100	200	—	150	−50	400	50
WED	200	150	200	200	—	750	100

Prices of reinforcers

Late night TV film ⎤
             ⎬ at weekend = 250
Cinema outing ⎦

Extra pocket money 5p = 100
Choice of TV programme = 150

Choice of Sunday pudding = 100
Choice of Sunday meat = 150
Cooked breakfast on Saturday = 150
Cocoa and cake at bedtime = 150
Play one record = 100

*Chores e.g. wash dishes, dry dishes, tidy kitchen, empty rubbish, carpet sweeper over floor, make tea or cocoa.

Some further advice on points systems: firstly, ensure that the person gains overall: he must be better off with the programme than he was before it began.

Secondly, you must give some thought as to how to dispense with the system after it has done its job. As with other operant programmes, it must be phased out gradually. To begin with, you should raise the criteria for reinforcement, and also reduce the frequency of awarding points and of the times when they can be spent. McAuley and McAuley (1977) suggest using the system on alternative days for a while, then reducing this further. It can be reinstated if there is any falling-off in the improved behaviour. A points system usually teaches the 'mediator' to cue and reinforce appropriate behaviours, and the client to behave in ways which are intrinsically reinforcing (e.g. acting in a more controlled or 'grown-up' manner) or which obtain natural reinforcement and make for improved family relations. Nevertheless, the client should not find himself getting less pocket-money or fewer treats. In residential settings, this is generally managed by giving clients who have achieved their behavioural change goals all the privileges free that they have previously had to purchase with points, and in families an equivalent arrangement can be made. It is important to consider this matter at the onset: for example, will father be willing to go on taking his son to football matches? If not, then do not use football matches as a reinforcer in the points system. Likewise, reinforcers that cost money should not be so expensive that parents have difficulty in affording them – it is wrong to suggest that this will only be a short period while the system is in operation.

'Interpersonal' approaches

Clearly, most behavioural procedures involve more than one person. Dividing off behavioural family therapy and couple therapy from other kinds of behavioural work is a somewhat artificial exercise as this is a model of treatment applied to the family rather than a model of family treatment. There are three major marital-family approaches, usually combined with each other: contracting or negotiation; communication-training; and decision-making or problem-solving training.

Several well-designed studies have produced encouraging results (for a review see Rachman and Wilson, 1980) but there is some debate as to whether behavioural approaches in this field work better than modern present- and systems-orientated therapies of other schools (Gurman and Kniskern, 1978).

Contracting (negotiation-training)

This is the simplest of the 'family' approaches. The worker and the clients together draw up a specific, written agreement about changes in behaviour, with duties and privileges spelled out in detail. The worker acts as negotiator, and the family members are behaviour modifiers for each other using positive reinforcements as their main tool. The behaviours chosen must be specific, repeatable and acceptable to all. The key message is 'Exchange actions, not just words'.

Contracts have numerous advantages in promoting behaviour change. People usually dislike breaking promises, especially if they are written and public. In making a contract you ensure that people understand clearly what is being asked of them and you do away with the problem of 'misremembering' which so often leads to failure with behavioural assignments. Lastly, contracts provide for consistent positive reinforcement where social reinforcement is not a strong enough or reliable enough consequence.

Against this, some experienced marital therapists argue that the written contract can be counter-productive, in that when one partner breaks his or her commitment the other partner becomes even more upset and angry. A clear plan of behaviour change with just a written reminder for both people of what they have undertaken to do is therefore more appropriate. This is usually called 'negotiation' rather than 'contracting'.

This approach is appropriate with a variety of problems, but it can be overused. It is not suitable with young children or severely mentally handicapped people. It will only help to change behaviours that can be recognised and monitored easily and that occur regularly but not at a very high rate (which excludes, for example, communication problems and 'habits') and problems that are not compulsive in nature (which excludes, for example, problems of anger-control, sexual deviation and addictions).

The basic steps in contract making or negotiation are (1) define the problem and the wishes of each person; (2) negotiate the behaviours and the contingencies; (3) write the contract; (4) monitor the contract.

Firstly, the family members produce individual lists of things they would like the others to do more of. It is almost invariably necessary to work hard at turning these items into positives as well as specifying them clearly. For example 'not be inconsiderate' becomes 'be considerate' becomes 'be ready on time in the mornings, share in getting breakfast ready, ask me about my day', and so on. Stern (1978) gives the example of a husband wanting his wife to be 'more feminine' which turned out to mean 'allow me to touch her breasts'.

In the negotiating phase, the worker should support the weaker party, ensure that everyone ends up better off, and feed in information about norms for the behaviours requested, for example times for teenagers to get home at night, or pocket-money requirements.

Here is an example of a contract between a single parent and his fourteen-year-old daughter.

Contract between Mary Wilson and Mr Wilson

Mary agrees to:	*Mr Wilson agrees to:*
(1) Be ready for school by 8.30 am.	Drive Mary to school, making sure she gets there by 9.00 am.
(2) Wash car/vacuum car/mow lawn/clean downstairs windows on Saturday (father to choose).	Give Mary £2 pocket money on Saturday evening.
(3) Be home by 9.30 pm Sunday to Thursday and 10.15 pm Friday and Saturday.	Allow Mary to stay out till agreed times without arguing.

Bonus Clause: If Mary keeps her side of the contract for 4 weeks she will receive an extra £1 pocket-money.

Penalty Clause: If Mary fails to carry out item (1) or (2) she will forfeit 50p. For every 15 minutes late coming home, she will forfeit 20 minutes from her next evening out.

If Mr Wilson causes Mary to be late for school or forgets to give her pocket-money or nags her about being out in the evening he will do her Saturday job the next week.

Re-negotiation: Any party can request re-negotiation at next meeting with Miss Higgs [social worker].

Signed ....

Note that each person's new, desirable behaviour is reinforced *independently* of the other person's new, desirable behaviour. In other words, the one does not depend on the other. This has been shown to be a more helpful approach than straight 'behaviour exchange'. For more detailed accounts of contracting and negotiation see Sheldon (1980), Stuart (1980), Jacobson and Margolin (1979).

Research on behavioural marital therapy strongly suggests that contracting by itelf is less effective than a package that also includes the two approaches we consider below, communication-training and decision-making or problem-solving (Jacobson, 1984); these three components together make up some of the most effective family therapy programmes, such as those of Alexander and Parsons (1973) for young delinquents and their families.

Communication training

Between severely distressed couples on the point of divorce proceedings, criticism and lack of acknowledgement are very common and
each spouse commonly complains of being misunderstood. Teenagers frequently complain of their parents lecturing and not listening.
Unpopular group members are often people who talk more and listen
less than their companions. All of these are examples of people who
could benefit from communication training.

Communication training is closely related to social skills training
(see pp. 160–4). It is often the main approach in work with families or
couples who complain of relationship difficulties: they feel they
cannot get their message across to one another, or else it is what their
relatives say or do not say to them that is a major cause of mutual
dissatisfaction. Note that the behavioural approach to family
problems does not *assume* that communication is necessarily the
crucial problem: people can be thoroughly unhappy with one another
even with perfect communication (the crucial problem may be in
what they *do* for or to each other).

Communication training plays a supporting role in other work
where more than one client is involved: for example, when setting up a
family contract it is usually necessary to teach people to express their
wishes in specific and positive terms and to decrease the amount of
nagging or criticism. Likewise, in teaching people decision-making
skills (see below) it is important to show them how to describe clearly
the issues at stake, to keep to the point and to listen to one another's
views.

This approach is also valuable in group work with people who are
not related to one another, and even in work with one person who can
use the social worker as a stand-in for re-enactment and rehearsal of
difficult interactions.

One of the most thorough studies of communication characteristic
of couples with marital problems is by Thomas (1977) who gives
forty-eight items to look for, count and modify. Our own experience
suggests that the following short checklist provides a useful start.

Overgeneralisation ('You're selfish' as against 'That hurt').
Focus on the past (harping upon old misdeeds by the partner).
Lack of acknowledgement of the other person's feelings.
Lack of positive reinforcement.

Too much punishment and negative reinforcement.
Mind-reading ('You're jealous'; 'You want me to be like your mother').
Talking too much.
Talking too little.
Interrupting and changing the subject.
Lack of empathy.

You should take a sample of talk – perhaps asking people to discuss a topic (we have used 'plans for next weekend' or an issue a couple disagree about). You then select some behaviours which are particularly frequent and which upset the other person – preferably behaviours by each of them. A baseline measure can be taken at this stage.

Then the worker uses modelling, practice and feedback in order to reduce the undesired behaviours and build up more acceptable alternatives.

Decision-making/problem-solving

A frequent source of discord is people's inability to decide on an agreed plan and carry it out; instead, they spend much time and energy arguing – often repeating their arguments, and returning to old arguments – and yet if asked, they are often quite unable to state what the alternative solutions are or what the other person wants and why. Part of the problem is communication, as we have discussed. However, it is also useful to learn a series of logical steps to be followed in order. The same procedures can be helpful with an individual who has one key decision to make, or who has generalised problems in decision-making.

It is worth noting here that much of social work with individuals as well as with families is concerned with decisions: a very common social work goal is to help a client to decide something – whether to continue with an unplanned pregnancy, whether to offer a home to an elderly relative, whether to change one's flat or job. In groupwork, the agenda frequently includes giving people experience of taking responsibility for decisions that affect them: often in simple things like what activities to choose or where to go on group outings.

The decision-making (or problem-solving) steps are as follows:

(1) Agree to work on a problem
(2) Specify the problem (or part of it)
(3) List all the possible solutions you can think of (brainstorming)
(4) Eliminate all obviously bad solutions
(5) Examine the remaining solutions one at a time
    (a) list all possible negative consequences
    (b) list all positive consequences
    (c) eliminate if generally negative
    (d) take next solution on the list and repeat (a)–(c)
    (e) compare remaining solutions
(6) Select solution with the most positive consequences
(7) Agree on details of implementing the chosen solution, using steps (3)–(6) as needed.

     (Adapted from the flow-chart by Turkat and Calhoun, 1980)

If clients have one decision to make once and for all, the worker's task is to see them through the various steps and ensure that they have covered every issue to their joint satisfaction.

However, when a couple's relationship is problematic, it is usually not a question of solving a single dilemma, but of learning a new pattern of joint decision-making. It is therefore a matter of taking them repeatedly through the steps, pointing out what each step comprises, and making rules about the process: no skipping steps, no returning to previous steps, remembering of course to avoid the communication faults mentioned in the communication training section of this chapter.

Lastly, we should note the value of decision-making training for depressed or chronically anxious people who may have as a 'symptom' severe difficulties in reaching quite ordinary decisions. Certainly such people often recover from this inability to make decisions when they recover from the anxiety or depression, but many who come to the attention of social workers are not in this category.

In both communication and decision-making training, the social worker is constantly modelling, giving feedback and reinforcing the client's mastery of each separate task.

Sex therapy

Sex therapy has become something of an industry divorced from 'generic' behavioural work, and is used by workers who would not describe themselves as behaviourally-orientated. We would suggest, however, that the sex therapist ought to be able to carry out a broad behavioural analysis and to intervene with problems other than those that are entirely sexual. He or she must also have sound knowledge of sexual functioning, and this is probably unusual among social workers who have not had further training in this field. Another caveat is that, in a few cases, sexual problems can have a (sometimes central) physical component, so that medical screening and back-up is often necessary; for example, certain kinds of medication and illnesses like diabetes can be implicated in problems of getting or maintaining an erection (though you can be sure that the man who experiences this difficulty with his wife but not with his mistress has a social-psychological, not a physical problem).

Sex therapy starts with a detailed and wide-ranging assessment of the couple's current sexual difficulty and their relationship and the history of both. Attention needs to be paid to attitudes and knowledge, as well as to feelings and overt behaviour.

Treatment usually begins with the instruction to refrain from intercourse and from touching breasts and genitals. Home assignments are prescribed, beginning with 'sensate focus' exercises in which the couple move through a series of tasks of increasing intimacy, concentrating on giving and getting enjoyment without any 'performance demands'. For example, they might be required to take turns to caress their partner's back (a typical assignment in the early part of the programme) or to have insertion take place with the woman above and without thrusting (a more advanced assignment). One way of conceptualising the process is as a form of desensitisation, developing an alternative response (pleasure/sexual arousal) in the place of anxiety.

Equally important components are learning how to please and arouse one's partner and to express one's own preferences. So it is also a training process, using feedback and reinforcement. The worker's role includes modelling of attitudes ('It's OK to enjoy sex . . . for the woman to make advances, etc.'); and a considerable amount of education about sexual functioning.

Towards the end of the programme, the tasks become more specific to the particular sexual difficulty: for example, where the woman experiences anxiety in intercourse, the couple use the 'woman above' position with the woman in control of the situation; where the man has problems keeping an erection, the 'stop-start' technique may be suggested, with the man repeatedly withdrawing and allowing his erection to subside and then being stimulated to erection once again. (For a more detailed account of the specific techniques of sex therapy, see, for example, Jehu, 1979; or Hawton, 1985).

There is promising evidence in favour of sex therapy. It is a specialist field, and referral to a sex therapy clinic may be the most appropriate help for the social worker to provide. (Even more specialised is the treatment of people with physical disabilities – a possibility that social workers should be aware of.) However, where clients cannot obtain specialist treatment, or if there is good reason to try to help them yourself, reading a detailed textbook plus consultation with an expert may enable you to offer the right kind of help. An example from our experience: a social worker asked for advice regarding a mentally handicapped couple whom she had known for some years. Exceedingly shy, the couple were unwilling to talk to their GP about their problem, and the social worker was sure they would not find their way to a sex therapist by the complicated route of GP – psychiatrist – therapist. Medical involvement seemed unnecessary, since the husband had no problem in getting an erection. But he understood little about sexual arousal, and his wife was equally unclear about the process and said she felt nothing. In this case, the social worker read some of the literature, used a sex therapist as a consultant and was able to instruct the couple and adapt sex therapy techniques in a programme suited to their needs.

Social skills training

Social skills training seems to have had more success in attracting social workers' interest than any other behavioural method and it is used in work with the unemployed (job interview training) and with offenders. But it has many other applications, with clients in every age group and with a wide range of problems.

The skills that are taught are non-verbal, such as gaze, posture or voice volume; verbal, such as asking questions or expressing interest; and also cognitive, such as knowing the rules of social situations and thinking logically and constructively about social interactions.

'Assertiveness training' is an American variant, with more stress on expressing one's own feelings, both positive and negative, and standing up for oneself and exercising one's rights without encroaching on the rights of others. However, the differences between the approaches are slight nowadays, and we shall use the term 'social skills training' to refer to them both.

The people who most need social skills training include the very shy, who look uncomfortable, speak too quietly and do not look at others; those who appear aggressive, standing too close, too straight, looking others too firmly in the eye and speaking too loudly; and those who do not show any interest in others, not looking at them, talking too much and only about themselves. Many psychiatric patients have one or more of these difficulties. A somewhat different group are people who get into trouble through inability to work out effective strategies in problem situations, such as the claimant at the social security office or the young person being interviewed by the police. They have the basic skills but don't use them appropriately.

Social skills training can also be helpful to people who do not have habitual difficulties with social interaction. It may form just an adjunct to other help with problems not defined as 'lack of social skills'. For example, Mrs Evans, whose difficulties were summed up by her psychiatrist as 'inadequate personality', used newly-learned social skills to deal with neighbours and relatives, and her husband, with coaching from her, learned a way of tackling his boss about low wages (Hudson, 1975). Parents using time-out are given training in how best to give instructions to their children (McAuley, 1982). Thus, social skills training is just as relevant for a single situation that someone finds hard to cope with as for general problems of 'social inadequacy'. A woman whose mother interferes with child-management, a teenager who dreads meeting his friends again after discharge from a psychiatric unit, someone with a difficult apology to make or upsetting information to impart: these are further examples of potential users of short episodes of social skills training. The procedures can also be very helpful to social workers themselves: preparing for a confrontation with a client or another professional, indeed for any unaccustomed or worrying interchange.

Assessment of social skills

Whether the client is thought to need general social skills training or just help with a small piece of social interaction, it is necessary to check what skills are already present and what skills are lacking. There are many ready-made instruments – checklists, rating scales and questionnaires – for assessing performance in problematic interchanges, 'micro behaviours', discomfort, and how the person thinks he would actually behave in particular situations. Role-plays, preferably video-taped, are another useful way of getting a picture of the person's assets and deficits.

For one-off situations all that is necessary is to analyse what will be required and to check what parts are missing from the person's repertoire. If at all possible, real-life observation is ideal. Failing that, it is useful to get the person to re-enact or rehearse a difficult interchange.

Intervention

In formal social skills groups, assessment is often followed by one or two general teaching sessions conveying the skills and the principles of learning. Training proper consists of modelling, prompting (or coaching), practice, feedback and reinforcement, further modelling and prompting further practice and so on in that order, until the client reaches an acceptable standard and feels able to repeat his practice in real life.

Among the key points to remember in social skills training are the following:

(1) Initially, people may seem to get worse at the tasks. This is a recognised phenomenon (which you may have experienced yourself in interview training at college). The disruption will pass, and it will be less severe if the training focuses on one behaviour at a time – for example, just gaze, or just posture.

(2) Sessions must be carefully timed. A most serious error is to have people perform a single role-play and go away feeling they have done badly: they must go away feeling they have achieved something.

(3) People have their own style. You can accommodate this by considering a variety of possible approaches to a given situation and helping the person select the one he feels most comfortable with. (This is not, of course, the same as

accepting every style as appropriate or effective: a young offender in one of our groups thought that saying 'F— off' was a good way of getting the police off his back.)

(4) Arrange homework assignments for practice in the 'real world'.

Cognitive aspects of social skills training

Lastly, some suggestions about the thoughts, beliefs and feelings that may underlie or accompany social skills deficits. It is advisable to consider this aspect during the initial assessment; and if thoughts and feelings appear very influential then they should be a major focus of the work. For example, a youth may think that accepting criticism from anyone in authority is equivalent to 'losing face', or may expect to find himself friendless if he refuses to join in illegal activities; a shy woman may interpret a single 'brush-off' as evidence that she is totally unattractive to men. But if these covert elements are only part of the picture, it is probably best to work on overt behaviour first. When the person gains the necessary skills and uses them, it is likely that feelings and thoughts will change. On the other hand, if training does not have much effect, it may be necessary to return to these matters and introduce cognitive techniques. Preparing lists of one's assets (a common feature of job-interview training) may help overcome excessive modesty. Role reversal can help people understand the other person's point of view. Social rules may need to be spelled out and discussed. Problem-solving and modelling of attitudes are other elements that may be required. Interest in the cognitive aspects of social interaction is growing, and it is clear that some clients require a more cognitive style of intervention such as rational-emotive therapy or formal problem-solving training with a lesser input of social skills training proper.

Social skills is a multi-component approach that relies heavily on modelling, prompting, shaping and sometimes on cognitive procedures. It further requires a knowledge of the components of social skills which have been described by social psychologists (see, for example, Furnham and Argyle, 1981).

The effectiveness of social skills training is much argued over by researchers. Their current consensus, insofar as consensus can be said to exist, is that the training is effective in changing specific behaviours in the short term, but will only produce lasting results that generalise to new situations if plans for maintenance and generalisation are carefully worked out, and not simply left to chance.

Such planning includes homework assignments; helping clients organise their social activities; trying to ensure that other people reinforce their efforts; and teaching people general social rules and problem-solving skills as well as how to cope with specific social situations.

Another important issue: what are the appropriate skills the client needs? A number of studies have appeared describing 'normal' or 'effective' social behaviour for different groups of people, but such research is still in its infancy. At present, our best insurance against attempting to teach behaviours that are not natural or suitable for the client's age or social setting is to work with a group of clients, in the hope that other members will contribute the necessary knowledge. ('Peers' can also be brought in as co-trainers.) We discuss groupwork in the next chapter.

7

Groupwork and Community Work

Behavioural groupwork is a growth industry. By contrast, there is a dearth of literature on behaviourally-orientated community work, despite the efforts of a small number of community psychologists and an even smaller number of social workers interested in developing this field.

Groupwork

Behavioural groupwork is an area where the social work profession has made major contributions. The approach draws on group-process principles as well as behavioural principles.

Groupwork has many advantages. To begin with, the group can be a useful setting for observation and assessment of individual clients. This is, of course, true only to the extent that the group activity provides a representative sample of relevant behaviour. Thus, it is useful for assessing how people behave in a talking group, a team game, or whatever, but tells us little or nothing about how, for example, children get on with their parents or adults with their spouses or employers. In terms of helping people change, groupwork offers the following:

(1) clients' feelings of distress and aspects of unconstructive 'self-talk' may be reduced by the knowledge that they are not alone in facing their difficulties;
(2) people get information and learn skills from other members of the group;
(3) meeting with other clients may be more enjoyable than meeting with a social worker only;
(4) the wider range of models and of potential social reinforcement may facilitate the learning of new behaviours;

(5) the group may provide a closer approximation to people's natural environment and thus increase the likelihood of new learning being generalised and maintained;
(6) watching others learn and helping them to do so may further extend the range of new learning and the likelihood of generalisation.

A fast-increasing number of control group studies show behavioural groups to be more effective than other kinds of groups, and a great many single case (or, rather 'single system') studies demonstrate the power of behavioural procedures used in the group setting. Among the wide range of clients and problems represented in these studies are the elderly (Linsk and Pinkston, 1982); parents of hard-to-handle children (Tams and Eyberg, 1976) and of mentally handicapped children (Tavormina, 1975); patients with phobias (Hand *et al.*, 1974); battering husbands (Saunders, 1984); and many others. These are in addition to the even larger number of studies on social skills training.

The pre-group phase, as with any other kind of group, is of very great importance. The worker spends time preparing the ground in the agency, prompting and reinforcing colleagues' referrals, and setting up an agreement to provide them regularly with information about their clients' progress. Special emphasis is laid on clarifying the theoretical rationale for the enterprise and drawing on empirical research when it comes to planning group composition and likely intervention procedures. Methods of evaluating the effects of the group are built into the plan, preferably a mix of the relatively objective (for example, parents' or teachers' records of children's behaviour) and of the more subjective (for example, the members' ratings of their progress and how useful they find each session). It is crucial to take time over this and not allow oneself to be hassled into starting the group before this issue has been settled: all too many groupworkers come to regret their lack of evaluative procedures – especially when they feel that their group has gone well!

Then there will be pre-group meetings with the people who have been referred, to ensure that the group will suit their needs and to prepare them for the experience. The worker–client agreement is made as explicit as possible, with details of number of sessions, type of activity (role-play, outings, games, use of tokens etc.) and what is expected in terms of attendance, behaviour in the group, and homework assignments.

Some groupworkers arrange for members of a previous group to meet with the new members (see for example, Zander and Kindy, 1980). Sometimes there is a signed agreement, or else the client writes a letter accepting the offer after he has had time to consider.

From disappointing personal experience we also recommend some attention to very practical matters such as how people will get to the premises. A social phobics' group almost didn't happen because some of its members got lost in the hospital and were too shy to ask for directions; another member turned out to suffer from crippling anxiety about bus travel. A group planned for severely handicapped schizophrenic patients did flop because none of the clients could face the journey.

The behavioural groupwork has two interrelated general aims. The first is obvious: to help achieve behaviour change that will generalise to the natural environment and to future as well as current situations; the second is to facilitate group cohesion and to reinforce attendance and co-operation.

Liberman (1971) has given an elegant demonstration of how operant principles can be applied to the task of promoting group cohesion. The group therapists prompted and reinforced cohesive-type contributions by the members ('we' statements, showing interest in others, etc.). Not only did this procedure increase the number of such contributions, it also resulted in clients expressing more satisfaction with the group and showing more positive change than clients in groups where the leaders did not do this. For children's groups, Rose (1972) suggests providing material and activity reinfor-cers for attendance and co-operation, having the members choose a special name for their group, and – a useful idea from the many points of view – being quite systematic about giving members responsibility for assisting each other's progress. Extracts from a transcript may help to clarify these points:

(From the middle of the fourth of fourteen meetings of the 'Panthers': six boys, aged eleven to twelve, with social interaction problems.)

Leader: Well, it's great! Everyone seems to have done his homework. Everyone got his card signed. (Names each member and the task he has completed) . . .

Dinny: And you brought the stickers.

Leader: So I did! Let me give them out. Now put the points on the thermometer. I think we're almost to the top. (Members put points on large thermometer for completing assignments.)

....

Leader: Who's going to help the others to review their diaries?

Joey: It's my turn.

Leader: OK, Joey, and I'll sit behind you in case you need me. And of course you get the leader's card with the helpful hints ...

Joey: Ronnie, what did you write in your diary?

Ronnie: I was visiting my aunt, the old one I told you about last week with the cat, the one I was afraid to talk to. She asked me about the club.

Joey: What did you say?

Ronnie: I sort of muttered 'OK'. I really wanted to answer her but I still couldn't say anything.

Joey: That's a good diary example. (Pauses)

Leader: (Whispering) We can work on it later, on to the next ...

Joey: And, if you like, we can work on it later, and see if we can help you to figure out what to do ...
          (Joey goes round the room asking each person for their diary reports which are descriptions of stressful situations. They had been trained the previous two weeks on the criteria for selection of a good situation).

Joey: OK, now, everyone except Dinny brought in something from their diary. So that gives us 25 points. I'll just put that on the thermometer.

Leader: Joey, thank you for doing my job. What do you guys think he did well?

Toby: He kept on the track! And he didn't have to look at the cue-card much.

....

Source: Rose (1981).

Others ways of involving clients in the group and making the experience a rewarding one include group savings towards an outing, individual reinforcers in tokens or in kind, refreshments and shared activities.

The worker's role is to a large extent – perhaps even more than in individual behavioural work – that of a teacher, aiming to teach learning principles and to give the members practice in applying the principles to their own and others' problems. At first, the worker takes a directive stance, but gradually transfers the leadership tasks to the clients. Thus, in the early sessions the worker uses behavioural skills to model, prompt and reinforce the kinds of behaviour that will enable the work to proceed effectively and efficiently: staying 'on task', offering specific and positive feedback to other members, describing problems in concrete terms. In due course, the members will have learned enough to take over and allow the worker to take a back seat.

Like any behavioural intervention, groupwork goes through several well-defined stages. What follows is a typical programme.

Problem assessment. The members learn to describe their problems in behavioural language, and to count and measure and analyse in terms of antecedents and consequences. Each person selects an initial target behaviour and, if possible, baseline measurements are obtained.

Goals are set: 'I will be attending some outside social event or educational facility at least once a week'; 'I will have reduced my anxiety rating when shopping in the supermarket'; 'Jimmy will have fewer than three tantrums per week'.

Discussion of strategies, as suggested by the analysis of current conditions. If the main problem is a behavioural deficit, ways of developing the required behaviour, such as a programme of positive reinforcement, shaping or chaining, are planned; if a behaviour is to be reduced in frequency, the group plans an extinction or punishment programme combined with increasing an acceptable alternative.

Modelling and rehearsal. The behaviour involved in carrying out the plan is modelled by the worker or by other members and rehearsed by the individual concerned.

Homework assignments These are usually real-life repeats of the rehearsals, or else just the task of recording key events during the intervening period. For example, to keep a diary of a child's refusals to go to bed and the surrounding circumstances, to note 'tricky' interpersonal encounters, to ignore delusional talk on the part of a relative and respond with enthusiasm to sensible talk, to make three telephone calls to other members of the group. The assignments should be written down, and some groupworkers have members get them signed by some reliable witness when completed: this might be a 'buddy' from the group or a parent or teacher. Homework assignments in some groups include reading, for example from a self-help book on depression (for example, Lewinsohn *et al.*, 1978) or child behaviour problems (for example, Patterson, 1975) or a specially prepared hand-out as used frequently with social skills and phobics' groups.

Subsequent sessions. After the first meeting the sessions begin with a report-back on the homework: good efforts receive positive reinforcement, problems are re-analysed, lack of effort is passed over rather than being allowed to attract interest and sympathy.

Many groups have an activity other than talking or role-play as a setting in which to work on problems. Some provide relaxation training, particularly where anger-control or anxiety is a problem shared by all the members. Others include practice off the premises, for example for agoraphobics or social phobics. Children's groups include games that are not only fun but also show up behavioural problems such as shyness, pushiness or rudeness, and offer the opportunity to try out an alternative behaviour and have it reinforced by all present. Thus it is perfectly possible for a behaviourally-oriented social worker to utilise his methods during a football game or a camping trip.

To sum up; obviously, the worker uses behavioural principles as he guides the behavioural analysis and the behavioural change programmes tailored to clients' individual needs. Less obviously, he uses behavioural procedures in the following ways: positive reinforcement for helpful contributions; non-reinforcement for unhelpful contributions (in 'unruly' groups such as some groups of young offenders or hard-to-handle children it may also be necessary to employ sanctions at first); arranging modelling, prompting and immediate reinforcement of cohesive behaviour and efforts by members to help themselves and each other; and training the group to make their own decisions and to solve both individual and group problems (for example, dealing with the over-talkative member or leader or stopping others messing around). There is a wealth of practical ideas in the behavioural groupwork literature as to how these things can be achieved.

Varieties of behavioural groupwork

We have considered social skills training elsewhere (pp.160–4) and have tried to draw attention in this chapter to some of the other uses of groups. Nevertheless, almost every behavioural group contains some element of social skills training: using modelling, rehearsal and feedback in order to develop skills in the interpersonal situations.

More recently, behavioural groupwork has been 'going cognitive'. It has also been moving into the field of prevention (as against remedial work), and the fast progress and encouraging results from this body of work are impressive. The groups in question combine a variety of cognitive procedures with behavioural principles.

For example, Barth *et al.*, (in press) describe a 'coping skills' group for teenage mothers, which began by identifying situations causing distress to these clients, such as coping with criticism, asking for help and managing tension. Saunders (1984) has developed a cognitive–behavioural groupwork approach for husbands who batter their wives, which includes systematic desensitisation to anger-provoking stimuli and 'consciousness-raising' about the pressures on men, as well as women, to conform to social stereotypes. Barth *et al.*, 1983) used a wide range of social skills and self-control techniques and relaxation training with a group of parents of children at risk of abuse. In all of these examples, the findings on a variety of measures suggest that the group was achieving some success in helping these rather hard-to-help clients.

Specifically preventive work has focused on teenage smoking and pregnancy. The social workers in this field have developed intervention packages that are a combination of education (for example, about the effects of smoking on health, or the physiology of sex); attitude change methods (producing a TV programme about smoking risks or an advertising campaign for contraceptives); and skills-building (learning stress-management and other self-control techniques, practising saying no to sex without contraceptives or to cigarettes offered at a party).

The series of studies by Schinke and his colleagues (Schinke, 1984) with school-age mothers and children aged from fourteen to eighteen have demonstrated improvements in knowledge of sex, attitudes to contraception, problem-solving ability and assertiveness in role-plays. Further research will tell whether the programme cuts the rate of unwanted pregnancies.

The smoking prevention research by the same workers (for example, Schinke and Gilchrist, 1983) has shown that these groups do increase members' knowledge, ability to deal with problems related to smoking and social skills in 'tobacco use' situations. Even better, they have shown that a year later group members are smoking less than their contemporaries. Another interesting finding from this group is that the skills-building procedures seem to be crucial to success (no surprise to behavioural practitioners!).

Alcohol abuse is another potential target for preventive group-work. Research on relapse in problem drinkers by Marlatt (1982) supports an emphasis on learning to control feelings of frustration and anger in interpersonal encounters and to resist social pressures. Wodarski and Lenhart (1982) have begun a study of cognitive–behavioural groupwork with adolescents with the aim of teaching them about alcohol, and developing self-management and assertiveness skills. There are some similarities with the 'alcohol education' groups offered in a number of British probation departments, but we think the more structured behavioural and cognitive procedures used by the American social workers could be introduced to these groups with advantage. Other areas where this type of work might be tried include glue-sniffing and drug abuse.

Preventive groupwork of the sort we have described is part of a continuum from the remedial at one end to the self-help/community group at the other. We turn now, briefly, to consider behavioural intervention within community work.

COMMUNITY WORK

First, we would stress the value of social skills training techniques in community work. Examples from the American literature include the use of modelling, coaching and rehearsal in order to prepare members of a residents' association to act as chairperson and to represent their membership to other official bodies (Fellin, *et al.*, 1967); training a board of directors of a poverty programme in decision-making skills (Briscoe, *et al.*, 1975) and training door-to-door canvassers (Weisner and Silver, 1981).

Community workers have a special interest in helping low-power groups to achieve more influence, and assertiveness training tailored to their particular concerns can sometimes be a helpful addition to the services offered. It has been used to help women with low incomes

(Berman and Rickel, 1979), elderly people (Gambrill, 1985), battered women (Jansen and Meyers Abell, 1981) and clients on public welfare (Galinsky *et al.*, 1978) to stand up for their rights and make appropriate requests of others.

Rothman (1980) points out the relevance of a variety of other behavioural techniques in community work: analysis of antecedents and consequences; baselining; formulating goals and sub-goals in, measurable terms; systematic use of reinforcement; and built-in evaluation procedures. But despite his advocacy of behavioural methods in community work, there is little sign of their introduction in any formal sense. We wonder if this is due in part to the fact that many community work projects already do adhere to principles that the behavioural worker holds dear, such as setting specific goals and evaluating outcomes.

Finally, some of the newer cognitive theories might usefully be added to the community worker's conceptual repertoire, in particular Learned Helplessness theory (Seligman, 1975) for the light it throws on the difficulties many disadvantaged people have in believing in the possibility of changing some things about their lives or their environment; and for the practical suggestions this work has to offer about ways of breaking up the helplessness set that develops in the wake of experience of uncontrollability.

Part 2

In Part 1 we have described the main elements of the behavioural approach. In the chapters that follow, we detail the procedures most commonly used with particular types of clients and target problems. These should provide you with some preliminary ideas. But more important is your careful analysis of each individual case, your own and your client's ingenuity and persistence, and the resources you can muster.

8

Parents and Younger Children

Work with children is often more accurately described as work with their parents who typically play an important part in the maintenance, if not the onset, of children's problems. The bulk of this chapter will deal with work with children in their own homes, but we also discuss the relevance of a behavioural approach when working with children in substitute families and with children living outside their parental home when the aim is rehabilitation. Many of the techniques mentioned lend themselves to use within the school setting, and sometimes it is important to tackle behaviour at both home and school. (Some references dealing with school behaviour problems are given in the Appendix.) We begin with a brief summary of the findings of behavioural research into the factors which seem to distinguish families with conduct-disordered children. These are families who typically complain that their children's behaviour is beyond their control; sometimes referred to in American literature as 'the brat syndrome'.

Problem analysis

Several studies have examined the differences between families labelled 'problematic' and normal families (Delfini *et al.*, 1976; Forehand *et al.*, 1975; Lobitz and Johnson, 1975; Patterson, 1976). The results can be summarised as follows.

Children labelled 'aggressive' display higher rates of 'coercive behaviours' generally, such as hitting, issuing commands, yelling, humiliating and teasing, and non-compliance. Conduct-disordered children exhibit a corresponding lack of desirable behaviours such as laughing and talking, independent activity and 'positive attention' e.g. listening interestedly, admiring.

Parents of children referred for help give more commands than their non-referred counterparts; engage in more criticism of their children's behaviour and issue more commands in a threatening, angry or nagging way. They respond to their children with more negative behaviours in general (e.g. shouting) and more often supply negative consequences to their children's behaviour, whether deviant or not. The picture is aptly summed up by Patterson (1976) as one in which the families of 'problem' children are characterised by a high rate of coercive interaction. This conjures up all too clearly a large number of the families known to social work departments. Some writers suggest that at the extreme end of the spectrum, where behaviour problems occur in several children (even though only one may be presented as problematic) and parents experience difficulties in other areas besides child management, successful intervention could require years of co-ordinated professional intervention, with no guarantee of success (McAuley and McAuley, 1977).

Behavioural interventions

Whilst case studies can be found in the literature describing successful treatment of an immense range of problem behaviours from stammering to head-banging, this chapter will focus on those problems commonly complained of by parents known to social services. Typically the complaint is that one or more children in a family are 'beyond parental control' or that they engage in a number of behaviours that the parent finds objectionable or 'aversive'. A clustering of problems is the rule rather than the exception, comprising a combination of the following: aggressiveness, destructiveness, temper tantrums, non-compliance, high-rate annoying behaviours such as whining, screaming, demanding, teasing, and a high degree of activity and poor concentration.

Behavioural practitioners use the parent as change agent for several reasons. Parents are usually in the position of greatest control over their child and his environment. They are, therefore, in the best position to alter the antecedents and consequences maintaining the problem behaviour. The child's behaviour may sometimes be maintained – or triggered – by the behaviour of siblings, over whom the parent also has some control. Most important, the parent's own behaviour is often instrumental in maintaining the child's problem behaviour.

Programmes aimed at changing children's behaviour thus typically involve changing parental behaviour first, and such intervention is referred to generically as 'parent training'. Three procedures are commonly used in these programmes: differential attention; time-out; and points systems. McAuley and McAuley (1977) say they commonly use differential attention and time-out with children under seven, roughly speaking, and points systems with children between the ages of seven and twelve years. Our own experience supports this (although any combination of procedures may of course be used depending on the individual circumstance); certainly time-out becomes increasingly difficult to implement as children get older . . . and bigger!

Conduct disorder

In general, studies indicate that parent training, using the three strategies we have referred to, has good results with a wide range of child behaviour problems, and remains the treatment of choice (Wells and Forehand, 1981). But there are problems. First the success rate is not 100%. Second, there are, in many cases, quite high drop-out rates and a failure of successful results to last for any appreciable length of time beyond the end of intervention or to generalise to new problems. (Follow-up periods are often a matter of months and sometimes only weeks.) Reasons for these failures are increasingly the subject of investigation. Some writers note that families most vulnerable are those where one or more of the following pertain:
—poor parental adjustment, particularly maternal depression (McMahon *et al.*, 1981b);
—social isolation of mother (Wahler and Afton, 1980);
—marital disharmony (Reisinger *et al.*, 1976);
—extrafamilial conflict (Wahler, 1980);
—the problems are longstanding (McAuley and McAuley, 1980);
—parental misperception of the deviance of their children's behaviour (Wahler and Afton, 1980).
In our discussion 'parental misperception' will be used to refer to the failure of some parents' perceptions of their children's behaviour to shift in parallel with behaviour change resulting from intervention. (It

would be inappropriate to construct and implement a parent training programme where the problem was one of parental perception of non-existent deviance.)

We would emphasise that these are contraindications for adopting *simply* a parent training response to child behaviour problems, not contraindications for adopting a behavioural approach *per se*. Recent research and literature (e.g. Griest and Wells, 1983) suggest that what is needed is a broadening of the behavioural aproach into what is perhaps more accurately described as behavioural family therapy. The behavioural worker will need to be more skilled to work with these 'multiproblem families' than was once thought necessary, but this is in keeping with experience of social work intervention generally and should be regarded as a hopeful development.

Child abuse

Little evaluative research has been conducted on behavioural work with parents who abuse or neglect their children, and what has been conducted is subject to a number of methodological flaws which limit the conclusions one can draw (for a review of these together with a more detailed discussion of this area, read Gambrill, 1983a). However the results so far are more promising than those from the psychodynamic literature, in terms both of understanding the phenomenon and of intervention (Sweet and Resick, 1979), and it is an area currently receiving a great deal of attention.

Increasingly the multiplicity of factors responsible for abuse is being recognised, together with the need to intervene on a number of fronts ranging from environmental stress (e.g. poor housing and social isolation) to impulse control (i.e. teaching parents to identify and control angry impulses). Often parent training will not be appropriate until other areas such as maternal depression, marital problems or other sources of stress have been worked on, but in all probability it will have a major role at some stage. Gambrill summarises this need:

> Abusive parents must acquire nonviolent alternatives to physical punishment, such as ignoring and time-out, and reassess when punishment is warranted. They must learn to avoid coercive interactions, acquire more constructive ways to handle conflicts, and develop more realistic expectations of themselves and of their children. (1983a p.15)

We shall examine two of the areas identified above which seem to be of particular pertinence: anger control and child management skills. We begin with child management skills in the context of parent training and discuss some extensions.

PARENT TRAINING PROGRAMMES

Indications: (1) when behaviour problems reported by parents are confirmed by your assessment and the parent is the appropriate change agent; (2) when an instance of child abuse has been assessed as resulting from the parent's reaction to aversive child behaviour which could be eliminated, or brought within the parent's tolerance threshold, with different or additional management skills.
Contraindications: the presence of factors which would interfere with parent training such as those indicated earlier (p.179) and others e.g. severe mental illness, educational subnormality. If and when these factors have been addressed satisfactorily then it would be appropriate to proceed to parent training.

What follows is a list of the special considerations that apply to the assessment of and intervention in child behaviour problems. The general format for assessment and intervention given in Chapters 3, 4, 5 and 6 should be followed.

Assessment

Be familiar with child development. Without this knowledge you will not be able to assess the 'normality' of a child's behaviour and, of course, the appropriateness of the parents' complaints or expectations.

Involve everyone whose behaviour impinges on – or is impinged on by – the child's. Especially beware grandmothers, boyfriends and fathers whom you can never get hold of: the saboteurs of many a good programme. Mrs M's attempts to 'regain control' of her youngest daughter (Chapter 2) were constantly thwarted by her boyfriend who ignored her requests not to give in to the children's demands, particularly for sweets and ice-cream. Besides undermining her every effort, his actions 'devalued' her reinforcement 'currency'.

Attend to parents' perceptions, their expectations and beliefs. Parental perceptions of their children's behaviour do not always change in accordance with overt behaviour change, and some authors (Griest and Wells, 1983) think this may be one reason why successful treatment changes so often fail to last; the parents' unchanged perceptions ('his behaviour is no better') become a self-fulfilling prophecy.

Identify lack of relevant skills. For instance, in order to implement a procedure such as time-out you may first need to shape up the mother's use of instructions. Does she use praise at all? If not, can she? You may need to give her lots of rehearsal, taking the part of the child yourself, before she can praise her child. Or perhaps she seems to be able to praise her other children but not the 'target' child. It may be necessary to facilitate and build up the parent's ability to interact with the child, ranging from providing nappy-changing skills to play skills (Reavley *et al.*, 1978).

Identify parent and child assets. Find out what the parent likes about the child (there is usually something). Besides being able to build on this in one's intervention it usually introduces a note of hope into an otherwise desperate picture of aversive interaction.

Intervention

Maximise the chances of success. In order to persevere with any programme people need early reinforcement for their efforts, and this is nowhere more true than in this area where parents are often utterly worn down and where they are likely to have to endure a startling worsening of the problem behaviour before improvement begins. If possible choose a problem which is limited in nature (i.e. has a beginning and an end) and which occurs at a reasonably high frequency (e.g. going to bed).

Whatever the list of problems drawn up, several of them are likely to fall within the general category of non-compliance. Unless there are more urgent considerations it is from these behaviours that you should select your first target behaviour. This is because compliance is a necessary prerequisite for other more complex behaviours, such as using the toilet and getting ready for school.

If possible the problem you select should be one whose resolution would achieve the maximum benefit for both parent and child. Bedtime is often a difficult time for families and establishing a bedtime routine (that ends with the child in bed!) is often a good starting point. A good night's sleep can have a knock-on effect for both parent and child, enabling the one to execute the demands of a training programme and the other's behaviour to improve, tired children being generally more irritable and troublesome than well-rested ones (Buchanan and Webster, 1982).

Attend to your client's environment. If you are tackling problems of non-compliance or temper tantrums your intervention strategy is likely to generate a lot of noise, at least initially. A parent may have failed to obtain their child's compliance in part because of 'what the neighbours would say' if little Johnny were left screaming. You may need to cope with this first, either by persuading the parent that this isn't too important or simply by arranging that the parent tell the neighbours that she is going to tackle Johnny's bedtime problem behaviour, and for a few nights there may be a few hours' noise but she hopes they'll bear with her.

Prepare the parent. Warn her of the likely worsening of the problem following implementation of the programme ('extinction burst') and encourage her with the information that this is a sign of success. Particularly warn her of the possible trauma – for her – of implementing time-out, if using it.

Be available. Don't embark on a programme without scheduling time in your diary to execute it. Besides time for teaching, modelling and behaviour rehearsal you will need to visit in order to monitor progress, to reinforce parents and to offer advice and information (regardless of the amount of preparation it seems inevitable that something will have been misunderstood, at least at the commencement of the programme). Also you may be a valued source of support and authority.

Involve the child. That is, tell him what you are going to do – or, better still, get the parent to explain in terms he will understand and that will be attractive to him e.g. 'I'm going to try to help you do things right so that we'll get on better and not have so many rows and temper tantrums'. If he's old enough, involve him in assessment and intervention, e.g. monitoring his parent's behaviour and choosing some of his own reinforcers. Even a three-year-old that one of the authors was working with was heard to tell her mother 'you're not supposed to do that' when her mother failed to carry out an agreed and rehearsed procedure.

Include as much teaching of behavioural principles as the parent is capable of understanding. Parents are more likely to use procedures whose rationale they understand, and this may increase the capacity of some parents to apply what they have learned in one situation to another, i.e with different problems and with different children.

McAuley and McAuley (1977) point out that for some 'multi-problem' families the problems presented may require years of professional involvement, perhaps from a multiplicity of sources. Certainly some of the failures encountered by one of the authors working with such families were due in part to a decision to 'go it alone'. This did not mean a rejection of available help; rather it was the omission, in the course of a busy timetable, to recruit and train one or two volunteers. Initially such recruitment is time-consuming but, in our opinion, well worth the effort.

Given the length of time some families are on our books, it is worth trying to implement change endeavours when possible: either way these families will consume huge amounts of agency time and over the years something may 'rub off'. And some sense of going somewhere is important to the worker too.

Maintenance and generalisation

Good behavioural programmes consider at the outset the problems of maintenance and generalisation. Broadly speaking this means building into the programme factors which will ensure that treatment effects will endure (maintenance) and that parents will be able to apply their newly acquired skills to different problems and in different settings with different people e.g. siblings (generalisation). To date this has usually been attempted by pairing social reinforcers with the tangible ones (material rewards, points) so often necessary at the outset of intervention, gradually fading out the latter; and this, in turn, often requires an educational enterprise aimed at establishing positive reinforcement within the behavioural repertoires of parents particularly. Unfortunately these endeavours have not proved sufficient to the task and other solutions are now being explored.

We have already referred to the possible contribution to *generalisation* of teaching parents the principles of behaviour change. Whilst the results are mixed, there is also some evidence that such teaching may enhance *maintenance* (McMahon *et al.*, 1981a). Various manuals have been produced for use with parents both in groups and in individual casework (Becker, 1971; Patterson, 1975; Peine and Howarth, 1975). If such texts are beyond the capacity of your clients, it might be possible to write a tailor-made, simple text. Alternatively, you could simply build into your interaction with the parent as many examples as possible from which she might grasp a more general picture than would otherwise result from simply focusing on one problem behaviour. Getting parents to apply what they have learned to other problems with other siblings and/or in other settings may help. It should be stressed that these suggestions lack an established empirical base but seem sensible and promising avenues for further investigation.

APPLICATIONS BEYOND PARENT TRAINING

The ability to deal effectively with child behaviour problems should be part of the competence of every generic social worker; at the least within each area team there should be some workers thus equipped to tackle these problems which produce, in one way or another, a sizeable amount of the work of any social services department. Besides being an essential part of work with abusive parents and parents deemed to be at risk of abusing their children this ability is also essential to other areas of work.

Foster care

Behaviour problems have been identified as one reason for the failure to move children from residential to foster care (Rowe and Lambert, 1973) and for the high incidence of foster placement breakdown (George, 1970). Behavioural research suggests these problems can be resolved, and the prognosis for children in both residential and foster care considerably enhanced. Insufficient attention has been given to these areas in the literature and in practice. One exception is the work of Fahlberg (1981) who suggests that behavioural programmes should be incorporated in work with foster parents and children in order to deal with the many behavioural problems that may make the placement difficult for both parties.

This would complement the other two areas of work currently recognised as crucial to successful foster placements – 'matching' foster parents and children, and adequately preparing the child – for these are demonstrably not sufficient to the task. We need to equip foster parents to do the difficult tasks we nowadays expect of them.

Rehabilitation

Social workers expend creditable amounts of time and energy in trying to rehabilitate children in care to their natural parents. Typically this is little more than a phased return to full-time parental care, following a period in residential care or a foster home, beginning with short day visits which are gradually increased. The parents are offered support and advice. There is no evidence to suggest this is enough, and it is not uncommon to encounter seemingly endless cycles of breakdown – rehabilitation – breakdown. If rehabilitation is taken seriously then so must remediation of the precipitating causes, whether these are tied up with the child's behaviour or comprise parent problems which impinge on his welfare e.g. inadequate care or supervision, or a drink problem. The results of such enterprises are encouraging.

Services consisting mainly of behavioural interventions were offered to the natural parents of some 227 children who were in foster care in Alameda. The usual county services were provided for a control group of 201 children also in foster care. The overall goal, selected by the parents, was the return of their child; and specific objectives were set by parents and workers in order to achieve that goal. A multiplicity of behavioural interventions were used by project workers, including parent training. At the end of the intervention period 114 of the experimental children (behavioural methods used) were 'headed out of foster care'. Of these, 70 were restored to natural parents; 29 were placed with adoptive parents; and 15 were made subjects of guardianship. Only 59 of the control group left or were leaving foster care at the end of the project (Gambrill, 1983a, see also Stein *et al.*, 1978).

Where endeavours to rehabilitate children have failed, or when efforts to prevent breakdown have proved unsuccessful, the behavioural worker typically has a sounder and more objective base from which to make other decisions than some of his colleagues. The information he has collected, perhaps over a length of time, will place him in a strong position when preparing reports for courts or for social services committees, and when speaking to those reports.

ANGER CONTROL

As we indicated earlier, families in which child abuse is a problem are often characterised by low levels of pleasant exchanges and high rates of aggressive behaviour on the part of parent and child. This often results in the all too common 'spiralling' in which, in response to a child's misdemeanour, his mother shouts; he continues, she threatens; he goes on in either the same way or (typically) his behaviour gets worse; mother smacks him, he retaliates with verbal and/or physical aggression; mother 'lets fly'. One of the aims of intervention is to break this chain of events at the earliest possible stage. Equipping the parent with effective means of child management is one way which simultaneously reduces the amount of punishment used, both physical punishment (because it relies heavily on procedures such as time-out) and verbal/affective punishment (because if you break the chain earlier the amount of everything is automatically reduced). However, sometimes the child's behaviour is not particularly abnormal or the parent is unable to refrain from being drawn into this cycle. In these circumstances a different approach is needed, probably in addition to parent training: impulse or anger control.

Put simply, you endeavour to equip parents with various means of self-control (specifically anger control) which they seem to lack. The problem is not angry feelings – which are widely reported across abusing and non-abusing parents alike – but angry actions. One factor in child abuse is the failure on the part of certain parents to develop or exercise the restraints that most of us use to control our violent impulses. Anger control training does not yet enjoy the empirical support that parent training does, but offers a promising avenue for continued research (Barth *et al.*, 1983).

Training typically involves the following steps:

(1) The parent learns to identify cues that signal anger. These may be *physiological*: tension, shaking, 'going hot'; or *situational*: provocative situations such as the supermarket, where the parent feels particularly vulnerable. Some cues overlap both such as tiredness, premenstrual tension, financial worry.
(2) The parent learns to relax when these cues are identified and to use various coping strategies. These might include: deep breathing; engaging in an alternative activity; changing the way he or she thinks about the situation. Details of the latter technique can be found on pp. 146–9.

Helping parents reconstruct their perceptions of situations often entails providing them with information about age-appropriate expectations of children. One of the authors whose baby was prone to wake every hour found it helpful to tell herself, before she got out of bed, that eight-week-old babies could not, in fact, wake themselves up with malevolent intent.

It also seems to help some parents if they are coached to engage in constructive self-talk, giving themselves positive feedback on their performance whilst handling a situation:

> That was a good answer, now just make sure you stick to what you've said. You know what his next move will be, don't you, going to the tin as soon as your back's turned, so what will you do then? Yes, that's a good idea, put the tin out of reach now.

Choosing alternative courses of action presupposes the ability to think constructively about a situation, to decide what courses of action could be taken and to choose which would be best. Often, abusing parents are unable to resolve not only problems with their children, but more general difficulties, and the resulting stress and frustration contribute to their general outbursts. Problem-solving can be taught, and this has been one component that several self-control training programmes have used. Unfortunately, because programmes with abusing parents so often include a *number* of intervention strategies (reflecting an appreciation of the urgency and multifaceted nature of the problem) it is impossible to say which procedures are in fact (the most) effective or responsible for the successful outcomes reported.

One other question worth considering is whether or not intervention with these clients is enhanced by adopting a group approach rather than, or in addition to, individual help. Reports of such an approach suggest it is (Nomellini and Katz, 1983; Barth *et al.*, 1983). It seems that groups may be a valuable source of social contact for these clients. Reducing social isolation was one of the aims of the second study, and is supported by Wahler (1980) who ascertained that parents' child–directed punitive behaviour was significantly correlated with the number of extrafamilial contracts they enjoyed with friends on any day i.e. the more such contacts the fewer the incidents of punishment. The group setting also gives an opportunity to provide parents with a variety of coping models, and feedback and support for change endeavours.

ENURESIS

We end this chapter with a discussion of a very specific, but important, behaviour.

> There is a clear role for the social worker in the management and treatment of enuresis. . . .
>
> (Morgan, 1982)

This is the conclusion of one authority on this all too common childhood problem. There are a number of competing explanatory hypotheses but the evidence overwhelmingly supports the view that, while there may be a biological predisposition to enuresis, a learning-based intervention is almost always appropriate. In a small minority of cases enuresis can be caused by, or treatment hampered by, infection or physical abnormality and so it is important that children are examined by a doctor before any treatment is undertaken.

In order to use the toilet a child needs to recognise signs of a full bladder, caused by the rhythmic contractions of the bladder wall and which are experienced as urgency. To avoid wetting the bed, he must also exercise control over excessive bladder contractions (preventing urination), and wake up. Some children seem less sensitive than others to such stimuli, failing to acquire the skills necessary for emptying their bladders in the toilet. Others lose these skills. The reasons for secondary enuresis, as the latter problem is called, are unknown and in any case the treatment remains the same: teaching the child to recognise and respond to bladder fullness.

There are, broadly speaking, three kinds of treatment strategy: drug treatment; intensive operant programmes such as that developed by Azrin and his colleagues (1974); and the enuresis alarm (bell and pad). Most commonly used in this country is the enuresis alarm, usually administered by the health authority under the direction of health visitors or an enuresis clinic. We shall give a brief outline of how the alarm is thought to work and then detail why it is important that social workers are familiar with this problem and able and willing to advise and intervene on their client's behalf. Any worker seeking to advise on the problem of enuresis or embark on treatment must acquire further information (such as that offered by Morgan, 1981; or Doleys, 1979) both regarding the nature of the problem and the important detail of treatment.

The enuresis alarm is essentially a respondent intervention and works as follows. When a child begins to urinate the urine completes an electrical circuit which sets off an alarm. The alarm wakes the child who realises he needs to urinate, gets up, turns off the alarm and goes to the toilet to finish urinating. Besides waking the child, the alarm also produces tension in the pelvic floor, closing the bladder outlet. As treatment progresses the child learns to associate these two responses – waking and closure of the bladder outlet (holding on) – with the stimulus of bladder contractions. One of the most common mistakes made is for parents to turn off the alarm before waking child, who has then 'missed' this learning opportunity.

Along with the proper use of the equipment, many other procedures are necessary: careful explanation, record-keeping, provision of reinforcement for the child and anyone else involved in assisting him, and, of course, a good deal of trouble-shooting, such as anticipating mechanical problems and misunderstandings, or preparing the family to cope with complaints from another child whose sleep is being disturbed.

When used correctly the alarm has an across the board success rate of 80% with an average relapse rate of 12.8%. This increases to 35.6% amongst children in care, because this client group is more prone to factors correlated with relapse, such as stress or change of circumstances. Parents should be told of the possiblity of relapse and advised that this is not an indication of failure, but merely signals the need for a booster programme.

Often clients (and other professionals) think enuresis is something that children will grow out of or, at the other extreme, that it is symptomatic of some underlying psychopathology. Such faulty information prevents clients from seeking and getting the help they need. There is no evidence of symptom substitution following behavioural interventions, and, though it does diminish, research does not suggest the problem disappears with age. There are enough teenagers and not a few adults who still bedwet.

Behaviourally-trained social workers, familiar with the literature, are well placed to provide sound advice and to supervise both operant and respondent programmes. Enuresis is a problem they frequently encounter and they are well aware of the other problems it entails: cost and effort involved in laundry; as a precipitant of parental anger; social isolation of 'smelly' children; foster-home breakdown. Given the high success rate of treatment it is a pity that more is not commonly undertaken by social workers, either in attempting intervention themselves (with medical approval) or referring to an appropriate agency. A lot is made of the phenomenon in terms of its alleged emotional correlates e.g. it is cited as a sign that some event or relationship is emotionally disturbing. As Morgan concludes, this is to:

> overrate the significance of enuresis in indicating anything other than poor bladder control, and the social worker may greatly benefit a client by placing his enuresis in a more accurate perspective.
>
> (Morgan, 1982)

9

Older Children and Teenagers: With Special Reference to Delinquency

This chapter will be largely concerned with the problem of delinquency, for three reasons. Firstly, the size of the problem is such as to merit special consideration. Secondly, the term delinquency is used to encompass many problems which, alone, are not necessarily indicative of delinquency e.g. non-school attendance or family discord. Thirdly, many of these problems are found in teenagers who have not come before the courts, either through inconsistencies in the legal system or because of their age, that is, they are what Americans would term 'predelinquent'.

Some delinquent acts such as stealing are extremely common even amongst non-delinquent adolescents (some 63% of boys interviewed by Belson (1975) admitted theft of a non-trivial kind at school). In order to attach a label such as delinquency, which has well known social consequences, one must be able to decide when a young person's behaviour is outside the range of the 'normal'. Delinquency should therefore be defined in terms of the intensity and frequency with which certain behaviours are performed by an individual, rather than merely in terms of the behaviours themselves. And, writing from a behavioural point of view, it seems appropriate to include in this discussion all who perform certain antisocial behaviours, whether or not they are apprehended and adjudicated 'delinquent'.

Despite our focus on behavioural contributions, delinquency, like child abuse (and indeed the majority of the problems which social work faces), needs to be understood as a social problem, informed by a number of other disciplines besides social learning theory. Important amongst these are sociology and various strands of psy-

chological research such as attribution theory and moral development. The social learning approach in fact uses findings from these
other areas of psychological research, as will become apparent in the
course of this chapter.

BEHAVIOURAL CONTRIBUTIONS TO THE
UNDERSTANDING OF DELINQUENCY

Family interaction

Longitudinal studies demonstrate clearly that delinquents do not
develop 'overnight' but represent the end of a continuum of learning
which starts very early on indeed. Early (and unresolved) behaviour
problems of the type referred to in the previous chapter are highly
correlated with later delinquency. West and Farrington (1973)
compared children who became delinquent with those who did not on
a wide range of variables. They found that delinquents were more
likely than non-delinquents to come from large families, families with
low incomes, families with a record of parental criminality and/or low
intelligence. One composite variable they examined (i.e. an amalgam
of apparently related variables) which differentiated delinquents
from non-delinquents was 'poor parental behaviour'. This is particularly interesting in the light of other research such as that
conducted by Patterson and his colleagues at the Oregon Research
Institute (for a review of their findings, see Patterson, 1982). Whilst
the children they studied were under fourteen and most had not been
adjudicated 'delinquent', the problems they presented closely resem-
bled those of teenagers formally designated 'delinquent'.

These researchers have carried out impressive microanalyses of
family functioning which suggest that the parents of conduct-disordered children do not cue, nor do they reinforce, socially appropriate behaviour. They rarely set rules, they fail to give clear messages
about the rightness or wrongness of particular behaviours and are
poor supervisors of their children's activities.

At the same time, these families exhibit frequent and prolonged
coercive interchanges (see Chapter 8), in which parents use a great
deal of punishment and negative reinforcement (physical, verbal and
psychological) inconsistently and ineffectively. The significance of
these exchanges is thought to lie in the *affective* information they

convey. They are triggered not by specific misdemeanours on the part of the child but by feelings of irritation or annoyance on the part of the parent. The parent makes a comment or gives a command and immediately goes on to make a series of negative, increasingly general comments about the child's behaviour. If the child manages to say anything it is usually defensive and hostile and this simply fuels the onslaught. The parent's comments have little impact on the child's behaviour because, rather than communicating how the parent wants him to behave, the predominant message is anger and irritation.

This is accompanied by an apparent lack of affection for the child coupled with few shared (pleasurable) activities. It is hypothesised that such low rates of pleasant interaction reduce the reinforcing potential of the parent, who consequently has little influence over the child. Stuart (1970) has also emphasised the low rate of positive exchanges in the families of older delinquents.

These researchers report that there are consistent links between such negative behaviours as yelling, teasing, temper outbursts, non-compliance and fighting, and delinquent behaviours such as lying, stealing, running off and so on. The implication is that these lower frequency (delinquent) behaviours can be affected by interventions focusing on the higher frequency, family-oriented ones (Patterson, 1982). Whilst the empirical evidence to date is rather slender and the bulk of these analyses have been conducted with the families of aggressive adolescents, few of whom have passed through the courts, Rutter and Giller (1983, p.256), commenting critically but favourably on this body of research, write:

> The suggestion, in common with that in other social learning theories, that 'aggression' and 'delinquency' can be usefully broken down into hierarchies of interlinked behaviours is . . . critical in its provision of useful openings for therapeutic interventions.
>
> This approach seems to be one of the most important new developments in the field of family studies of delinquent youths, and further work of this type is much needed . . . [it] provides a most promising new way of tackling old, but still unresolved problems.

Socialisation and the development of internal control

Socialisation begins early, within the family, children being rewarded and punished for socially appropriate and inappropriate behaviour. Respondent conditioning is thought to be one aspect of this process.

Punishment is believed to cause considerable anxiety in the child as it is linked with (temporary) withdrawal of parental affection/approval. Over time, this anxiety becomes associated with the punished behaviour so that, faced with a similar situation, the child is prevented from misbehaving by the need to reduce his anxiety and to avoid the possible loss of parental affection.

A child's understanding of right and wrong is developed by giving him reasons for the prohibitions and exhortations he encounters, by using simple rules and principles (generalisation) and endowing these with appropriate feelings such as aversion to stealing or inflicting pain (maintenance). Internal control is established as the child learns to reinforce and punish his own behaviour in the absence of others.

These processes are thought to impinge on the development of delinquency in the following ways. First, if it is the case that the delinquent's background is often one in which there is a poor relationship between parent and child, then one important mechanism of socialisation and the development of internal control is automatically weakened, namely the threat of loss of love. This links with Patterson's suggestion that the reinforcing value of such parents is weak.

Further, in the absence of a positive relationship, the child who is punished is likely to respond with anger and aggression. Research suggests that these are in fact the 'normal' human responses to punishment which are inhibited by the anxiety aroused in a child with a close, loving relationship.

It has been suggested that the over-representation of delinquents amongst working class children may be partly due to the tendency of working class parents to expect their children to do what they say without lengthy explanations (Newson, 1972, cited in Herbert, 1978), thus providing them with fewer opportunities to develop the understanding of moral rules and concepts which play such an important part in internalising control. Finally, the failure to spell out to children the consequences of their actions may also contribute to a common characteristic of delinquents, namely their inability to empathise with others, to put themselves in other peoples's shoes and envisage what the consequences of their actions will be for them. This is sometimes referred to as a failure in role taking (Platt *et al.*, 1974).

Although much of this theory is either very speculative or rests on a slender empirical base there are, as Rutter and Giller suggest, sound implications for intervention, the foremost of which is the need for preventive work and early, family-based intervention. The relevance of skill deficits is discussed next. The need to equip adolescents who lack them with effective self-control strategies seems particularly important.

Additional learning models

Skill deficits. Another conceptualisation of delinquency that is informing behavioural interventions is of delinquency as situation-specific skill deficits (Freedman *et al.*, 1978). The basic idea is that delinquents lack the necessary skills to tackle satisfactorily the problems they encounter every day and instead generate solutions which bring them into conflict with society. These ideas are detailed below. According to these authors the chance of a boy being classed as delinquent increases as a function of three things:
(1) the extent of his inability to deal effectively with everyday problems;
(2) the frequency with which he encounters those situations;
(3) the degree to which his solutions depend on illegal behaviour.
Their research supports their claim and points clearly to the need for intervention strategies which will enhance the delinquent's ability to resolve everyday problems in socially acceptable ways.
Operant conditioning theory highlights the importance of considering the roles played by reinforcement and setting events (antecedents) in maintaining delinquency. Sources of reinforcement may be internal, such as arousal – the youth who steals, attacks or abuses solvents 'for kicks'; or external – the youth who steals in order to acquire goods which he could not otherwise acquire. Where intervention with an individual is possible these factors require special attention if it is to succeed. However, there are many sources of social reinforcement, some of which we may be unable to do anything about except by adopting a community approach. For instance, Stumphauzer *et al.*, (1979) identified such consequences as police attention, as well as attention from their peers, as highly reinforcing to delinquent gang members.

RESEARCH EVIDENCE: BEHAVIOURAL INTERVENTIONS

Twenty years ago when the first studies of behavioural interventions with delinquents were published, much optimism was generated that, at last, there was something practitioners could do to tackle this 'intractable' problem. Such optimism was relatively short-lived. Most of the early work was conducted with institutionalised adolescents; and follow-up studies soon showed that the changes that had been effected within the institution failed to generalise to the community to which the young people returned, and had little or no impact on their rates of re-offending. This latter fact highlighted another problem, namely that most of the behaviours selected for change were not criminal/delinquent behaviours and, further, had no empirically established relationship with delinquent behaviours. All too often they were behaviours which related to the smooth running of the institution, and so it is not surprising that such behaviours 'lapsed' when the young people found themselves back in an environment where there was no direct relationship between what they did and the consequences of their behaviour (institutional programmes typically specified 'do this' and 'this' will happen). Poor research methodologies completed this depressing picture, severely limiting the conclusions that could be drawn from even the most encouraging studies.

However, the present day picture is again a more promising one. More attention is being given to methodological problems, and research into community-based programmes is increasing. Behaviour analytic studies looking at the behavioural differences between delinquent and non-delinquent groups are producing validated hypotheses as to which behaviours are in fact correlated with delinquency and which, if changed, might bring about a decrease in delinquent behaviour. These studies are also shedding light on what behaviours (including cognitive behaviours) might account for the existence of non-delinquents in circumstances that would, ordinarily, predispose a young person to delinquency, such as living in a community with a high rate of juvenile crime or belonging to a large family in which there are several delinquent siblings (e.g. Aiken *et al.*, 1979; Stumphauzer *et al.*, 1979). Interventions are being developed to deal with delinquent behaviours such as theft and alcohol abuse (Stumphauzer, 1979, 1980; Wodarski and Lenhart, 1982).

Whilst it would be quite misleading to say behavioural practitioners have the answer to the problems of delinquency it is fair to say that they presently appear to offer more than their psychodynamic colleagues whose interventions have been shown to be sadly lacking (e.g. Cornish and Clarke, 1975; Feldman, 1977, 1983). Certain interventions seem particularly promising and well founded and there is some evidence that a number of areas of work repay attention.

APPROACHES TO INTERVENTION

Family work

Although family-based intervention becomes progressively harder as the child gets older, there is a growing body of evidence that such work can be done and some evidence that it can reduce the number of minor offences such as running away, using soft drugs and shoplifting, as well as reducing non-compliance and aggression within the family (Alexander and Parsons, 1973). As we have seen, the problems most commonly found in families experiencing unusual levels of difficulty with their older children are:
—an established cycle of unpleasant, very negative interaction
—a correspondingly low rate of pleasant exchanges
—an abundance of conflict with no give-and-take between family members
—a history of inconsistent disciplining of the young person concerned.
Typically parents, in a desperate attempt to regain control, heap sanction upon sanction on the youngster. It is often impossible for parents to carry out these sanctions and, more significantly, they fail to inform him of what he must do in order that these sanctions be removed. The older child often feels he has nothing more to lose and simply disregards them. In fact he may have one more thing to lose – his place in the family – and it is often at this point that he arrives at the social worker's office.

With older children, parent training, as described in the previous chapter, ceases to be either appropriate or sufficient, and is superseded by an approach which is most accurately described as behavioural family therapy. The aims of behavioural family therapy are, broadly speaking, to resolve conflict and to bring about changes in family patterns of interaction, teaching negotiation skills and endeavouring to increase the rate of pleasant exchanges. Progress depends on clarity of communication and one of the first steps is to get parents to stipulate their expectations of their offspring.

In order to break the impasse reached between parent and teenager the social worker often needs to assume a directive role initially, getting all parties to spell out their grievances and wishes and arbitrating a negotiated settlement in which everyone stands to gain something and, if possible, does not lose too much. In doing this the worker is modelling negotiation behaviours and, in all probability, introducing (and rendering acceptable) the idea of negotiation to parents who fail to see why they should yield anything to someone as unreasonable as their teenager. The most common medium for this procedure is the behavioural contract discussed in Chapter 6. Having broken this impasse, the next step is to equip the parties with negotiation skills, if these are what they lack.

In order to negotiate problems and resolve conflict people need several skills including the ability to:

(1) see things from another's point of view;
(2) define the problem (What I want is X but what you want is Y);
(3) generate alternative solutions;
(4) evaluate those solutions in terms of their consequences (good and bad);
(5) select the alternative that gives as much recognition to everyone's interests as possible (and/or which is most acceptable to most people);
(6) implement the solution selected.

Skills (2) to (6) have been taught to families experiencing difficulties with their teenage members. There is a marked resemblance to the procedures used to teach individuals problem-solving skills, the difference being the emphasis on communication and negotiation components. Methods found to be useful in training communication and negotiation skills are shaping, prompting, modelling, behaviour rehearsal (lots of it) and feedback. Role reversal within role-plays might be one way of enhancing the role taking ability (empathy) of family members who seem unable to appreciate how their actions will affect other parties. Giving all parties equal amounts of time to put their point of view (Alexander and Parsons, 1973) and shaping the communications they make so that they are complete and presented in the most acceptable light (Kifer *et al.*, 1974) also seem promising ways of establishing the give-and-take relationships upon which family harmony rests.

The research in this area is promising although the results are, at best, mixed. Kifer *et al.*, (1974) reported substantial increases in negotiation skills which generalised beyond the training sessions to

new conflicts (cf. Robin *et al.*, 1977). However, in a more sophisticated study by Foster *et al.* (1983), significant improvements were
noted at the end of training, on a range of outcome measures, but not
all of these were maintained at follow-up some six to eight weeks
later. Amongst the possible reasons for their results the authors
consider the following. Whereas Kifer's programme used a proportion of hypothetical conflict situations, Foster *et al.* used the problem
situations brought by the families themselves throughout training.
Apart from the possibility that these problems may actually have
been more difficult to solve, the authors suggest that:

> the content and distress associated with these problems may have
> inadvertently diverted the families and/or instructors from the
> instructional aspects of the program, thus sacrificing skill acquisi-
> tion for workable solutions to problematic situations   (p. 19).

It was not that families failed to solve their present problems but that
the 'principles' of problem-solving got lost amongst the specific issues
in which everyone had such a vested interest. Posing hypothetical
problems may therefore enhance generalisation by enhancing skill
acquisition. Most participants (both adult and adolescent) rated the
programme highly and reported improvements which were not, in
fact, borne out by the behavioural data; this discrepant finding is not
uncommon (e.g. Eyberg and Johnson, 1974).

The most exciting results to date are those reported by Alexander
and Parsons (1973). Their behavioural approach to family therapy
produced both positive changes in family interaction and significant
reductions (statistically and economically) in recidivism rates in the
referred adolescent and his or her siblings. This major, controlled
study was undertaken with young offenders aged thirteen to sixteen
years who had been convicted of minor offences, such as possessing
soft drugs and alcohol, shop-lifting and running away: however,
more recent work by this group with much more serious offenders has
also proved extremely promising (Barton, 1980; cited in Lane and
Burchard, 1983).

The apparent connection between family functioning and delinquency is one good reason for working with families whenever
possible. Also, in order to counter peer influence it is necessary to
establish some community-based sources of control and reinforcement for socially appropriate behaviour: the family remains one of

the most obvious candidates for this role given the amount of time the adolescent spends there (when not with his peers this is where he is likely to be). And unless relationships are in tatters, one or both parents is likely to remain a 'significant' other.

Non-school attendance

This is an important problem to tackle because there is evidence that suggests a strong relationship between truancy and delinquency, the majority of delinquents having a history of truancy (Glueck and Glueck (1950) report the proportion of the delinquents they studied with a record of truancy to be some 95%). Precisely what the link is is uncertain. It may be that the patterns of punishment and negative reinforcement experienced by the child at home are repeated at school, which becomes a place to be avoided. Looking at the experience of all too many adolescents, it is reasonable to hypothesise that school is somewhere where a sense of failure is fostered and where there is little in the way of incentive to attend. Certainly the amount of unstructured time which results from truancy is a significant factor in the performance of delinquent (and law-breaking) behaviours, many of which occur in the time the teenager should be in school. Robins (1970) revealed that 82% of his sample of male truants had frequently been absent in the first two years of their school life. Together these factors point again to the importance of preventive work: breaking the chain of events at the earliest possible point.

We need to distinguish between the school refuser whose refusal is based upon some form of anxiety – sometimes school-based but often some form of separation anxiety – and the truant who absents himself regularly and frequently without good reason. Whereas the 'school phobic', as the first sort of non-school attender is often called, stays at home with the knowledge (and often approval) of his parents, the truant's parents rarely know of their offspring's absences until they are contacted by the school. In all probability these 'types' represent two ends of a continuum: often one is faced with a non-school attender whose behaviour has elements of both problems. A behavioural assessment will soon clarify which problems are present: each has different implications for intervention.

Where non-school attendance is related to anxiety, the most usual forms of intervention are desensitisation and the gradual re-establishment of school attendance, and these have a high success rate. (See

Chapters 5 and 11). When faced with the persistent truant one is back to contingency management (Herbert, 1978). The Leeds experiment, in which magistrates made the non-making of care orders contingent upon regular school attendance (sentence being deferred to allow the young person to improve/re-establish school attendance), was an extreme form of contingency management relying upon negative reinforcement; but there is continuing debate about the full consequences of its detailed implementation. The more usual form is a contractual agreement between the parents and the child based largely, though not exclusively, on the use of positive reinforcement. The aim is to establish regular school attendance as soon as possible. Where appropriate the social worker and/or school staff are parties to the agreement.

A functional analysis of the young person's non-school attendance is crucial: what factors maintain it? Is there someone to wake him up and supervise his going off to school? If he leaves on time but doesn't get to school, at which point does he decide not to go and what does he do with his time? Legal constraints mean that school attendance is not negotiable and it may be necessary to eliminate sources of positive reinforcement for non-attendance wherever possible. More common, however, is the establishment of incentives for the teenager's return to school, such as outings, extra pocket-money, permission to stay out late and so on. Negative reinforcement does play a role in so far as one might persuade parents to relax sanctions already in existence, contingent upon school attendance. Similarly social workers could make a reduction in their visits contingent upon school attendance.

How does the young person explain his non-attendance? Are his complaints valid and is there something you could do to improve the situation? Some teachers are willing to make school as attractive as possible for the non-attender, although without fundamental changes in the education system such endeavours are extremely limited. It is interesting to note that some of the young people who began attending school in Leeds following their court appearances, reported that once attendance had been re-established their opinion of school shifted favourably: going to school, like not going to school, is habit forming.

It is often possible to minimise the unpleasant consequences that tend to follow the truant's return to school. For instance teachers can be prevailed upon not to thank pupils sarcastically for 'gracing the school with their presence' when they appear, and can take steps to minimise the taunts of classmates, perhaps by behaving as if the non-attender had not been absent and ignoring contrary behaviour on the part of other pupils.

Social skills and problem-solving

There is still a paucity of research examining normal adolescent behaviour. Its importance cannot be overstated, partly because of the wide range of the 'normal' but largely because we need to know which skills are correlated with non-delinquent behaviours if we are to implement appropriate changes within the skill repertoires of delinquents. Further, skills taught to adolescents need to be adolescent-appropriate and not based solely on adult conceptions of prosocial behaviour. Given the importance of the peer group, it is only by establishing behaviours that will not be ridiculed or rejected by other adolescents that their survival beyond training will be ensured.

Social skills

Skills deficits could be due to an inhibiting anxiety (i.e. the skills are there but are not being used), to an absence of behavioural skills, both verbal and non-verbal, or to maladaptive or inadequate cognitive processes. Much of the work reported with adolescents to date has focused on the behavioural components of skill performance, such as increasing eye-contact or being assertive (but polite) as an alternative response to anger. (For a useful guide to procedures in this area of work, see for example the manuals by Liberman *et al.*, 1975; or Spence, 1980). There has been an emphasis on teaching conversational skills (Minkin *et al.*, 1976) and much work has been done on addressing and talking with authority figures such as policemen. This last has a two-fold rationale and/or source of empirical support. First, communication has been demonstrated to be an integral part of interpersonal problem-solving (e.g. Platt *et al.*, 1974). Secondly, a person's mode of communication has a direct bearing on the way people respond to him. Pilavin and Briar (1964) for instance, showed that the differences that one so often encounters in the handling of offenders by the police (e.g. middle class boys being less likely to be prosecuted) is largely due to the discretion exercised by the arresting officer. This is determined, in large part, by the young person's behaviour and attitudes to the officer.

Problem-solving

Inadequate cognitive skills have been identified in delinquents' inability to satisfactorily resolve problems (Platt *et al.*, 1974). The research by Freedman *et al.* (1978) demonstrated that delinquent adolescents performed better on their Adolescent Problems Inventory when it was presented to them in a multiple-choice form. That is to say, they could recognise more appropriate courses of action than the ones they themselves suggested, but were not very good at thinking them up unaided.

The reported difference in problem-solving skills has obvious implications for work with delinquents. There is a clear format for teaching these skills (and plenty of evidence that they can be learned) but one must not lose sight of the situation-specificity of skill deficits. It takes a different style of interaction, and requires different sorts of strategies, to resolve conflict with the police than conflict with a classmate. Each individual requires a personal assessment of his skill deficits across the range of situations which seem to cause him problems. This remains the case even though the group medium is the usual forum for the implementation of skills training. It is in fact an ideal medium of change for this population. Besides offering workers the chance to observe the behaviour of their clients within a peer group, it provides the opportunity for sharing ideas which are most likely to be acceptable to the adolescents concerned, and for modelling and behaviour rehearsal which are important change procedures.

Social skills training has rather 'taken off' both in the UK and in the USA and is one of the more acceptable faces of behavioural work. But despite an impressive track record with regard to demonstrable behaviour change, there has been little evidence to date that it has significantly helped teenagers with the problems they face or reduced the rate of offending associated with delinquency. We have suggested that one probable reason has been the mismatch between the skills taught and those teenagers actually need to solve the problems they face. Improvements on this front are reviving the faith that has been placed in this important area of work.

Anger and Aggression

As we indicated earlier one important skill (or set of skills) which delinquents often lack is self-control. There is growing interest in teaching anger control techniques to adolescents (Goldstein *et al.*, 1978), and the approaches used are largely similar to those described on pp. 186–7, with considerable attention being paid to how adolescents talk to themselves and the attributions they make. The adolescent who turns on an innocent bystander (or social worker) and says: 'What are you looking at me like that for?' when the person concerned wasn't 'looking at them' at all is an example of the 'attributional errors' commonly made by problem adolescents. The consequences of such mistakes are familiar to anyone who has worked with teenagers: either the accused person reacts antagonistically, in which case an unpleasant exchange commences; or they withdraw or apologise, which the adolescent construes as evidence in favour of his perception.

Focus on 'setting events' is central to establishing self-control, as the person needs to be able to identify the situations likely to 'spark him off' as early as possible in order to put into practice the techniques he has learned. There is some indication that if a person can be helped to understand the sequence of events which precipitates his behaviour he can develop a degree of 'immunity' to those stimuli, although there is no indication that such understanding is sufficient in itself.

Cowie (1982) reports the successful placement with foster parents of a difficult and violent girl who 'had demolished all of the possible CH(E)s (Community Homes with Education), stabbed several policemen and care workers and was turned down by the secure unit on the grounds of being too violent'. A simple contract was set up in which, at the request of the foster parents, the girl promised to go to her room whenever they thought she was about to lose her temper, whether she agreed with them or not. Contingent upon her compliance certain reinforcers were provided at the end of the week (together with small sanctions for non-compliance). The girl was helped to identify the things which triggered her outbursts, such as being criticised, being bossed about and being tired. With the foster mother's help, she practised alternative strategies such as counting to ten and punching a bean bag, and role-played appropriate reactions to criticisms. Cowie points out that the foster parents were very skilled and the girl herself had a lot to lose (was at risk of being sent to a psychiatric prison) and was therefore highly motivated. However, these results are still impressive. Apart from one minor hiccup (which could have been disastrous had her foster parents not fought for her

to have 'one more chance') she went 'from strength to strength' and
Cowie reports that the girl secured a job in a local nursery and, when
last seen, was 'changed out of all recognition'.

Theft

On the whole, behavioural interventions with stealing have had
disappointing results: with significant reductions being made but not
maintained. However, in 1981 Henderson reported successful intervention to eliminate the stealing behaviours of ten boys between
the ages of eight and fifteen years, who had been stealing for periods
ranging from six months to eight years. At the time he published, all
of the boys had had two years without stealing; eight of the ten
stopped stealing at the commencement of intervention, despite varied
histories.

This is an interesting report in that it attends not only to the
external factors apparently maintaining the stealing but to the
internal factors which simultaneously cue and reinforce behaviour
i.e. arousal. Henderson hypothesises (on the basis of other research)
that the feelings and thoughts which accompany theft acquire
stimulus control over stealing behaviour and, at the same time,
provide a source of immediate reinforcement. For example, a study of
the interactions of families of children who steal, conducted by Reid
and Hendricks (1973), suggests that there is a low rate of both positive
and negative interchanges, which motivates youngsters to seek
excitement and positive reinforcement outside the home.

Henderson's intervention was threefold and comprised:

Internal/self-control. Clients were taught to identify internal stimuli
(e.g. arousal) and to control these via relaxation. Self-talk was taught
as a means of thought-stopping and initiating alternative responses
e.g. to walk away rather than steal, praising oneself for so doing.
Procedures were first practised in the clinic and then in the
environment where 'traps' were set for the client (with his agreement).

External/other control. With a view to increasing non-stealing
behaviour, each boy kept a note-book in which his parents and/or
teachers recorded all periods during which they knew he had not

stolen (whilst observed). They also recorded the length of time it took him to travel from A to B: if his travel time coincided with the length of time they would expect him to take (many journeys were timed for this purpose) he was deemed not to have stolen (an activity which would have lengthened the journey). The total time was converted into minutes per day which were then exchanged for back-up reinforcers.

Individualising the back-up reinforcers. The worker ascertained what the child did with goods stolen and endeavoured to provide the same sort of gains for not stealing. Three categories were used: stealing for *friendship* (e.g. buys presents); for *adult attention* (e.g. is easily caught); and for *'kicks'* (e.g. does nothing with the goods).

Henderson rightly describes this approach as 'a proposal for treatment based on ten cases'. But his results are impressive and, whilst he describes this intervention as suitable only for clients who wish to stop stealing, he also reports that most, in fact, do wish this.

Sexuality

In a concise summary of the available evidence (1984, USA) Schinke reports that the rates of contraceptive use have lagged behind the very significant rise in sexual activity reported amongst teenagers; the age at which intercourse first occurs is dropping; the rise in the rate of abortion has not halted the rise in the number of children born to teenage mothers. The children of adolescent parents, and the parents themselves, fare badly on a whole host of social, psychological and educational variables.

Schinke and his colleagues have developed a cognitive–behavioural approach to the prevention of teenage pregnancy which can be used both within institutions and in the community. Based on survey and correlational data these workers hypothesised that effective contraceptive behaviour depended on *cognitive skills* enabling informed decision-making, the resolution of interpersonal problems and implementation of solutions; and *behavioural skills*, such as the ability to discuss contraception with a prospective partner (research indicates contraceptive use to be higher amongst couples who have discussed contraception prior to intercourse than amongst those who have not).

In order to equip adolescents with the necessary cognitive skills clients are provided with factual material on reproduction and birth control and are helped to relate this material to their own situations e.g. to move from 'unwanted intercourse leads to pregnancy' to 'when Rick and I have sex without using anything, I could get pregnant' (Schinke, 1984, p.49). Problem-solving training is then provided following the procedures discussed earlier. Modelling and behaviour rehearsal are used to teach verbal and non-verbal components of effective interpersonal communication e.g. approach, refusal and request responses. Homework assignments are used (written and practical) and include: getting information about birth control; pricing contraceptives; discussing birth control with dating partners and significant adults.

Several controlled studies (comparing these procedures with both wait-list controls and other methods e.g. education alone/placebo) have now been conducted with large numbers of adolescents of both sexes. Results consistently indicate that at post-test and follow-up teenagers who have participated in such programmes know more about human sexuality, have better attitudes and intentions towards birth control, and are better able to raise and discuss sexual and contraceptive matters with an opposite-sexed partner, and arrive at negotiated decisions (e.g. Gilchrist and Schinke, 1983). Whilst more evidence is needed (particularly more and longer follow-up periods) several studies so far suggest that members of prevention groups go on to use birth control more regularly, and use more effective methods, than members of control groups. Such intervention has received very positive acclaim by adolescents, parents and teachers.

These authors have used the same approach to tackle health problems such as smoking (Gilchrist *et al.*, 1979). Results are similarly encouraging.

COMMUNITY-BASED PROJECTS

In this section we shall outline two community-based residential projects and one non-residential approach with young offenders. The residential projects provide promising models of structured intervention; the non-residential approach, known as Intermediate Treatment, highlights the need for such structure and one such attempt is identified.

Achievement Place (USA)

Achievement Place was a small group-home set up in 1967 which was run on behavioural lines by two teaching parents who were more akin to professional foster parents than residential workers, in that they were a married couple and comprised the entire staff. The residents were local boys who could therefore continue to attend their own schools and maintain contact with their parents. Rehabilitation home was the overall aim. Operant programmes using social and token reinforcement; self-government; and social skills training, were the three main strategies used.

Both the total programme and the interventions relating to particular target behaviours were stringently evaluated. Early results (Braukmann *et al.*, 1975) suggested improvements in the educational and social skills of boys at Achievement Place whose re-conviction rate was 19% as opposed to over 50% for boys placed in other institutions or on probation. Conclusions could not be firmly drawn as there had not been a random allocation of boys to Achievement Place, so that these boys might in any case have been less likely to re-offend (more likely to improve), more socially skilled, from more supportive families and so on. More serious problems appeared in follow-up data and in attempts to replicate the original Achievement Place project. The dramatic difference in re-conviction almost disappeared after several years, and many other homes based on this model have failed to produce the same results (Kirigin *et al.*, 1982). However the research orientation of Achievement Place means that problem selection and intervention are constantly being refined, and as our understanding of delinquency improves, it is hoped that future work will be more effective.

Achievement Place pioneered the move away from institutional care in the USA, and one thing that can be said with some certainty is that, whatever the limitations of community-based programmes, such a move does not lead to the upsurge in offending dreaded by some members of the populace (Webb and Scanlon, 1981).

Shape (UK)

Shape aims to provide living accommodation, work and work-skills training. By doing so in conditions approximating those of the local community from which clients come, and to which they are likely to return, it is hoped to minimise the problems of maintenance and generalisation that usually beset rehabilitative projects (Ostapuik and Reid, 1981)

Clients are offenders in their late teens and early twenties. The Shape programme is a phased one in which clients move from hostel accommodation, with around-the-clock supervision, to independent, non-shared flats via semi-independent accommodation (Ostapuik and Reid, 1981; Stallard, 1983) Besides the goals common to all residents, careful analyses are conducted of individuals' needs, and interventions are designed to tackle specific skill deficits and offence behaviours. Workers at Shape hope to teach coping behaviours which will be acceptable and appropriate alternatives, strong enough to replace previous responses, and which will receive sufficient reinforcement to ensure maintenance and generalisation.

There are to date no published results of individual programmes, but initial results of the project as a whole, using reconviction rates, are most encouraging. In the course of a thirteen-month follow-up 60% of Shape clients had not re-offended: an impressive result given that these clients had an average of 3.3 previous court appearances and 2.4 previous institutional placements (Stallard, 1983). Those who do re-offend appear to do so in the first six months.

Increasing attention is being paid to equipping Shape clients to survive 'out of work'. This illustrates the refreshingly down-to-earth nature of this project whose interventions are firmly tied to empirically identified and validated needs. They make innovative use of the community in which they (and their clients) must live and function, cultivating good relationships with agencies like the police and neighbourhood groups. Not only does this benefit their clients by providing sources of help, good modelling and valid feedback on behaviour change, it highlights the importance of community support for the success of such ventures. These sentiments are being echoed elsewhere, not least of all regarding the success of Achievement Place establishments (Kirigin *et al.*, 1982).

Intermediate treatment (IT)

Intermediate treatment was a political response to a dual concern in the UK: the failure of institutional treatment or ordinary community supervision to effect changes in adolescent offending, and the demonstrable undesirability and cost of institutional care. IT was conceived as a community-based alternative to incarceration which would leave the adolescent in his own home but which required him to engage in certain activities or 'treatment' which, it was hoped, would 'enrich (his) environment and assist with his development' (DHSS Guidelines, 1972). Unfortunately neither activities nor treatment were specified, reflecting the absence of any underlying model of delinquent behaviour. The result has been a mish-mash of projects into which have been poured much money, much ingenuity and much manpower but which, to date, have failed to demonstrate their effectiveness in tackling juvenile offending (or making more than a transient impact, if any, on the young person's quality of life).

The reasons for this are several. Much work has simply not been evaluated. Where evaluation has been tried the methodologies have been such as to pre-empt any conclusions; in particular, aims have been too global. There is an absence of empirically-based interventions. Often groups are simply activity-based, and whilst these may improve adolescent functioning, work to date does not substantiate this, nor does it indicate which components, if any, are effective. There is a tendency to channel predelinquent 'at risk' juveniles into IT which means that the population it was intended to help, i.e. offenders quite high up the penal 'tariff' (and at risk of custodial sentences, or removal from parental care to that of the local authority), is rarely provided for. Finally, there has been a failure to tackle offending behaviour (Preston, 1982).

The behavioural approach has much to offer this form of intervention. Besides its contributions to the understanding of problems detailed earlier, it provides a rationale for intervention and empirically-based guidelines for working with groups, the primary mode of intervention in Intermediate Treatment (see Chapter 7). One often comes across 'bits' of behavioural work within IT projects; often social skills training, often a parody of the real thing, but there have been few attempts to use a behavioural approach systematically for assessment and intervention purposes. One praiseworthy example was the Birmingham (UK) Action for Youth project.

The Birmingham Action for Youth

A day-care centre, this project took up to thirty young persons who fulfilled the following criteria: they were between the ages of fifteen and sixteen years; there was an immediate probability that they would be taken into residential care; there was some (albeit minimal) support from a parent. It aimed to provide work, social, and general survival skills (Preston, 1982). Upon entering the programme adolescents engaged in a three-week induction period in which their general skills, work skills, social and overall self-management skills were assessed using behavioural check-lists, observation, and educational tests. At the end of this period a contract was drawn up between the young person, the centre staff, the social worker and the parents: short- and long-term goals were specified where possible. (These were reviewed, along with progress, every two to three months). Adolescents then embarked on a three-stage programme.

Stage 1. Run in conjunction with individual education schemes (six to eight weeks average). Participants earned points for achieving a variety of set targets e.g. self-management and work behaviours. Points were exchangeable daily for a variety of activities.

Stage 2. When earning points consistently, adolescents moved on to an individual programme focusing on establishing work and social skills. A points system remained in operation but an emphasis was now placed on long-term reinforcers to encourage the budgeting and saving of points.

Stage 3. Work experience: an opportunity to generalise acquired skills and sample an actual working situation. Adolescents were now on a weekly points system. Preston (1982) reports that this gave participants, many of whom had criminal records, more realistic expectations of work.

The control group were twenty-six people who had been through the centre in the year prior to intervention. Results at three months' follow-up suggested that young people in both groups had done better at getting jobs than the average sixteen-year-old in Birmingham, and that adolescents in the treatment (behaviourally-based) group had had a better employment rate than the control group. However these differences disappeared at six months. Similar results were found when re-offending was examined. The conclusions drawn are that more follow-up supervision and support is needed in order to maintain changes, perhaps in the form of a drop-in facility. Rightly, Preston points to the need to focus more on family variables and family involvement, bridging the gap that presently exists between the IT workers who deal with the young person and the social worker who works with the family. She presents persuasive figures about the cost-effectiveness of this day-care programme.

Conclusion

Adolescents are an unwilling population on the whole and this, together with the enormous influence of an often inaccessible peer group, makes work with them difficult, to say the least. Further, the fact that delinquency is a social and not just a psychological problem, places very definite limits on what can be done on an individual or small group basis.

Special attention needs to be given to motivation. Some changes in family interaction will be sufficiently important for some adolescents to work for, if they can be persuaded they are possible. It is worth trying negative reinforcement (e.g. 'achieve this and I will apply to rescind an order/visit less frequently') or making some 'goodies' (e.g. IT activities) contingent upon change in other areas.

Even when you lack access to IT facilities (or similar) and find yourself face to face with an adolescent whose family is simply not interested in working with you (the other problem!) the material in this chapter can inform your intervention. Supervisory meetings can shift from the 'How are you getting on?' and the 'Why did you do that?' to the more profitable 'What is happening?' and 'What else could you have done?'. One-to-one situations are less advantageous in dealing with the sorts of problems we have mentioned, but more constructive use could be made of them than is often the case at present. Focused work also helps to sustain social workers' morale.

On the topic of the overall importance of behavioural work in these areas we give the last word to reviewers of considerable standing with no behavioural axe to grind:

Behavioural interventions . . . [seem] to offer most promise of effective methods of dealing with delinquent behaviour. Research in this field has been marked by care in detailed measurements of behaviours and in the steps taken to check whether changes in behaviour are functionally related to the mode of intervention. The results leave no doubt that important changes can be brought about. . . . so far as can be assessed, behavioural methods do appear to be more effective than most other approaches in the short term . . . The problem is not so much in bringing about change as in *maintaining* change . . . [and in] gaining people's involvement in those modes of intervention (a problem shared with all other methods).   (Rutter and Giller, 1983, p.283.)

10
Mental Handicap

CHILDREN

The mentally handicapped are most accurately described as developmentally, rather than mentally, retarded. Whilst there continues to be disagreement on the nature of mental retardation the present consensus is that the mentally retarded develop in the same way – sequentially – as the non-retarded, but do so at a much slower rate. Therefore it is more important to be familiar with the course of normal development than to use age-related norms in assessment and intervention. Regardless of age, the handicapped person's level of functioning needs to be seen against a background of what, in the normal course of events, it would be reasonable to expect him to do next, rather than what, given his age (be it eight or thirty-eight) one would expect him to do. Such a background will inform assessment and intervention in such a way as to prevent goal setting from being too ambitious and, more important, minimise intervention failures.

Areas of need: support, information and practical help

After recovering from the shock of discovering themselves the parents of a mentally handicapped child, the vast majority of parents are beset by two major concerns. First, how to cope with the extra demands and stress associated with caring for a mentally handicapped family member; in this respect their needs are for such things as knowledge of welfare rights and supportive services from professional bodies and from friends and family. Secondly, they are concerned to do 'the right thing'; that is to maximise the developmental chances of their son or daughter, and to provide as rich an environment as possible. A behavioural approach is especially suited to helping parents with this second concern.

The mentally handicapped child is, by dint of his handicap, deprived of many sources of reinforcement which are naturally available to his non-handicapped sibling: on the one hand he may be generally less responsive and so get less pleasure than a normal child from day to day interactions with those around him. On the other hand, his mental retardation (and the physical handicaps so often linked with it), may mean he is less able to avail himself of the pleasures afforded by, for instance, play activities or motor activities, that are generally recognised as important to developmental progress. This environmental deprivation is thought to be one of the factors contributing to the common phenomena of self-injury and self-stimulation in mentally handicapped children and adults. Both are thought to provide intrinsic sensory reinforcement. Sometimes enriching the child's environment will reduce such activity but, more usually, it is difficult to find an alternative reinforcer which is more attractive to the child. And, it must be said, the problem of self-injury is certainly much more complex than simply a matter of reinforcement or lack of it.

The behavioural approach has a major contribution to make to the quality of life of the mentally handicapped person, simply because of its concern with the role of antecedents and consequences in eliciting and maintaining behaviour. The behavioural worker will look to see in what ways the mentally handicapped person's environment can be changed in order to compensate for the missing stimuli and rewards, improving life generally and enhancing his chances to develop.

The developmental problems faced by the mentally handicapped mean that if they are to achieve their full potential, their environments must be specifically designed to facilitate this. The impressive record of behavioural interventions with the mentally handicapped testifies to the appropriateness of this view. Even when the developmental 'ceiling' that can reasonably be expected is quite low (some severely mentally handicapped persons will not develop beyond the level usually associated with a two-year-old) the scope for developing certain basic skills now exists that was thought impossible fifteen or twenty years ago.

The behavioural contribution

The bulk of intervention strategies with the mentally handicapped are derived from the operant model, particularly important being shaping, chaining, prompting, fading and the use of reinforcement. These are now commonplace in educational programmes with the mentally handicapped and are used to teach self-help skills (washing, dressing, eating, toileting), communication, work and social skills.

It is not possible adequately to cover the scope of behavioural interventions with the mentally handicapped. There is a rich and exciting literature and various suggestions for further reading are given in the Appendix. We hope to give a flavour of those areas of work most likely to be encountered by the fieldworker and give some idea as to how work should be structured. On the whole management problems will be appropriately dealt with by the procedures discussed in Chapter 7. Particular problems presented by the mentally handicapped are discussed below. We begin with a consideration of the procedures used to deal with skill deficits.

Making up for skill deficits

Two phrases sum up the behavioural approach to work in this area: 'task analysis' and 'precision teaching'.

Task analysis

Having selected the behaviour to be taught (e.g. dressing), break it down into its component parts and list them in the order in which they need to occur. There are many manuals written for the parents of mentally handicapped children which provide useful ready-made analyses of numerous skills from washing to tying shoelaces (the ultimate in task analysis!). However, comparing these, one is made immediately aware of several problems.

Different authors include different behaviours in the same task analysis, for instance some include drying as part of learning to wash one's hands while others regard this as a separate skill to be separately taught. There is immense variation in how many 'mini-behaviours' the same task is broken into and each task analysis presupposes one particular way of doing something. There are often several and it is important to ascertain (a) how the caretaker and their family perform that skill and (b) what constraints might be imposed by the physical limitations of the child, the incidence of physical handicap being quite high amongst the severely handicapped. An illustration: one of the authors had always assumed that you took off a jumper by crossing your arms across your chest, pulling the bottom of the jumper up and over your head, removing one arm and then the other. She eventually realised this was impossible for one young man with a somewhat round back whose hand co-ordination was poor. The only way he could pull a jumper off was to reach behind his neck and tug at the jumper from there – even though this meant early damage to jumpers in the form of holes under the arms! Having said this, these manuals are useful as models to work from: it is often easier to adapt something than it is to work it out oneself. Several of these are referenced in the Appendix.

Let us consider one possible task analysis for tooth brushing:

Task analysis A
   (1) Turn on tap.
   (2) Pick up glass.
   (3) Fill glass with water.
   (4) Put glass down.
   (5) Turn off tap.
   (6) Remove top from tooth-paste.
   (7) Take tooth-paste in one hand and toothbrush in the other.
   (8) Squeeze tooth-paste on to brush.
   (9) Put tooth-paste down.
(10) Place toothbrush in the mouth and begin brushing up and down.
(11) Brush the outside surfaces of the teeth, from one side of the mouth to the other.
(12) Brush the cutting edges of the teeth, first the top and then the bottom.
(13) Brush the inside surfaces of the teeth from one side of the mouth to the other.
(14) Put the toothbrush down.
(15) Pick up the glass.
(16) Rinse the mouth.
(17) Put the glass down.
(18) Dry the mouth.
(19) Turn the tap on.
(20) Rinse the toothbrush.
(21) Rinse the glass.
(22) Turn the tap off.
(23) Place the cap on the tooth-paste.

For a more able child it might well be sufficient to have a list which went something like this:

Task analysis B
  (1) Fill a glass with water.
  (2) Put tooth-paste on the brush.
  (3) Brush teeth, inside and outside.
  (4) Rinse mouth.
  (5) Clean brush and glass.
  (6) Tidy sink.

Some children are physically incapable of doing certain things, so you might have to put the tooth-paste on the brush and put the cap back on the tube. Others, more severely retarded, might need even the small steps listed above broken down even more e.g. in order to teach step A (1) you might need to teach the child to:

Task analysis C
  (i)   lift his arm
  (ii) extend his arm
  (iii) extend his arm towards the tap
  (iv) grip the tap
  (v) twist the tap
  (vi) release grip.

We return to this later. In fact, teaching toothbrushing is quite an advanced skill and most children embarking on it would probably have learned several of the component skills in the course of other teaching e.g. learning to wash (turning on taps) and eat (gripping spoons and so on).

Reinforcers

As we have stressed elsewhere it is very important that any tangible reinforcers used are paired with social rewards, such as praise. It takes a lot of imagination to identify effective primary reinforcers with which such praise can be paired. Edible treats are commonplace, but it has often been found necessary to use other physical reinforcers such as sounds, touch (e.g. stroking the face), tickling and, occasionally, making an activity the child engages in of choice (rocking or sitting staring out of the window) contingent upon compliance with the task required.

You will need to get the parent to spell out to the child the link between the reinforcer and the behaviour performed. Typically this will have to be done in a quite exaggerated way, as comprehension and/or attention is more limited than with normal children. Similarly, praise needs to be delivered enthusiastically, in a very unBritish manner. Secondary reinforcers such as stars, points and ticks in books, have all been used successfully with the mentally handicapped. Tokens have been used in institutions where it has often been necessary to begin by shaping the learners' token-using (not to mention token-keeping) behaviour.

It is best to use as many different reinforcers as possible to prevent satiation, a problem when very frequent reinforcement is needed, as is the case in the early stages of this teaching. Social rewards are less likely to reach satiation point; another reason for using them in conjunction with other reinforcers.

Precision teaching

This is no more or less than the systematic application of operant procedures to teach the target behaviour. The steps in the task analysis constitute a chain of behaviours that make up the target behaviour. The next step is to ascertain which of the component behaviours the child can presently perform, if any. You can do this by asking him to 'do' the target behaviour, e.g. 'John, clean your teeth please.' If he does not respond you then give particular instructions, such as 'John, turn on the tap', and proceed until John either fails to respond or responds incorrectly. It is at this point that teaching commences.

You can teach the chain in a forward or a backward way (see p. 128–9). There is little evidence in favour of one or the other but many workers prefer backward chaining because the child then constantly experiences a sense of achievement and because the endings of some behaviours are intrinsically rewarding e.g. eating a meal, washing hands (many children like putting their hands in water). Either way the teaching components are the same. The steps to follow are these.

(1) Begin by instructing the child to perform the target behaviour (or subskill: see below).

(2) If he complies and performs adequately, reward immediately.
(3) If he fails to comply or performs inadequately, repeat the instruction and demonstrate the skill.
(4) If he then complies and performs adequately, reward immediately.
(5) If he still fails to comply or performs inadequately, repeat the instruction and physically guide the child though the action (prompting).
(6) If he performs the behaviour adequately, reward immediately.
(7) Repeat, gradually fading physical guidance until the child eventually responds to the instruction alone.

If he still fails to perform the behaviour, or clearly finds it very difficult even with your help, or if your attempts to fade out prompts fail, then it is probably necessary to break this particular task into even smaller subtasks and apply steps (1)–(6) to each. This will often involve shaping. Consider the example given in task analysis C above.

Shaping

Shaping has been described as an art (Bricker, 1975): it is the creative art of getting a child to produce a new response (Tsoi and Yule, 1982). You start by reinforcing the child for something he can already do which can conceivably be used as the first approximation to the required response: for turning on the tap this could be simply arm movement, for example.

Having established arm raising by reinforcing the child every time he does this, the next step is to withold reinforcement until the child has raised his arm and extended it in the direction of the tap. And so on, until reinforcement is given only when the tap is turned on. At this point you can return (or proceed) to task analysis A and continue teaching. Because modelling is a very quick means of learning and teaching, it may be worthwhile shaping imitative behaviour – if this is absent – before embarking on other projects. Shaping also plays an important part in language acquisition and development, for instance with autistic children.

Fading and generalisation

Fading prompts and verbal cues must be done gradually and, as verbal prompts can be particularly difficult to fade, some workers use just the global instruction concerning the target behaviour, e.g. 'John, brush your teeth', throughout training, gradually chaining more and more steps together under this umbrella prompt. Guidance about fading physical guidance/prompts can be found on pp.130–1.

The mentally handicapped seem particularly vulnerable to the extinction of newly acquired behaviour. Similarly they seem very susceptible to stimulus control, and unless one is careful a newly-acquired behaviour might come to be performed only in the context of the training situation (be that the person training, the room used or the time of day). It is necessary to programme against these eventualities from the outset. Using different people, different settings and different materials (e.g. a variety of cups when teaching to drink) will help with regard to generalisation. Training all those who interact with the child to behave consistently, placing a great emphasis on praise and varying the situations in which behaviour is reinforced, will help with maintenance, as will changing the strength and the schedules of reinforcement (Kazdin, 1975).

Further considerations

The mentally handicapped, given an ordinary environment not geared to their needs, are often set to fail, and many social workers will come across families of mentally handicapped children whose sense of failure is immense. A behavioural approach, based on a sound assessment, is in a good position to change this but care must be taken nonetheless. It is important to engage parents as co-workers if progress is to be sustained. The mentally handicapped often have only short concentration spans, and the work can be taxing: this suggests that frequent but brief bursts of teaching are to be preferred to extended interventions. Indeed family commitments may pre-empt the latter. It is important to end on a note of success and, whatever happens, training must not be allowed to deteriorate into a battle for control. Programming for success might also involve such things as using food a child likes when teaching feeding skills (one stands a better chance with ice-cream than with cabbage – usually); using clothes that are one or two sizes too big when teaching dressing skills (they are easier to manipulate) and gradually 'shrinking them' to his own size, and so on.

This brings us to a final point: the gradualness of change is vital for most of these children. A nice example of this is to be found in Yule and Carr (1982) who quote the treatment of a strong attachment of a four-year-old boy to a blanket which he carried to such an extent that it interfered with his learning of hand-eye co-ordination skills. Over a period of a month or more the authors (Marchant *et al.*, 1974) instructed his mother to cut small pieces off the blanket. Eventually, with no trauma, the boy discarded the bundle of threads with which he was left and proceeded to make large learning gains.

Toilet training

This is a particularly important skill upon whose acquisition depend a number of things including social acceptability, health (absence of sores) and access to resources such as some day care facilities. Continued incontinence can prove to be the breaking point for many parents, leading to long-term institutional care. Incontinence is more prevalent among the handicapped than amongst the general population and sadly it is often assumed to be inevitable. This is rarely true. For these reasons we include a brief discussion of some of the basic principles of toilet training the mentally handicapped.

There are several programmes for toilet training. Wilson (1982) presents two; an intensive programme and a 'habit training' programme which she suggests will be adequate in a large number of cases. Both require continual recording of the following behaviours: urination in the toilet, wet pants, bowel movements in the toilet, bowel movements in the pants, incidence of dry pants (checked every half-hour). It may initially be necessary to reward the child for associated behaviours such as going to the bathroom, sitting on the toilet and so on. Similarly, skills such as pulling down pants (depending on the child's age) and sitting on the toilet may have to be shaped before toilet training can commence.

Habit training

(1) Take the child to the toilet (or potty) every half-hour or thereabouts.
(2) If he urinates, reinforce him; if he does not, say nothing and return him to whatever he was doing.
(3) As 'accidents' between toileting reduce, gradually extend the periods between visits to the toilet.

This is basically the sort of routine followed by most mothers when they toilet train their infants, and may prove sufficient to the task with the handicapped child. When not sufficient to the task Wilson suggests an intensive programme based on the work of Azrin and Foxx (1971).

Intensive toilet training

(1) Give the child as much liquid as he will drink.
(2) Place him on the toilet (for up to twenty minutes) every half-hour.
(3) If he urinates, reward him and return him to his play.
(4) If he fails to urinate remove him after twenty minutes; do not reinforce him.
(5) Every five minutes or so get the child to feel his pants. If he is dry, reward him profusely with comments like 'Good boy, John, dry pants', hugs and so on. If he is wet either say nothing and change him (or direct him to change himself) or say 'Wet pants, bad boy' (if he does not find this reinforcing).
(6) Gradually fade the programme out. This will involve reducing the fluids given to the child, taking him to the toilet less frequently and checking his pants less often.

In their hospital-based programme, Wilson and her colleagues also vary the caretakers throughout the programme and gradually move the child from the special 'toileting area' in which training occurs to the 'normal' hospital environment, and then extend the programme to the child's home with the parent in control. Variations on this programme could include musical potties – which give immediate reinforcement to some children and cue the trainer/parent to reinforce; and the use of pants alarms which alert the trainer/parent to inappropriate urination. *A useful tip*: because of the susceptibility to stimulus control it is wise (even if laborious) to take the child to the bathroom, even if using a potty. This will pre-empt the often more laborious task of transferring the learned potty-using skill from the kitchen or living room to the toilet.

The Portage Project

Behavioural work with mentally handicapped children has been accorded respectability in numerous teaching programmes such as the well known Portage Project (Shearer and Shearer, 1972) which was developed as a model of early intervention with pre-school developmentally retarded children some ten years ago. It basically sets out to train parents (and other caretakers such as nursery staff) as behaviour therapists for their children, so as to maximise their chances and pace of development.

It is now a very sophisticated and well produced product which facilitates the sorts of task analyses and precision teaching we have discussed. Guidance is given on all areas of normal development and evaluation is built into the programme. Portage is administered by home teachers under the auspices of a multidisciplinary team. They visit families weekly, thus overcoming many of the problems encountered in clinic-based work, and offering a lot of support and encouragement. It rates high on consumer satisfaction:

> The acceptance rate by parents of all socio-economic statuses and the reports of satisfaction are very impressive . . . This probably occurs because the service uniquely celebrates the existing skills and achievements of child, parent, professional and manager and goes on to build on these by clear, monitorable procedures. (Kushlick, 1984)

Along with other contributors to a recent volume concerned with Portage (1984) Kushlick points to a number of problems it faces, some of which arise out of its very success. Because of the frequency of their visits, the service they provide and the relationships they consequently establish with families, home teachers are often presented with numerous other family problems which most readers would identify as the bread and butter of traditional social work. This is indicative of the human face of behavioural work. These authors are consequently struggling with role definitions and the heavily felt responsibility to respond to these clients without interminably 'referring on'. The social worker with a knowledge of behavioural techniques, and with access to expert help, will be in a particularly good position to offer the all-round help so often needed by families with handicapped members, and in a similarly strong position to work alongside such workers as home teachers.

We turn now to the mentally handicapped adult.

MENTALLY HANDICAPPED ADULTS

The behavioural programmes that work for children and teenagers can often be adapted for use with older handicapped people. For example, parents of mentally handicapped people aged between twenty and thirty-five have benefited from training in behavioural principles and from learning to plan and carry out programmes (in the form of contracts) to modify such behaviours as conversation skills, self-care, and household tasks, using social, tangible and activity reinforcers (Molick *et al.*, 1982).

Increasing the frequency of behaviour

Given that the client already has certain skills, it may be necessary to increase the use he makes of them by straighforward prompting and social reinforcement. You will usually need to make greater use of these procedures with mentally handicapped people than with other adult clients in order to encourage them to persevere with tasks. Porterfield *et al.* (1980) increased levels of recreational activity using a consistent routine. The clients were given materials, and offered an alternative if they finished a task or appeared to get tired of it, and were prompted briefly if they did not start to use the materials right away; the worker chatted only to those clients who were occupied, commenting on their work or joining in. The same system can be used for engaging clients in any sort of activity, for example housework or gardening.

New practical skills

Equally important is the teaching of new behaviours, and there have been large numbers of studies showing clearly that behavioural programmes can provide mentally handicapped people with the skills they need in order to live independently.

First, two examples of work done by social workers. Lomas (*personal communication*, 17 November, 1984) has described how he and his colleagues set up a new hostel adhering closely to the principle of normalisation (the client's lifestyle should be like that of any other person of the same age except where there is good reason for there to be a difference) as well as to behavioural principles. Thus, despite staff misgivings, residents received their own keys. As expected, some keys got lost, but the natural contingencies (inconvenience to all concerned) soon ensured that this problem ceased to occur.

Instead of using special transport, the residents were to travel to their training centre by ordinary buses. Learning to do this required a long drawn-out programme of modelling and shaping. At one stage the social worker was watching anxiously while a group of residents waited to change buses, letting the right bus go past them time and again. Lomas discovered that they were unable to identify the correct destination written on the front and so the original task analysis had to be extended. Later on, some of these residents moved out to flats, and Lomas ensured that they received visits at times other than 'times of crisis', in order to reinforce coping successfully in the community as against 'crisis behaviour'.

A social work student, Ainsworth (1980) ran a group to teach money and shopping skills. The group members spent part of each session on basic money-handling, using materials designed for primary schools, and the rest of the time learning how to buy things in shops. Later the members went out with the worker to carry out the tasks in real life. Homework assignments, with help from the clients' parents, formed an important component of the training.

There is a large literature giving detailed accounts of training programmes, as well as plentiful evidence of their effectiveness. We have chosen some examples of recent developments that may be of particular interest to social workers either preparing their clients for community living or else helping mentally handicapped people already there.

The handbook by Mori and Masters (1980) gives outlines of programmes for teaching both very basic self-care skills and more 'advanced' ones as well. For example, bus travel. Mori and Masters quoting Laus (1977) report the finding that even people with a very low IQ can learn to use buses. The initial task analysis lists the following:

(1) Identify bus-stop sign
(2) Stand by bus-stop sign
(3) Identify bus
(4) Face driver
(5) Pay driver

And so on. These may themselves have to be further broken down, for example: (1) remove wallet (2) display pass to driver/give correct money to driver; etc.

One serious handicap that can make it difficult for a mentally handicapped person to leave hospital is bed-wetting. Success has been reported rather infrequently; however Smith (1981) has shown that the bell and pad method can succeed, but that with this client group the treatment will take much longer than for ordinary problems of childhood enuresis (Smith's clients needed between 18 and 92 weeks, mean length of time: 47.6 weeks).

Social skills

Matson (1982) has developed and evaluated training in telephone skills. Telephone conversation skills included introducing oneself and saying hello, talking in an audible voice, answering a series of questions, acknowledging the end of the conversation and saying goodbye. Matson's training consisted of modelling and instructions, practice, feedback, and social reinforcement; in addition, he asked clients to give a rating of their own and other group members' performance after each practice. This is an example of a variation of social skills training. Matson also used this method for teaching clients how to telephone for help in an emergency (Matson, 1980).

There have been numerous other studies of social skills training with mentally handicapped people, including work on job interviews (Kelly *et al.*, 1980; Grinnell and Lieberman, 1981).

In view of the fact that many handicapped people do lack social skills – or indeed, have been 'taught' inappropriate social behaviours by well-meaning staff or relatives (such as hugging strangers, holding hands in the street), social skills training is often a key form of intervention.

Budgeting and meals

Apart from basic self-care and social skills, ability to get around, and use the telephone, it is important that people who live in the community should be able to manage their money and feed themselves sensibly. Ballard *et al.* (1983) describe a programme to teach a mildly retarded young man how to manage his money. They note the prerequisites: being able to read and write well enough to record expenditure; to calculate and handle money; and to use shops and a bank. They describe the budgeting skills (thirteen in all) beginning with drawing the columns in a notebook for date, item and amount, and including 'write the date and the correct amount of money in the appropriate column', 'write in the appropriate column the item on which money is spent', and so on. Similar programmes (appropriately modified) can be used with less able clients.

In the study by Sarber and Cuvo (1983) the clients received even more ambitious training: they learned to plan nutritious meals and make up grocery lists as well as locating the food on the supermarket shelves. With the help of a nutritionist, printed instructions were prepared, and the clients learned to identify food groups (bread, milk, fruit and vegetables and meat) in order to work out a well-balanced menu. Other workers have devised programmes for additional meal-related tasks: buying the food (Wheeler *et al.*, 1980; Matson, 1981a), and cooking (Johnson and Cuvo, 1981).

Familiarity with some of this literature will give you the guiding principles and a wealth of ideas for devising programmes with your own particular clients in mind. The key ideas are:

(1) Build on existing skills.
(2) Break down the task into components that can be learned one by one.
(3) Use modelling, verbal instruction and feedback.
(4) Provide plentiful reinforcement.

Grinnell and Lieberman (1981) suggest that it is helpful to include money reinforcers, and they mention the 'motivating' effect of using video.

Psychological problems

Social skills training, shaping and chaining, are certainly not the only behavioural approaches that are helpful for mentally handicapped clients. Obviously these clients can suffer from any of the personal problems that beset the rest of us. A particularly common problem is anxiety, often taking the form of phobias. Matson (1981b) has evaluated group *in vivo* exposure treatment of a phobia of going into shops. First the group learned about the rationale for the approach: what a fear is, why it is a problem, and how the worker expected to be able to help them. The worker demonstrated in role-play and talked about the tasks involved, and the members rehearsed. They then went to a store: first just driving to the place, then parking, then entering the store. Prompts, reinforcement and plentiful reassurance were provided throughout.

Conclusion

The literature on mental handicap gives the clearest demonstration of how very effective behavioural intervention can be where no other treatment approach is suitable. You will find a plethora of programme suggestions. But it is extremely sad that so few mentally handicapped people receive the behavioural assistance that would make it easier for them to join in with the rest of the community more successfully.

11

Depression and Anxiety

Depression and anxiety are exceedingly common outside of psychiatric settings, and the behaviourally-oriented social worker has much to offer, either in addition to medical treatment or where medical treatment is not considered appropriate. It is essential, however, to discuss your intervention with the doctor if you feel your client is seriously distressed.

We shall describe how behavioural and cognitive-behavioural theorists construe these problems; and offer some guidelines as to how to assess them; and how to select a method of intervention.

DEPRESSION

Models of depression

There are several quite closely related learning and cognitive–learning models of depression. These are compatible with one another, and the style of intervention derived from one model may be similar or even identical to that derived from another model. For the sake of clarity we shall look at the models separately, but we suggest that it will be helpful to combine them into a multidimensional model for assessment and intervention planning.

Operant or reinforcement model

This is the earliest behavioural formulation of depression (Ferster, 1973). Depression is seen in terms of overt behaviours such as crying or complaining, and in terms of behavioural deficits, such as the typical apathy of the depressed person. The person's repertoire of 'adaptive' behaviours is deemed to be low because of lack or loss of positive reinforcement or because of punishment. A husband or wife dies, a person moves house away from family and friends or becomes unemployed, and as a result loses major sources of positive reinforcement: extinction ensues. A woman's efforts to control her children and to 'be a good housewife' are criticised or derided: punishment. On the other hand, crying, complaining, or staying in bed may receive lots of attention of various sorts: positive reinforcement. This is not a description of 'manipulative' behaviour in the usual sense of the word, neither is it unsympathetic. Such skewed patterns of punishment and reinforcement usually evolve unwittingly. The situation is then exacerbated, because any 'comforting' effects of the reinforcement tend to be short-lived, and as the depressive behaviours take over they make matters worse by concentrating the person's attention on miserable thoughts and feelings.

Skills

Associated with the reinforcement model which emphasises the non-performance of behaviours the person is capable of, is the notion of a lack of skills: an inability to do things that lead to positive reinforcement. Lewinsohn and his colleagues (1976) have emphasised the part played by lack of social skills. The depressed person may be unskilled at beginning new relationships or asking people for things he wants. Other types of skills may also be lacking: organising an outing, controlling a disruptive child, cooking a meal for friends – the list of potentially crucial skills is endless.

Both the 'operant' and the 'skills' conceptualisations emphasise the idea that the depressed person is on a weak schedule of positive reinforcement and suggest that the goal of intervention should be to increase the amount of positive reinforcement he obtains.

Eliciting stimuli

Another behavioural approach focuses especially on the emotional component of depression and suggests that depressive feelings are triggered by particular settings or antecedent events: the recently divorced person upset by visits to happily married friends, the woman who has lost her baby bursting into tears at the sight of other people's babies. Different settings elicit different emotional states. This formulation suggests that the person should either be encouraged to avoid distressing situations or else taught to cope with these by means of techniques similar to those used for coping with anxiety.

Cognitive–behavioural approaches

More recently, there has been increasing interest in the cognitive aspects of depression. Seligman (1975; Garber and Seligman, 1980) proposes that depressed feelings and behaviour result from the expectation that one can do nothing to improve one's situation and that this is caused by the experience of uncontrollable aversive events. Learned helplessness can be precipitated by a single traumatic event or series of events, but a history of lack of control may make some people particularly vulnerable. Construing depression in this way leads to an emphasis on the client's own efforts, encouraging him to undertake manageable tasks (behavioural element) and helping him to appreciate his own achievements (cognitive element). Central to this model is the importance of ensuring that clients attain control over their own lives, for example involving elderly people in decisions about whether they should enter a home and encouraging them to participate in the organisation of the place. Thus, this 'cognitive' model has 'behavioural' implications for intervention.

Other workers in the cognitive–behavioural group, in particular Beck and his colleagues (1979), place even more emphasis on cognitive factors. They maintain that it is the content of the depressed person's thoughts that leads to depressive feelings and behaviour. Depressed people, according to this model, hold negative and unrealistic views about the world, about themselves, and about their future. It is crucial to correct these thoughts before the person can begin to feel and act differently. The approach associated with this model of depression requires detailed examination of unconstructive thoughts, monitoring of these, and a systematic effort to weaken them via logical discussion and disconfirming experiences.

Lewinsohn in his recent work has combined the several models (Lewisohn *et al.*, 1978). Assessment covers the person's behaviour, thoughts and feelings, and then the client and worker together decide where it might be best to start, recognising the to-and-fro interaction between all the different aspects but focusing on one aspect at a time.

Since the evidence for the various models remains thin, (although there is a growing body of research on Beck's cognitive therapy with some promising results), we recommend Lewinsohn's composite approach: it 'starts where the client is' and allows intervention to proceed at the simplest level that makes sense. In many cases, this will involve a series of tasks designed to provide higher levels of reinforcement and increased feelings of mastery.

Assessment of depression

As always, assessment begins with the client's own account of what is wrong. When the client seems depressed it is particularly important to explore all the various parameters of this problem: is he coping with everyday tasks as he would wish? Does anything give him pleasure and/or provide a feeling of mastery? What are his feelings and thoughts? How would an outside observer know he was depressed?

One or two detailed interviews will be needed, including a 'typical day' account, and preferably also an interview with a close associate of the client. The interviews are best supplemented with a diary or 'ABC'-type record (see pp. 87–9), including ratings of mood, so as to discover what sets off or worsens depressed feelings and thoughts, and – most important – what tends to make the client feel better. A questionnaire (we suggest the Beck Depression Inventory, reprinted in Lewinsohn *et al.*, 1978) is useful to assess the severity of depression and to measure subsequent progress.

The composite picture that emerges will give clues as to where to focus the work. As we indicated earlier, it could be that the person is getting very little positive reinforcement; is constantly finding himself in settings that trigger depressed feelings; or is 'making himself miserable' with repetitive gloomy thoughts. Using the data the client has provided, you can explain your formulation and check that he accepts it or is willing to try it as a working hypothesis. Does he agree that he does very few things that give him satisfaction? Or that certain experiences or thoughts are making him feel low? Depressed people may dispute some of your suggestions: for example, they may claim their gloomy thoughts are realistic or deny that anything could give them pleasure. In particular, the proposition that their depressive behaviours might be maintained by other people around them may be taken badly (no one likes to think they are feeling depressed because their complaints get attention). Clear and sympathetic discussion of the basis for your formulation will usually lead to an agreement about where to begin; if this proves difficult, focusing on a different aspect of the problem at least initially may lead to some encouraging changes. You may have to work hard to convince your client to join you in experimenting with an attempt to modify his problem.

Intervention with depression

If you have elected to follow the reinforcement model, you and the client will plan an increase in reinforcing events and activities, using a task-centred approach. Mr and Mrs Arthur, referred initially for sex problems, were both assessed by their psychiatrist as mildly depressed. They described aimless weekends, but recalled happier times: trips to other towns, walks in the country, and cooking special meals together. This couple needed encouragement, but not the skills, to obtain these reinforcers again; and the social worker (quite directively!) got them to agree to do increasingly more of these things week by week, monitoring their mood, and reporting back at their weekly sessions. A probation client, Mr Potts, bought himself a diary and entered his plans in it in consultation with his probation officer: this was unusually successful in that his first outing to a football game ended with him being invited to the pub, where he met Miss Johnson who later became his girlfriend!

Miss Hope was a single lady who had lived with her sister for many years and had depended on her to organise outings and social life; two years after her sister's death, she remained depressed, and it emerged that she did not possess the skills to do any entertaining or organising for herself, and indeed had never learned how to find her way around London. Miss Hope required a considerable amount of skills training as well as encouragement before she could cope with a lunch club, invite a new neighbour to tea and visit an old friend on the other side of town.

If settings and triggers are the focus you and the client have chosen, planning activities will again form the main content of the sessions. One young widow, Mary Moore, cried a great deal when she was with her mother-in-law, who spent much of the time dwelling on Mary's husband's death and his disappointed hopes, and predicting a continued sad and lonely life for Mary. Another woman, Rosalind, had lost touch with her friends, except for one couple who seemed to consider it their duty to provide some kind of 'therapy' for her, getting her to talk about her feelings of loneliness and failure, urging her to 'have a good cry'. Both these women could identify situations where the opposite occurred: in Mary's case, visits to old friends who liked to do the things she and her husband had enjoyed, watching 'bad' television and playing darts at the local pub; in Rosalind's case, meetings with new acquaintances who were interested in her job and her ideas about local politics and did not see her as someone who needed a shoulder to cry on. The social worker's role was to encourage them to increase time spent in these settings, and to help them overcome guilt feelings resulting from beliefs they appeared to hold about 'having a duty' to spend time with people who made them feel depressed; Rosalind also needed some help to conquer her shyness about meeting new people.

Modifying depressive thoughts is the most complex type of intervention. Beck's (Beck *et al.*, 1979) cognitive approach is the most frequently used and has the strongest research backing of the behavioural and cognitive–behavioural approaches to depression (Rachman and Wilson, 1980). As we have mentioned elsewhere (p. 146) it requires lengthy discussions, and demanding homework tasks (detailed self-monitoring, and learning to challenge unconstructive thoughts with logical argument, in addition to behavioural assignments). Rational-emotive therapy (Ellis and Grieger, 1977) makes similar demands in terms of intellectual work, and carries perhaps some risk of making the client feel in some sense to blame. Both of these approaches and (perhaps to a lesser extent) Meichenbaum's (1977) self-instructional method may present difficulties for clients who are not verbally skilled or well educated. We also think the worker needs special training in addition to basic behavioural training. There is little evidence that these approaches work better in those cases where the simpler approaches are feasible; but cognitive–behavioural approaches do seem to do better, overall (Rachman and Wilson, 1980). And depression is one area where it can be difficult or impossible to avoid focusing on thoughts. Nevertheless, it is important not to allow the 'cognitive–behavioural' approach to become exclusively 'talking treatment': not only must the client monitor his thoughts and learn to analyse and dispute them, he must also undertake tasks to test out beliefs against experience. Beck *et al.* (1979) state that the behavioural techniques are generally more powerful than the cognitive techniques; Ellis (1979) stresses that he does not in fact spend the bulk of his time on combating irrational beliefs, but on arranging other procedures including operant conditioning, desensitisation and skills training.

In view of the present uncertainty as to what works best with whom, we propose that you use the simplest procedures that make sense to your client, make a particular effort to evaluate progress, and consider additional cognitive refinements if progress is disappointing. You might also find a more informal use of cognitive procedures helpful in the course of your work, drawing clients' attention to the way they may be 'doing themselves down' challenging unconstructive ideas and false assumptions.

Beck (Beck *et al.*, 1979) emphasises the importance of increasing not only pleasurable but also mastery experiences. The idea of mastery or control, which is at the heart of the learned helplessness model, should act as a guiding principle in every intervention you undertake with a depressed person.

As we have indicated, evidence in favour of these various approaches to depression has only recently begun to accumulate; there remains some doubt whether they do better than well-tried antidepressant drugs and – in the case of the cognitive–behavioural approaches – whether the cognitive part adds anything valuable (Latimer and Sweet, 1984). But these approaches can, of course, be used alongside drugs, and if successful they may have more lasting beneficial consequences: providing the client with new skills and strategies to use in the future.

ANXIETY

Models of anxiety

Behaviour therapists have been doing research on the treatment of anxiety for much longer than is the case with depression; and there is extensive evidence to show that a behavioural approach is by far the most effective way to deal with anxiety focused on particular objects or situations (fears and phobias) (Rachman and Wilson, 1980). The development of techniques to help people with generalised (free-floating) anxiety is more recent, and it is apparent that this is a more difficult undertaking.

Behavioural and cognitive–behavioural models of phobias propose that anxiety be viewed as a learned (conditioned) reaction in vulnerable people, which has not extinguished, in the normal way, through repeated exposure to the feared situation. This is because the person avoids the situation, thus avoiding the anxiety (negative reinforcement of avoidance behaviour). The avoidance may be further strengthened by positive reinforcement, perhaps attention from other people. More recently, the person's thoughts or self-talk have been implicated too: telling himself he cannot cope or that the situation is very dangerous. As in depression, a vicious circle develops: anxious feelings intensify anxious thoughts which in turn strengthen avoidance behaviour; and so on, back and forth. The difficulties can be further compounded by subsequent events. For example, a school phobic child gets behind with his lessons and loses touch with his friends and some teachers may go out of their way to be unpleasant to the child on his return, while his mother may grow to like having him around at home. A woman with agoraphobia may not understand the new bus system and may no longer have any friends to visit.

Assessment of anxiety

Anxiety can be implicated in problems with other major headings such as alcohol abuse or child neglect. Careful analysis may uncover anxiety as an antecedent to drinking, over-eating or not handling a baby. Social anxiety can produce avoidance of key tasks such as visiting the social security office, complaining about a defective gas cooker, telephoning a child's teacher, volunteering to join a resident's committee. Not all of these will require intensive or complicated treatment; but some form of desensitisation, *in vivo* exposure or social skills training (with role-play as a means of gradually approaching the feared situation) will pay dividends.

You should first establish whether the client's anxiety is focused or free-floating. If focused, it is necessary to specify exactly what the focus is: places, objects, people. Then the composite term 'anxiety' needs 'unpacking': does the person avoid the situation, or does he enter it but suffer painful feelings and thoughts? Does he try to escape the situation? Does he panic?

Usually you should aim for a reduction in both avoidance and in physiological anxiety symptoms (feelings). It is debateable whether you need to tackle thoughts in every case, or whether this is only necessary when they prove to be obstructing the client's progress.

Then the antecedents and consequences must be identified. In particular, other people's behaviour both before and after the person faces the feared situation. Some husbands of agoraphobics urge their wives to go outside, while others suggest that this will make them feel bad; some provide sympathy after their wives refuse to go out (reinforcing avoidance). In some families, unfortunately, successful efforts are followed by criticism (punishing attempts to change): 'So you can do it when you want to!'

Intervention with anxiety

Specific fears

These respond well to exposure methods (see pp. 120–3). The crucial point is to get the client into the feared situation and to stay in it until his anxiety drops, rather than running away. At least daily practice is needed. This can best be achieved by means of graded exposure, perhaps facilitated by modelling. It may be helpful to add further procedures: self-management techniques, such as teaching the person to talk himself through the tasks and to counteract recurrent self-defeating thoughts, perhaps with the addition of relaxation as a coping device; and enlisting family or friends as co-workers to ensure that homework is carried out, and that the client's efforts are reinforced and avoidance is not reinforced (Gelder, 1979).

School phobia

Neale *et al.* (1982) describe a multifaceted intervention with a child who was terrified of school. Eight-year-old Robert received graded exposure for his phobia:

(1) his student therapist came to Robert's home daily half an hour before he was due to leave, talked soothingly to him, and went with him part of the way, getting closer to the school each time; (2) after a few days, they were going into the playground; (3) next they went together into the classroom; (4) after two weeks, Robert could get to the school by himself, and was met by the therapist in the playground; (5) two weeks after this, he was staying in class without the therapist, meeting him outside after lessons; (6) finally – seven weeks after the therapy began – Robert himself told the therapist he could manage entirely on his own.

Another aspect of Robert's problems which came up during the very thorough assessment was his 'perfectionist' attitude to school work: he was extremely worried at the prospect of making even a single mistake. For this he received 'talking treatment' along rational-emotive therapy lines (see p. 146).

A third aspect was his parents' own problems: marital difficulties and his mothers's dissatisfaction with her own life which (unawares) perhaps influenced her to be less firm about Robert's going off to school than was desirable. Robert's parents received marital therapy and advice and encouragement to maintain Robert's improved school attendance.

Neale *et al.*, comment that, possibly, equally good results could have been achieved with less professional input. For example, a volunteer could have carried out the exposure programme, and the additional components might not have been necessary.

Agoraphobia

This condition is very difficult to deal with, largely because sufferers typically have multiple fears and may experience panic attacks, diffuse unfocused anxiety and depression as well as fear of specific situations. Many studies suggest that graded exposure in real life is the most effective approach, and that it is particularly important to involve family members because of their potential for helping or hindering the client's progress. Some people with agoraphobia and those who suffer from free-floating anxiety may benefit from help in developing multipurpose coping strategies (see pp. 147–9).

Mrs Young's case illustrates a multiple package for agoraphobia:

(1) she worked through a hierarchy of 'going out' tasks, beginning with the short walk to the end of her road. Each task was carried out at least once a day, and she had to stay out until she felt all right. At first, her husband accompanied her, as time went on leaving her to cover an increasing distance by herself (2) she practised standing still whenever she felt the first physical stirrings of anxiety, and saying 'Be calm. I can cope with this. Just let it die away.' (3) Mr Young was provided with a booklet on how to overcome agoraphobia, and he rehearsed ways of providing attention and approval when his wife had done her assignment. He monitored his

performance and also his reactions to 'anxious talk' and failures to undertake assignments. (4) The couple were helped to organise repayment of some debts, and their welfare rights entitlement was checked.

Social anxiety

Social anxiety may require social skills training as well as exposure, since this problem can have a reality basis in that the client suffers in interpersonal situations because he lacks the necessary social skills. Indeed, social skills training that is geared to gradual exposure by providing practice with situations of increasing difficulty in an accepting group, followed by homework assignments, can be the most appropriate intervention method for this problem.

Mr Jackson was referred initially for what he described to his doctor as 'heavy sweating', which – he claimed – made it impossible for him to socialise. He would not accept that he might be anxious for reasons other than this, nor that it was anxiety that caused the sweating, but he did agree to give social skills training a try. At first he refused even to sit with the group, but was eventually persuaded to take part in role-play exercises and to carry out assignments. (The group was not cognitive in orientation, but this could be construed as a way of testing out his belief that his sweating would make others shun him.) Mr Jackson took on more and more demanding assignments, acting as an excellent model for the rest of the group, and eventually reported that the sweating had decreased. Furthermore, he managed to make some friends and improve his social life considerably (Hudson, 1976).

Generalised anxiety

Unlike the other clients we have described, Mr Perry could not name any particular situation that regularly brought on his anxiety attacks. He said they came out of the blue, and that between whiles he suffered from feelings of tension that he could not explain; at such times he found himself dwelling on all kinds of possible but improbable disasters that might befall him or his family. During the sessions, the worker persuaded him that he had some control over his symptoms by teaching him to relax while imagining any situation that could cause him anxiety, (a version of anxiety management training, see p. 148). Outside of the sessions he practised relaxing in response to the first sensations of tension or the first stirrings of 'anxious thoughts'. Mr Perry also received some self-instructional training. He learned to cope on a cognitive level by saying to himself such things as 'I can carry on . . . One step at a time . . . Take it easy . . .'

Though Mr Perry did get over his problem, it has to be said that the evidence in favour of these techniques for dealing with generalised anxiety is neither strong nor abundant, particularly with severely anxious people. However, they are worth trying with people whose problems are less severe, or those who have not responded to medical or psychiatric treatment.

To conclude: the evidence in favour of behavioural methods for focused anxiety is convincing, and in most cases the cognitive procedures appear to add little of value, except with very complicated problems. For generalised anxiety, cognitive–behavioural approaches seem to offer more hope than straightforward behavioural methods, though a lot more research is needed. For depression, the evidence in favour of a cognitive–behavioural combination is accumulating.

In all cases of anxiety and depression, it is essential assist with any other problems that may be adding to the client's misery: stressful personal relationships, financial hardship, housing problems or inability to take decisions. And it is important also to consider the person's general lifestyle after the anxiety or depression symptoms have gone, in order to ensure that new patterns of behaviour will be maintained in the future.

12

Older People

It is good to note the spread of behavioural treatment for this age group who are all too often left out and receive nothing like their fair share of skilled professional help. Any and every behavioural procedure used with younger adults can be applied in cases involving older people. But procedures suited to children must *not* be used and it is important to guard against the risk of infantilising the elderly and indeed to make a point of modelling respect and courtesy towards them. It takes skill and sensitivity to ensure that a behavioural programme does not seem to authoritarian or demeaning.

There are one or two interesting single case studies in the literature. For example, Gambrill (1983b) takes the reader step by step through the programme worked out for Mrs Ryan and her relatives, the Greens. Mrs Ryan was unable to provide much help in the home, and interaction between her and her daughter, son-in-law and teenage grandchildren was unpleasant for both sides, yet Mrs Ryan had few sources of satisfaction besides her immediate family. The outcomes agreed with the worker were (for Mrs Ryan): more social contacts, walks, letters, family conversations and household chores and, (for the Greens): information about ageing and more time to themselves. All agreed on the need to make a decision about the future and to share feelings constructively. The methods used in this case included shaping of various social and recreational activities, and a modified form of communication training to teach Mrs Ryan to ask questions about other people's interests and the Greens to express more empathy. Gambrill's case study offers an excellent illustration of how to assist an older person who feels that she is useless, while at the same time helping relatives who are under severe strain.

Many programmes in the family setting emphasise teaching the relatives (who are usually the 'complainants') how to modify their own behaviour. For example, the Whites learned how to rearrange the contingencies so that Mrs White's mother no longer obtained attention and solicitous questioning when she interrupted television programmes, but did get involved in a pleasant conversation when the set had been switched off. A very different situation – visits to a stroke victim in hospital – is the focus of a case study by Davies (1981). The patient's wife learned to change the content of her visits in parallel with a plan to provide Mr A with a greater number of enjoyable activities. When the intervention began, Mr A mostly complained and wept and abused Mrs A. Analysis of the visits showed that Mrs A consistently focused attention on Mr A's discomfort and disappointments, both past and present, but did not talk about outside events, or express approval or affection. Davies successfully taught Mrs A to elicit and reinforce positive statements by her husband.

In an aptly titled article, 'Not Too Old to Learn', Barraclough and Fleming (1984) describe a behavioural programme with a day centre client. After a fall, Mr Jones felt unable to go out unaccompanied. Assessment showed a large number of relevant assets: Mr Jones could walk, shop and prepare snacks, and he socialised well. His needs included walking more steadily, cooking meals, going out to the shops and to see friends, and developing more interests. They chose to work on 'going out alone without being afraid' because this was important to him and would facilitate the achievement of other goals. This goal was further specified: 'Mr Jones will go to the local shop and then meet one of his friends from the flats in the British Legion – almost next door to the shop – for a drink. He will do this twice a week at lunchtimes.' The end goal was divided into seven steps, beginning with the client being accompanied to and from the shops. The criterion for moving on from one step to the next was Mr Jones being able to carry out the step three out of four times. Detailed written instructions were provided for each step.

This programme took five months with two one-hour sessions per week. Barraclough and Fleming worked with the day care staff and note that despite having no prior knowledge of behavioural principles, they were well able to learn the goal-setting techniques.

Older people have benefited from social skills training. Such programmes are very similar to social skills programmes for younger clients, but usually include some variation in content to suit special needs. Thus, elderly people may be helped to counteract stereotypes held about their age group by younger people (including professionals) and to deal with difficult behaviour from others they live on close terms with, such as room-mates or neighbours in an old people's home. Despite the proliferation of this approach, the evidence for generalisation and longer term success remains thin; but the signs are hopeful (Toseland and Rose, 1978; Gambrill, 1986).

Another recent development is the use of cognitive–behavioural techniques with depressed older people in groups and individually. The evidence for effectiveness remains meagre–possibly less promising than in relation to younger clients (Steuer and Hammen, 1983). Whether this reflects the difficulty of the demands that cognitive–behavioural therapy makes on clients or the prevalence of endogenous types of depression among older people is not yet clear.

Some of the meticulous studies in residential establishments have implications for work in other settings, including clients' own homes. (Jenkins *et al.*, 1977; Powell *et al.*, 1979; and McClannahan and Risley, 1975). These researchers have demonstrated the power of discriminative stimuli, prompting and positive social reinforcement. Elderly clients' level of engagement in activities can be greatly increased via the two simple expedients of offering them materials to work with (discriminative stimuli) and ensuring that reinforcement in the form of social attention is contingent on activity and not on 'doing nothing'.

Other studies have shown the value of active questioning and frequent positive reinforcement for participation in group discussion (Linsk and Pinkston, 1982); the effectiveness of simply providing a setting that elicits social interaction such as a party or pub-like environment (Burrill *et al.*, 1974); and the effectiveness of a simple operant approach in encouraging people to write (and consequently receive) more letters (Goldstein and Baer, 1976).

Elderly people with dementia

The main problem that can be described as particularly a problem of old age is dementia. The behavioural approach to the loss of memory and 'confusion' in dementia is Reality Orientation, subdivided into 'classroom RO' and '24-hour RO' (Greene *et al.*, 1979). It relies mainly on operant procedures, and aims to re-establish such skills as finding one's way around, recalling the names of people and places and making appropriate comments. Classroom RO is usually given in small groups, with a notice board displaying the information to be learned. The sessions consist largely of questions and answers, with social reinforcement for correct answers, and intensive practice. The sessions need to be backed up by a team approach, so that everyone who interacts with the clients outside the group is informed of the behaviours to be prompted and reinforced. 24-hour RO involves a broad-based plan to provide an environment that cues and reinforces the appropriate behaviours: notice boards, signs, calendars and menus act as cues; and carefully trained staff supplement these and give consistent and immediate positive reinforcement. Despite efforts to achieve generalisation the evidence that the behaviours that have been re-learned do generalise from classroom sessions to the rest of the person's day is mixed (Powell-Proctor and Miller, 1982). It is clear that classroom RO and 24-hour RO should both be provided (Holden and Woods, 1982). There is also reason to believe that RO is mainly helpful for people whose mental function is only mildly impaired.

RO has been developed in residential establishments, but it is possible to introduce the procedures in people's own homes if there are relatives willing and able to carry them out. Greene *et al.* (1983) have shown that teaching RO skills to care-givers increases their feeling of coping. Brockett (1981) discusses the possibility of RO in adult foster care homes. He suggests that the main carer could be taught the procedures and that the whole foster family could be involved in the programme.

Another problem that can be troublesome for the very old is loss of bladder or bowel control. The results from various studies with people in residential care are only moderately encouraging. Treatment depends on a very detailed behaviour analysis to pinpoint which part of the total chain of 'toilet-using' behaviour has broken down: remembering to set out for the toilet with enough time, ability to find it and to walk there, get undressed, recognise the toilet bowl, use it, get dressed again. Some of these behaviours are amenable to prompting, Reality Orientation, or chaining. Medical checks are of course essential with this age group. The bell and pad method is rarely of any value if dementia is a complicating factor.

Straightforward (but intensive) operant programmes can be helpful with old people with dementia. They have proved capable of re-learning a variety of skills, such as using eating utensils, dressing, and self-care. But they require very frequent prompting, immediate and often tangible reinforcement, and a continued maintenance programme once the targets have been achieved.

Most of the work referred to above has taken place in hospital settings. For those still living in the community, with less severe dementia, a social worker and/or the client's family can use prompting and chaining or shaping methods to help re-establish behaviours that are important to client and family alike.

For example, one of us successfully used backward chaining with a woman of seventy-three suffering from dementia, who had become 'de-skilled' after a period in hospital. Both Mrs T and the relatives with whom she lived felt that re-learning how to make breakfast in her own bedsitter would constitute a highly desirable goal. Her usual breakfast was boiled egg, bread and butter and tea. The worker divided 'making breakfast' into sub-tasks, herself carrying out the earlier items in each chain at first. The order was as follows:

(1) *Making tea:* fill kettle, switch on kettle, put tea in pot, pour on boiling water.
(2) *Boiling egg:* put egg in water, boil for three minutes (laying table meanwhile), water off, put egg in egg-cup.
(3) *Bread and butter:* put bread on plate, butter bread.

The relatives set out the ingredients ready for Mrs T when she got up.

Each part of each little chain was practised many times, with much reassurance and positive reinforcement for success. The programme took three weeks of daily sessions at breakfast time. Despite increasing dementia Mrs T continued to prepare breakfast for two years after the programme ended.

Many types of behavioural deficits can be modified in a similar manner. Our own experiences include getting an elderly lady to go for walks after a hip replacement operation, gradually increasing the distance and withdrawing the support; and helping another to re-learn to dress herself and do her hair. Where dementia is a factor, there is no sense in hoping for more than a temporary respite – but it is possible that the changes achieved can improve the quality of the person's life and that of the relatives for a worthwhile period of time. We would stress, though, that the anxiety and sometimes querulousness that can accompany the dementing process make behavioural work with clients with this disorder particularly demanding in terms of patience and persistence.

Finally, we would suggest that Seligman's Learned Helplessness theory (Seligman, 1975; Garber and Seligman, 1980) provides valuable guiding principles to help us to think creatively about working with older people. You will recall that this theory suggests that depression, or at least a syndrome that looks very like it, is caused by the experience of uncontrollability, leading to apathy, the belief that one can do nothing to change one's situation, and inability to learn. Seligman (1975) suggests that old people, largely because of the way they are treated in our society, are especially prone to helplessness. In a later book (Garber and Seligman, 1980) Schulz describes a series of experiments with strategies designed to give elderly people a sense of mastery. The strategies included giving them control of when and for how long they would receive visitors, information about their home, and encouragement to feel that they were responsible for themselves rather than merely being 'looked after'. All of these experiences had than merely being 'looked after'. All of these experiences had measurable effects on how the old people saw themselves and how they rated their health and mood. Using these ideas, a field social worker with a brief to help elderly people in the community should seek in every case to give the client choice and influence over as many aspects of his life as possible: from major decisions, such as whether to go and live with relatives, to minor choices of everyday life such as what to have for tea and when to go to bed, in addition to making efforts to keep clients actively doing as opposed to being 'done for'. The concept of learned helplessness and how to prevent it can guide social work on a broader scale too, so that policies as well as individual case plans are scrutinised with a view to whether they broaden or narrow the clients' range of mastery.

13

Work and Money Problems

It would be absurd to claim that behavioural procedures can do anything to solve macro-level economic problems. But we suggest that they can make a modest contribution in helping some disadvantaged people.

WORK

Job finding

It must be said first of all that some behavioural practitioners who once concentrated heavily on job finding have since turned their attention to ways of preparing clients for unemployment; for example, the workers at the Shape Project for young offenders (Stallard 1983) now concentrate on providing their clients with the skills to obtain for themselves a more comfortable living standard and more satisfying leisure with less risk of being incarcerated. Even if a job-finding programme is successful for the clients involved, it can be argued that their success is at the expense of other unemployed people who have not had this assistance. Others take a different view, arguing that job-finding skills assume even greater importance for particularly disadvantaged clients such as ex-prisoners and psychiatric patients at a time when competition is fiercer.

'Job clubs' modelled upon those devised by Azrin and his colleagues (Azrin *et al.*, 1975, 1980) have spread throughout the USA. The programme is based mainly on operant principles. The clients spend their time on the premises when not out job hunting. Working in small groups and in pairs they learn how to look for a job (scanning advertisements, following leads, making check-lists of suitable firms and so on), how to make personal or telephone enquiries and written applications, and how to present themselves at interviews. The leader is a hard task-master, demanding that people are continually active, setting assignments, reinforcing efforts, and ensuring that maximum support is forthcoming both from the group and from the members' families. Material help is given as well: access to telephones, stationery, newspapers – even a bicycle for emergency transport to interviews.

The results from these clubs are encouraging – so much so that it is surprising that their methods have so rarely been adopted on this side of the Atlantic. For example, in the study of job-seekers in Harlem, New York, the club members were more likely to get work than clients receiving normal job-centre assistance, and furthermore, they got their jobs more quickly and the jobs were better paid (Azrin *et al.*, 1980).

Other job-finding programmes have usually been less intensive. Some focus on the job application and the job interview, many on the interview alone. Client groups have included teenagers still at school, teenage mothers, high school drop-outs, delinquents and adult offenders, psychiatric patients and mentally handicapped people. The results are consistently positive (for a review see Gillen and Heimberg, 1980).

Most base the content of their training on research into the criteria used by employers in selecting staff, and a number of generally useful skills have been identified. For example, the trainees' manual produced by Heimberg *et al.* (1982) has detailed instructions and scripts of inappropriate and appropriate verbal and non-verbal behaviour for the following aspects of the interview: arriving at the workplace, greeting the interviewer, talking about previous experience and qualifications, answering various common questions, asking questions about the job, and how to behave at the close of interview. As in other social skills training, the procedure goes through several stages: setting up the situation; modelling suitable behaviour; role-play; the client evaluates his own performance; the leader and other group members give further feedback; the role-play is repeated; and then more modelling, feedback and practice as required.

Job-related skills

But obtaining a job is not always enough. Some of our most disadvantaged clients, especially those who have little work experience and those who lack everyday social skills, perhaps in combination with a psychiatric history, may need additional skills if they are to settle happily at work. For this reason, behavioural approaches have been used to help people to develop other job-related behaviours. Some recent studies have begun to specify the components of important 'job social skills'. For example, Mathews *et al.* (1980) have identified the skills of accepting suggestions and criticism, explaining a problem to a supervisor, accepting compliments and filling in a tax form: each of these being subdivided into a sequence of discrete behaviours. Lindsay (1982) has made a detailed study of tea-break conversations, showing some striking differences between the conversation of a group of manual workers and a group of psychiatric patients labelled socially unskilled. The patients asked few questions, failed to answer questions or responded with just one word, or a very long sentence. Such research is essential groundwork for the development of training programmes.

Apart from the social skills element, other work behaviours may be lacking. Rehabilitation programmes for mentally ill and mentally handicapped people use structured tasks and both social and material reinforcers in order to build up the ability to work regular hours, to maintain on-task behaviour, and of course to teach practical work skills. Some of these systems can be adapted to other settings, but they do raise problems, not the least of which is the need to fade out the highly structured, artificial procedures gradually, in order to make the transition to a normal work setting.

MONEY PROBLEMS

This subject has received very little attention in the behavioural literature, and the reasons are not far to seek: behaviour change in the poor person is scarcely likely to have much effect on his financial position, and behavioural techniques employed by a single worker do not lend themselves to modifying the behaviour of the correct targets, such as the government of the day and the social security agencies. One use of behavioural procedures in this field is in helping the social worker to acquire the assertiveness skills needed in order to intervene effectively with officials on the client's behalf. But assertiveness for social workers is matter for another book!

Social skills

Assertiveness skills taught to clients have helped them to stand up for their rights. We have already mentioned the man who rehearsed with his wife and then approached his employer for a pay rise, and the woman who learned the skills her social worker had been using in dealings with the social security department. In a 'Practical Problems Group' in a day care setting, the members worked on a number of problems that required social skills type help as well as an input of information about their rights: dealings with the tax office, the housing department, and the gas and electricity boards as well as social security. Just ensuring that your client can utter the simple statement 'If you can't help me I shall have to get the welfare rights people to take the matter up' (in a firm but polite manner) can have a beneficial effect. A visit to an MP's or local councillor's surgery may take some rehearsing; and we are sorry to report that a client in one of our social skills groups requested help in approaching his probation officer!

Clearly, social skills are not all that is needed: there must be a lot of effort put into informing people of what their rights are, and of the appropriate channels by which to pursue them.

Pressure groups

An unusual example of work on a broader scale undertaken in the USA in the 1960s is given by Miller and Miller (1970). They studied grass-roots organisations set up to enable disadvantaged people to exercise an influence over welfare provision. Noting that these groups were poorly attended, and hypothesising that this was related to the fact that the benefits they promised were distant and vague, Miller and Miller designed an experiment to evaluate different methods of increasing attendance at meetings of recipients of Aid to Dependent Children, which had been set up in order to tackle common issues such as the amount of allowances and delays in receiving payment. Just informing people of forthcoming meetings was considerably less effective than a reinforcement programme which provided extra benefits for those who attended: toys, clothing and individual advice. Interestingly, those who came to these meetings were also more likely to become frequent attenders at other kinds of community meetings. No doubt these results come as no surprise to experienced community workers. Nevertheless, we suggest that 'behavioural thinking' in such endeavours ought to be more common than it actually is.

Budgeting

Though we would not want to suggest that poor budgeting ability is anything like as crucial or as widespread a concern as inadequate benefit or earnings levels, behavioural procedures can help people who have difficulty in budgeting what few financial resources they do possess. In Chapter 4 we mentioned the programme devised for systematically teaching a mentally handicapped young man to manage his allowance, a procedure that can be used with other clients (more commonly done than written about, we suspect). Sheldon (1982) reports a programme that encompassed keeping records on income and expenditure, reading the electricity meter and converting the result into cash terms, and paying off arrears. In a controversial article, Bennett (1971) described his work with a family threatened with eviction who had had rent arrears continuously for twenty years. The aims included job-finding and increasing the use of positive reinforcement between family members as well as paying rent regularly and reducing arrears. In essence, Bennett's approach consisted of positive reinforcement in the form of attention, praise, and cigarettes when his clients talked constructively about ways of solving their problems and paid their rent, and witholding reinforcement (filling his pipe, petting the dog) when inappropriate behaviours occurred, such as negative comments about getting work or non-production of the rent. Bennett drew a brightly coloured graph on which he marked the family's intermediate and long-term goals for the rent arrears payments, and produced and filled this in ceremoniously when the rent money was given to him. Later, the rent was paid direct to the housing department, who responded with a note saying, 'The Housing Manager wishes to thank you for the prompt payment of your rent and assures you of his co-operation'. This case study demonstrates a variety of methods with a variety of severe, long-term problems. After six months' involvement the social worker withdrew, and at follow-up six months later, the husband had been in a steady job for eight months and the rent was no longer in arrears. Though we have no personal knowledge of this case, we strongly suspect that the social worker had an excellent relationship with the family and that the cold manipulativeness of which his critics accused him was very far from the reality.

As a final example, here is a worker–client agreement set up with a couple who had thousands of pounds' worth of debts and rent arrears and were on the point of being evicted. Mr and Mrs J. felt that their situation was beyond their control, and the housing department and housing committee of the local authority were unwilling to give them another chance.

This is a CONTRACT between MR AND MRS J and SOCIAL WORKER of .... Social Services.

GOALS   Preventing Eviction
        Reducing Rent Arrears
        Regaining Control of Finances

(a) MR and MRS J agree to make the following payments for the 12 weeks beginning Monday 3 July:
   (1) £28.60 to Housing Department every time they receive a cheque from the social security office on the day they cash it
   (2) £3 to Finance Company every week.
   (3) To have prepayment gas meter installed.
   (4) To give evidence to the Social Worker that the rent has been paid each week.

The SOCIAL WORKER agrees
   (1) To approach various charitable bodies in order to raise £150. This will be given to the Housing Department against Mr and Mrs J's rent arrears at the end of the 12 weeks if *and only if* Mr and Mrs J have unfailingly made the weekly payments as stated above.
   (2) To prepare a report to the Housing Department stating Mr and Mrs J's present circumstances and the plans they are making to clear their arrears; this will include a copy of this and subsequent contracts concerned with financial matters. If Mr and Mrs J default on their weekly payments they will forfeit any money so far raised by the Social Worker towards their rent arrears and the Housing Department will be informed: this will result in eviction.

(B) Mrs J agrees to seek work with Jones' Biscuit Factory.

Mr J agrees to seek work at Xton Hospital.

In return, the Social Worker agrees to arrange day care for John J in the event of Mrs J obtaining work.

If either Mrs J or Mr J find work, they agree to make weekly payments to an amount agreed with Social Worker/Housing Department off their arrears.

The CONTRACT will be reviewed on either 1/9/198.. or 18/7/198.. if the Housing Department does not accept these proposals.

Signed ....

....

....

The Housing Department accepted the contract and the couple kept to it. A tough contract, certainly; but the alternative was even tougher, and the Housing Department and the charitable bodies concerned took a lot of convincing. (We should add that this contract was just the 'public' part of this piece of work: the family also received behavioural assistance with other aspects of budgeting and with a variety of personal and interpersonal difficulties.)

Problems with money and unemployment cause and exacerbate all other kinds of problems. Contrary to the impression the behavioural literature can suggest, behavioural social workers cannot be just 'therapists', (whatever meaning one might give to that term), and have much to offer in helping clients with material problems.

Afterword

Throughout this book we have endeavoured to convey some of our enthusiasm and optimism about the behavioural approach in social work. Perhaps it is appropriate that we should conclude with some words of caution.

First, on the limitations of the approach. No amount of behavioural theorising or experimentation will solve social problems, such as poverty and unemployment, that are beyond the scope of a psychologically-based intervention method. It is possible that this fact also explains the disappointments that behavioural workers have experienced in their work with delinquents and adult offenders. It may be, of course, that such problems are outside the scope of social work *per se*, but social problems on the macro scale do figure large in the social worker's professional view of the world. You will continue to need all your other social work knowledge and skills when you add behavioural skills to your repertoire; and even though in some areas you will be more effective than you were before, there will be many other areas where you will have to go on struggling to find ways of alleviating the hardships of disadvantaged clients.

Secondly, the vexed question of what constitutes acceptable training for behavioural practice. We might begin by noting that many of the best-respected practitioners in this field are largely self-taught (as is generally the case with new methods used by helping professionals). More positively, we believe that social workers have attitudes and key relationship skills that provide a firm foundation on which to build behavioural expertise. The best way to develop skills is by taking up training opportunities that provide demonstrations, practice and feedback – that is, not reading, not lectures, but small workshops and field experience with supervision or consultation.

These routes to skill development are open to social workers, and we hope that having read this book you will be encouraged to seek them out. Your efforts with a behavioural approach will be powerfully reinforced by the results you achieve with people who need your help.

Guidelines for Further Reading

General

Cormier, W. H. and Cormier, L. S. (1979) *Interviewing Strategies for Helpers*, Brooks/Cole, Monterey, California.

Gambrill, E. D. (1983) *Casework: a Competency-based Approach*, Prentice-Hall, Englewood Cliffs, New Jersey.

Sheldon, B. (1982) *Behaviour Modification: Theory, Practice and Philosophy*, Tavistock, London.

Stern, R. S. (1978) *Behavioural Techniques*, Academic Press, London.

Schinke, S. P. (1981) *Behavioral Methods in Social Welfare*, Aldine, New York.

Behavioural Abstracts (Journal) Carfax Publishing Company, PO Box 25, Abingdon, Oxfordshire, OX14 3EU, England.

The Behavioural Social Work Review (Editor: Carole Sutton) Free to members of the Behavioural Social Work Group. Details from 3 Galloway Close, Barwell, Leicestershire LE9 8HL, England.

Children

Herbert, M. (1981) *Behavioural Treatment of Problem Children*, Academic Press, London.

Herbert, M. (1985) *Caring for your Children: a Practical Guide*, Blackwell, Oxford.

McAuley, R. and McAuley, P. (1977) *Child Behaviour Problems*, Macmillan, London.

Morgan, R. T. T. (1984) *Behavioural Treatment of Children*, Heinemann, London.

Patterson, G. R. (1975) *Families: Applications of Social Learning to Family Life*, Research Press, Champaign, Illinois.

Ross, A. (1981) *Child Behavior Therapy*, John Wiley & Sons, New York.

Forehand, R. and McMahon, R. J. (1981) *Helping the noncompliant child: A clinician's guide to effective parent training*, Guilford Press, New York.

In residential care

Brown, B. J. and Christie, M. (1981) *Social Learning Practice in Residential Child Care*, Pergamon, Oxford.

School behaviour

Buckley, N. and Walker, H. (1978) *Modifying Classroom Behavior*, Research Press, Champaign, Illinois.
Goldstein, A. P., Apter, S. J. and Harootunian, B. (1983) *School Violence*, Prentice-Hall, Englewood Cliffs, New Jersey.
Yule, W., Berger, M. and Wigley, V. (1984) 'Behaviour Modification and Classroom Management' in N. Frude and H. Gault (eds), *Disruptive Behaviour in Schools*, John Wiley & Sons, Chichester.

Contracts/agreements

DeRisi, W. J. and Butz, G. (1975) *Writing Behavioral Contracts*, Research Press, Champaign, Illinois.
Sheldon, B. (1980) *The Use of Contracts in Social Work*, BASW, Birmingham.

Depression

Lewinsohn, P. M., Munoz, K. F., Youngren, M. A. and Zeiss, A. M. (1978) *Control Your Depression*, Prentice-Hall, Englewood Cliffs, New Jersey.
Williams, J. M. G. (1984) *The Psychological Treatment of Depression*, Croom Helm, London.

Drinking problems

Miller, P. M. (1976) *Behavioural Treatment of Alcoholism*, Pergamon, Oxford.

Enuresis

Doleys, D. M. (1979) 'Assessment and treatment of childhood enuresis', in A. J. Finch Jr. and P. C. Kendall (eds), *Clinical Treatment and Research in Child Psychotherapy*, Spectrum, New York.
Morgan, R. T. T. (1981) *Childhood Incontinence*, Heinemann, London.

Groupwork

Behavior Group Therapy Newsletter sponsored by the Interpersonal Skill Training and Research Project of the University of Wisconsin-Madison, 425 Henry Mall, Madison, Wisconsin 53706, USA.

Rose, S. D. (1972) *Treating Children in Groups*, Jossey-Bass, San Francisco.

Rose, S. D. (1977) *Group Therapy: A Behavioral Approach*, Prentice-Hall, Englewood Cliffs, New Jersey.

Rose, S. D. (1980) *A Casebook in Group Therapy*, Prentice-Hall, Englewood Cliffs, New Jersey.

Marital work

Jacobson, N. and Margolin, G. (1979) *Marital Therapy: Strategies based on Social Learning and Behavior Exchange Principles*, Brunner/Mazel, New York.

Stuart, R. (1980) *Helping Couples Change*, Guilford, New York.

Measuring instruments and evaluation

Cautela, J. R. (1977) *Behavior Analysis Forms for Clinical Intervention*, Research Press, Champaign, Illinois.

Bloom, M. and Fischer, J. (1982) *Evaluating Practice: Guidelines for the Accountable Professional*, Prentice-Hall, Englewood Cliffs, New Jersey.

Levitt, J. L. and Reid, W. J. (1981) 'Rapid Assessment Instruments for Practice', *Social Work Research and Abstracts*, 17, 1, pp. 13–20.

Reid, J. (1981) *Observation in Home Settings*, Castalia Publishing Company, Eugene, Oregon.

Mental handicap

Shearer, M. S. and Shearer, D. E. (1972) 'The Portage Project: A model for early childhood education', *Exceptional Children*, 38, pp. 210–17.

Watson, L. S. (1973) *Child Behavior Modification: A Manual for Teachers, Nurses and Parents*, Pergamon, New York.

Yule, W. and Carr, J. (1980, reprinted 1982) *Behaviour Modification for the Mentally Handicapped*, Croom Helm, London.

Older people

Hanley, I. and Hodge, J. (1984) *Psychological Approaches to the Care of the Elderly*, Croom Helm, London.

Holden, U. P. and Woods, R. T. (1982) *Reality Orientation*, Churchill-Livingstone, Edinburgh.

Pinkston, E. M. and Linsk, N. L. (1984) *Care of the Elderly; a Family Approach*, Pergamon, New York.

Sex therapy

Hawton, K. (1985) *Sex Therapy: A Practical Guide*, Oxford University Press, Oxford.
Jehu, D. (1979) *Sexual Dysfunction*, John Wiley & Sons, Chichester.

Social skills training

Liberman, R. P., King, L. W., DeRisi, W. J. and McCann, M. (1975) *Personal Effectiveness*, Research Press, Champaign, Illinois.
Spence, S. (1980) *Social Skills Training with Children and Adolescents*, NFER, London.
Wilkinson, J. and Canter, S. (1982) *Social Skills Training Manual*, John Wiley & Sons, Chichester.

Teenagers and offending

Herbert, M. (1978) *Conduct Disorders of Childhood and Adolescence*, John Wiley & Sons, Chichester.
Feldman, M. P. (1977) *Criminal Behaviour: A Psychological Analysis*, John Wiley & Sons, London.
Feldman, M. P. (1983) 'Juvenile Offending: Behavioural Approaches to Prevention and Intervention', *Child and Family Behavior Therapy*, 5, 1, pp. 37–50.
Nursey, A. (1985) *Skill Training with Offenders*, Social Work Monographs, University of East Anglia, Norwich.
Schinke, S. P. and Gilchrist, L. D. (1984) *Life Skills Counseling with Adolescents*, University Park Press, Baltimore.
Stumphauzer, J. S. (1979) *Progress in Behavior Therapy with Delinquents*, Charles C. Thomas, Springfield, Illinois.

Bibliography

Abramson, L. Y., Garber, J. and Seligman, M. E. P. (1980) 'Learned Helplessness in Humans: An Attributional Analysis', in Garber, J. and Seligman, M. E. P. (eds), *Human Helplessness: Theory and Applications*, Academic Press, New York.

Agras, W. S. Kazdin, A. and Wilson, G. T. (1979) *Behavior Therapy*, Freeman, San Francisco.

Aiken, T. W., Stumphauzer, J. S. and Veloz, E. V. (1979) 'Behavioral Analysis of Non-delinquent Brothers in a High Juvenile Crime Community', in Stumphauzer, J. S. (ed.), *Progress in Behavior Therapy with Delinquents*, Charles C. Thomas, Springfield, Illinois.

Ainsworth, S. (1980) 'Description of a Group to Teach Money and Shopping Skills', unpublished report.

Alden, L. and Cappi, R. (1981) 'Nonassertiveness: Skill-deficit or Selective Self-evaluation?', *Behavior Therapy*, 12, pp. 107–14.

Alexander, J. F. and Parsons, B. (1973) 'Short-term behavioral intervention with delinquent families: impact on family process and recidivism', *Journal of Abnormal Psychology*, 81, pp. 219–25.

Ayllon, T. and Michael, J. (1959) 'The psychiatric nurse as a behavioral engineer', *Journal of the Experimental Analysis of Behavior*, 2, pp. 232–334.

Azrin, N. H. (1976) 'Improvements in the community-reinforcement approach to alcoholism', *Behaviour Research and Therapy*, 14, pp. 339–48.

Azrin, N. H., Flores, T. and Kaplan, S, J. (1975) 'Job-finding club: a group assisted program for obtaining employment', *Behaviour Research and Therapy*, 13, (1), pp. 17–26.

Azrin, N. H. and Foxx, R. M. (1971) 'A rapid method of toilet training for the institutionalised retarded', *Journal of Applied Behavior Analysis*, 4, pp. 89–99.

Azrin, N. H., Philip, R. A., Thienes-Hontos, P. and Besalel, V. A. (1980) 'Comparative evaluation of the job club program with welfare recipients', *Journal of Vocational Behavior*, 16, pp. 133–45.

Azrin, N., Sneed, T. J. and Foxx, R. M. (1974) 'Dry bed training: rapid elimination of childhood enuresis', *Behaviour Research and Therapy*, 12, pp. 147–56.

Ballard, K. D., Gilmore, B., Christie, R. G. and Vanbiervliet, A. (1983) 'A format for writing teaching programmes for handicapped persons, with a budgeting skills example', *Australia and New Zealand Journal of Developmental Disabilities*, 9, 1, pp. 16–22.

Bandura, A. (1965) 'Influence of a model's reinforcement contingencies on the acquisition of imitative responses', *Journal of Personality and Social Psychology*, 1, pp. 589–95.

Bandura, A., (1977) *Social Learning Theory*, Prentice-Hall, Englewood Cliffs, New Jersey.

Bandura, A. (1984) 'Recycling misconceptions of perceived self-efficacy', *Cognitive Therapy and Research*, 8, 3, pp. 231–55.

Bandura, A. and Walters, R. H. (1959) *Adolescent Aggression*, The Ronald Press Company, New York.

Barraclough, C. and Fleming, I. (1984) 'Not too old to learn', *Community Care*, 23 February, 500, pp. 16–17.

Barth, R., Schinke, S. P. and Maxwell, J. S. 'Coping Skills Training for School-Age Mothers', *Journal of Social Service Research*, in press.

Barth, R. P., Blythe, B. J., Schinke, S. P. and Schilling, R. F. II. (1983) 'Self-control training with maltreating parents', *Child Welfare*, LXII, 4, pp. 313–24.

Beck, A. T., Rush, A. J., Shaw, B. F. and Emery, G. (1979) *Cognitive Therapy of Depression*,. Guilford Press, New York.

Beck, A. T. (1976) *Cognitive Therapy and the Emotional Disorders*, International University Press, New York.

Beck, A. T., Rush, A. J., Shaw, B. F. and Energy, G. (1979) *Cognitive Therapy of Depression*,. Guilford Press, New York.

Becker, W. (1971) *Parents are Teachers: A Child Management Program*, Research Press, Champaign, Illinois.

Bellack, A. S. and Hersen, M. (1977) *Behavior Modification: an Introductory Textbook*, Williams & Wilkins Co, Baltimore.

Belson, W. A. (1975) *Juvenile Theft: The Causal Factors*, Harper & Row, London.

Bennett, G. (1971) 'Behavioural intervention to prevent eviction', *Social Work Today*, 1, 11, pp. 11–16.

Berman, S. and Rickel, A. (1979) 'Assertive training for low income black parents' *Clinical Social Work Journal*, 7, pp. 123–32.

Blackburn, I. M., Bishop, S., Glen, A. I. M., Whalley, L. J. and Christie, J. E. (1981) 'The efficacy of cognitive therapy in depression', *British Journal of Psychiatry*, 137, pp. 181–9.

Bloom, M. and Fischer, J. (1982) *Evaluating Practice: Guidelines for the Accountable Professional*, Prentice-Hall, Englewood Cliffs, New Jersey.

Braukmann, D. J., Fixsen, D. L., Phillips, E. L. and Wolf, M. M., (1975) 'Behavioural approaches to treatment in the crime and delinquency field', *Criminology*, 13, pp. 299–331.

Bricker, W. A. (1975) 'Identifying and modifying behavioral deficits', in

Graziano, A. M. (ed.), *Behavior Therapy with Children*, II, Aldene Atherton, New York.

Briscoe, R. V., Hoffman, D. B. and Bailey, J. S. (1975) 'Behavioral community psychology: training a community board to problem-solve', *Journal of Applied Behavior Analysis*, 8, 2, pp. 157–68.

Brockett, R. G. (1981) 'The use of reality orientation in adult foster care homes: a rationale', *Journal of Gerontological Social Work*, 3, 3, Spring, pp. 3–13.

Buchanan, A. and Webster, A. (1982) 'Bedtime without battles', *British Journal of Social Work*, 12, 2, pp. 197–204.

Burgess, R., Jewett, R., Sandham, J. and Hudson, B. L. (1980) 'Working with sex offenders: A social skills training group', *British Journal of Social Work*, 10, 2, pp. 133–42.

Burrill, R. H., McCourt, J. F. and Cutter, H. S. G. (1974) 'Beer: a social facilitator for PMI residents, *Gerontologist*, 14, pp. 430–31.

Carr, J. (1980) *Helping Your Handicapped Child: A Step-by-Step Guide to Everyday Problems*, Penguin, Harmondsworth.

Cautela, J. K. (1972) 'Rationale and Procedures for Covert Conditioning', in R. D. Rubin, H. Fensterheim, J. D. Henderson and L. P. Ullman (eds), *Advances in Behavior Therapy*, Academic Press, New York.

Chelfham Mill School, (1976) *Fewer Shades of Grey* (Film) Chelfham Mill School, Barnstaple, Devon.

Clark, J. V. and Arkowitz, H. (1975) 'Social anxiety and self-evaluation of interpersonal performance', *Psychological Reports*, 36, pp. 211–26.

Collins, J. (1982) *Self-Efficacy and Ability in Achievement Behavior*, paper presented at the meeting of the American Educational Research Association, New York.

Cone, J. D. and Hawkins, R. P. (1977) *Behavioral Assessment*, Brunner/Mazel, New York.

Cormier, W. H. and Cormier, L. S. (1979) *Interviewing Strategies for Helpers*, Brooks/Cole, Monterey, California.

Cornish, D. B. and Clarke, R. V. B. (1975) *Residential Treatment and its Effects on Delinquency*, Home Office Research Studies, No. 32, HMSO, London.

Cowie, Mary, (1982, 10 July) *Training Foster Parents to Use Behavioural Approaches with Difficult Adolescents*, paper presented at the Annual Conference of the British Association for Behavioural Psychotherapy, University of Sussex.

Coyne, J. C. and Gotlib, I. H. (1983) 'The role of cognition in depression: a critical appraisal, *Psychological Bulletin*, 94, 3, pp. 472–505.

Curran, J. P. (1979) 'Pandora's box reopened? The assessment of social skills' *Journal of Behavioral Assessment*, 1(1), pp. 55–71.

Davies, A. D. (1981) 'Neither wife nor widow: An intervention with the wife of a chronically handicapped man during hospital visits', *Behaviour Research and Therapy*, 19, 5, pp. 449–51.

Delfini, L. F., Bernal, M. E. and Rosen, P. M. (1976) 'Comparison of Deviant and Normal Boys in Home Settings' in E. J. Mash, L. A.

Hamerlynck and L. C. Handy (eds), *Behavior Modification and Families*, Brunner/Mazel, New York.

Department of Health and Social Security, (1972) *Intermediate Treatment*. HMSO, London.

Doleys, D. M. (1979) 'Assessment and treatment of childhood enuresis', in A. J. Finch Jr. and P. C. Kendall (eds), *Clinical Treatment and Research in Child Psychotherapy*, Spectrum, New York.

Ellis, A. (1979) 'A note on the treatment of agoraphobics with cognitive modification versus prolonged exposure *in vivo*', *Behaviour Research and Therapy*, 17, pp. 162–4.

Ellis, A. and Grieger, R. (eds), (1977) *Handbook of Rational-Emotive Therapy*, Springer, New York.

Eyberg, S. M. and Johnson, S. M. (1974) 'Multiple assessment of behavior modification with families: effects of contingency contracting and order of treated problems', *Journal of Consulting and Clinical Psychology*, 42, pp. 594–606.

Eyeberg, S. (1980) 'Child behaviour inventory', *Journal of Clinical Child Psychology*, Spring.

Fahlberg, V. (1981) *The Child in Placement: Common Behavioral Problems*, Michigan Department of Social Services, Michigan.

Feldman, M. P. (1977) *Criminal Behaviour: a Psychological Analysis*, John Wiley, London.

Feldman, P. (1983) 'Juvenile offending: behavior approaches to prevention and intervention', *Child and Family Behavior Therapy* 5, (1), pp. 37–50.

Fellin, P., Rothman, J. and Meyer, H. (1967) 'Implications of the Socio-behavioral Approach for Community Organization Practice', in E. Thomas (ed.), *The Socio-behavioral Approach and Applications to Social Work Practice*, Council for Social Work Education, New York.

Ferster, C. B. (1973) 'A functional analysis of depression', *American Psychologist*, 28, pp. 857–70.

Fischer, J. (1978) *Effective Casework Practice*, McGraw Hill, New York.

Fischer, J. (1981) 'The social work revolution', *Social Work*, May, pp. 199–207.

Fisher, M., Newton, C. and Sainsbury, E. (1984) *Mental Health Social Work Observed*, George Allen & Unwin, London.

Foa, E. B. and Emmelkamp, P. M. G. (1983) *Failures in Behavior Therapy*, John Wiley & Sons, New York.

Forehand, R., King, H., Peed, S. and Yoder, P. (1975) 'Mother-child interaction: comparison of a non-compliant clinic group and non-clinic group', *Behaviour Research and Therapy*, 13, pp. 79–84.

Foster, S. L., Prinz, R. J. and O'Leary, K. D. (1983) 'Impact of problem-solving communication training and generalization procedures on family conflict', *Child and Family Behavior Therapy*, 5, 1, pp. 1–23.

Freedman, B. J., Rosenthal, L., Donahoe, C. P. Jnr., Schlundt, D. G. and McFall, R. M. (1978) 'A social-behavioral analysis of skill deficits in delinquent and non-delinquent adolescent boys', *Journal of Consulting and Clinical Psychology*, 46, (6), pp. 1448–62.

Furnham, A. and Argyle, M. (1981) 'The theory, practice and application of social skills training', *International Journal of Behavioural Social Work and Abstracts*, 1, 2, pp. 125–44.

Galinsky, M. D., Schopler, J. H., Safier, E. J. and Gambrill, E. D. (1978) 'Assertion training for public welfare clients', *Social Work with Groups*, 1, 4, pp. 365–79.

Gambrill, E. D. (1977) *Behavior Modification*, Jossey-Bass, San Francisco.

Gambrill, E. D. (1983a) 'Behavioral Intervention with Child Abuse and Neglect', in M. Hersen, R. M. Eisler and P. M. Miller (eds), *Progress in Behavior Modification*, Vol. 15, Academic Press, New York.

Gambrill, E. D. (1983b) *Casework: A Competency-Based Approach*, Prentice-Hall, Englewood Cliffs, New Jersey.

Gambrill, E. D. (1986) 'Social skills and ageing' in C. Hollin and P. Trower (eds), *Handbook of Social Skills Training*, Pergamon, Oxford.

Gambrill, E. and Richey, C. (1975) 'An assertion inventory for use in assessment and research', *Behavior Therapy*, 6, pp. 550–61.

Garber, J. and Seligman, M. E. P. (eds), (1980) *Human Helplessness: Theory and Applications*, Academic Press, New York.

Gelder, M. (1979) 'Behaviour Therapy' in S. Bloch (ed.), *An Introduction to the Psychotherapies*, Oxford University Press, Oxford.

George, V. (1970) *Foster Care – Theory and Practice*, Routledge & Kegan Paul, London.

Gilchrist, L. D. and Schinke, S. P. (1983) 'Coping with contraception: cognitive and behavioral methods with adolescents', *Cognitive Therapy and Research* 7, (5), pp. 379–88.

Gilchrist, L. D., Schinke, S. P. and Blythe, B. J. (1979) 'Primary prevention services for children and youth', *Children and Youth Services Review*, 1, pp. 379–91.

Giles, T. R. (1983) 'Probable superiority of behavioral interventions – I: traditional comparative outcome', *Journal of Behavior Therapy and Experimental Psychiatry*, 14, 1, pp. 29–32.

Gillen, R. W. and Heimberg, R. G. (1980) 'Social Skills Training for the Job Interview: Review and Prospectus', in M. Hersen, R. Eisler and P. Miller (eds), *Progress in Behavior Modification*, Vol. 10, Academic Press, New York.

Glueck, S. and Glueck, E. T. (1950) *Unravelling Juvenile Delinquency*, Commonwealth Fund, New York.

Goldberg, E. M. and Warburton, R. W. (1979) *Ends and Means in Social Work*, George Allen & Unwin, London.

Goldfried, M. R., Decenteceo, E. and Weinberg, L. (1974) 'Systematic rational restructuring as a self-control technique', *Behavior Therapy*, 5, pp. 247–51.

Goldstein, A. P., Sherman, M., Gershaw, N. J., Sprafkin, K. P. and Glick, B., (1978) 'Training aggressive adolescents in prosocial behavior', *Journal of Youth and Adolescence* 7, 1, 73–92.

Goldstein, R. S. and Baer, D. M. (1976) 'R.S.V.P.: a procedure to increase the personal mail and number of correspondents for nursing home residents', *Behavior Therapy*, 7, pp. 348–54.

Greene, J. C., Nicol, R. and Jamieson, H. (1979) 'Reality orientation with psychogeriatric patients', *Behaviour Research and Therapy*, 17, pp. 618–21.

Greene, J. C., Timbury, G. C., Smith, R. and Gardiner, M. (1983) 'Reality orientation with elderly patients in the community: an empirical evaluation', *Age and Ageing*, 12, pp. 38–43.

Griest, D. L. and Wells, K. C. (1983) 'Behavioral family therapy with conduct disorders in children', *Behavior Therapy*, 14, pp. 37–53.

Grinnell, R. M. Jr. and Lieberman, A. (1981) 'Helping Mentally Retarded Persons Get Jobs', in S. P. Schinke (ed.), *Behavioral Methods in Social Welfare*, Aldine, New York.

Gurman, A. S. and Kniskern, D. P. (1978) 'Research on Marital and Family Therapy' in S. L. Garfield and A. E. Bergin (eds), *Handbook of Psychotherapy and Behavior Change*, (2nd ed.), John Wiley & Sons, New York.

Hand, I., Lamontagne, Y. and Marks, I. M. (1974) 'Group exposure (flooding) *in vivo* for agoraphobics', *British Journal of Psychiatry*, 124, pp. 588–602.

Hawton, K. (1985) *Sex Therapy: A Practical Guide*, Oxford University Press, Oxford.

Heider, F. (1958) *The Psychology of Interpersonal Relations*, John Wiley & Sons, New York.

Heimberg, R. G., Cunningham, J., Heimberg, J. S. and Blankenberg, R. (1982) 'Preparing unemployed youth for job interviews: a controlled evaluation', *Behavior Modification*, 6, 3, pp. 299–322.

Henderson, J. Q. (1981) 'A behavioral approach to stealing: a proposal for treatment based on ten cases', *Journal of Behavior Therapy and Experimental Psychiatry*, 12, (3), pp. 231–6.

Herbert, M. (1978) *Conduct Disorders of Childhood and Adolescence*, John Wiley & Sons, Chichester.

Herbert, M. (1979) *'Why Behavioural Social Work?'* Paper read at 1st annual conference of the Behavioural Social Work Group, Leicester, 16 June.

Herbert, M. (1981) *Behavioural Treatment of Problem Children*, Academic Press, London.

Holden, U. P. and Woods, R. T. (1982) *Reality Orientation*, Churchill-Livingstone, Edinburgh.

Hudson, B. L. (1975) 'An inadequate personality', *Social Work Today*, 6, 16, pp. 505–9.

Hudson, B. L. (1976) 'Behavioural Social Work in a Community Psychiatric Service'. in M. R. Olsen (ed.), *Differential Approaches in Social Work with the Mentally Disordered*, BASW, Birmingham.

Hudson, B. L. (1978) 'Behavioural social work with schizophrenic patients in the community', *British Journal of Social Work*, 8, 2, pp. 159–70.

Hutchings, J., Jones, D., Hibbs, P. and Fox, J. (1981) 'The Ynys Mons Intermediate Treatment Project', *International Journal of Behavioural Social Work and Abstracts*, 1, 3, pp. 187–98.

Isaacs, W., Thomas, J. and Goldiamond, I. (1960) 'Application of operant conditioning to reinstate verbal behavior in psychotics', *Journal of Speech and Hearing Disorders*, 25, pp. 8–12. Reprinted in L. P. Ullman and L.

Krasner (eds), (1965) *Studies in Behavior Modification*, Holt, Rinehart and Winston, New York.

Jacobson, N. S. (1984) 'A component analysis of behavioral marital therapy: the relative effectiveness of behavior exchange and communication/problem-solving training', *Journal of Consulting and Clinical Psychology*, 52, (2), pp. 295–305.

Jacobson, N. S. and Margolin, G. (1979) *Marital Therapy: Strategies Based on Social Learning and Behavior Exchange Principles*, Brunner/Mazel, New York.

Jansen, M. and Meyers-Abell, J. (1981) 'Assertive training for battered women: a pilot program', *Social Work*, 26, 2, pp. 164–5.

Jehu, D. (1979) *Sexual Dysfunction*, John Wiley & Sons, Chichester.

Jenkins, J., Felce, D., Lunt, B. and Powell, E. (1977) 'Increasing engagement in activity of residents in old people's homes by providing recreational materials', *Behaviour Research and Therapy*, 15, pp. 429–34.

Johnson, B. and Cuvo, A. J. (1981) 'Teaching cooking skills to mentally retarded adults', *Behavior Modification*, 5, pp. 187–202.

Kazdin, A. E. (1975) 'Issues in behavior modification with mentally retarded persons', in A. M. Graziano (ed.), *Behavior Therapy with Children* II, Aldine Atherton, New York.

Kazdin, A. E. and Smith, G. A. (1979) 'Covert conditioning: a review and evaluation', *Advances in Behaviour Research and Therapy* 2, pp. 57–98.

Kelly, J. A., Wildman, B. G. and Berler, E. S. (1980) 'Small group behavioral training to improve the job interview skills repertoire of mildly retarded adolescents', *Journal of Applied Behavior Analysis*, 13, pp. 461–71.

Kempe, R. S. and Kempe, C. (1978) *Child Abuse*, Harvard University Press, Cambridge, Massachusetts.

Kifer, R. N., Lewis, M. A., Green, D. R. and Phillips, E. L. (1974) 'Training predelinquent youths and their parents to negotiate conflict situations', *Journal of Applied Behavior Analysis*, 7, pp. 357–64.

Kirigin, K. A., Braukmann, C. J., Atwater, J. D. and Wolf, M. M. (1982) 'An evaluation of teaching family (Achievement Place) group homes for juvenile delinquents', *Journal of Applied Behavior Analysis*, 15, 1, pp. 1–16.

Kushlick, A. (1984) 'A national Portage association?', in Tony Dessent (ed.), *What is Important about Portage?*, NFER, Nelson.

Lamb, Barbara, (1984) 'The right way, the wrong way, and the Leeds way with truants', *The Guardian*, 4 September, p. 11.

Lane, T. W. and Burchard, J. D. (1983) 'Failure to modify delinquent behavior: a constructive analysis', in E. Foa and P. M. G. Emmelkamp (eds), *Failures in Behavior Therapy*, John Wiley & Sons, New York.

Latimer, P. and Sweet, A. (1984) 'Cognitive versus behavioral procedures: a critical review', *Journal of Behavior Therapy and Experimental Psychiatry*, 15, 1, pp. 9–22.

Laus, M. D. (1977) *Travel Instruction for the Handicapped*, Charles C. Thomas, Springfield, Illinois.

Lewinsohn, P. M., Biglan, A. and Zeiss, A. M. (1976) 'Behavioral Treatment of Depression', in P. O. Davidson (ed.), *The Behavioral Management of Anxiety, Depression and Pain*, Brunner/Mazel, New York.

Lewinsohn, P. M., Munoz, R. F., Youngren, M. A. and Zeiss, A. M. (1978) *Control Your Depression*, Prentice-Hall, Englewood Cliffs, New Jersey.

Lewinsohn, P. M., Steinmetz, J. L., Larsen, D. W. and Franklin, J. (1981) 'Depression-related cognitions: antecedent or consequence?' *Journal of Abnormal Psychology*, 90, pp. 213–19.

Liberman, R. (1971) 'Reinforcement of cohesiveness in group therapy', *Archives of General Psychiatry*, 25, pp. 168–77.

Liberman, R. P., King, L. W., Derisi, W. J. and McCann, M. (1975) *Personal Effectiveness*, Research Press, Champaign, Illinois.

Lindsay, W. R. (1982) 'Some normative goals for conversation training', *Behavioural Psychotherapy*, 10, pp. 253–72.

Linsk, N. and Pinkston, E. (1982) 'Applying Behavior Analysis to Social Group Work with the Elderly', in E. Pinkston, J. Levitt, G. Green, N. Linsk and T. Rzepnicki (eds), *Effective Social Work Practice*, Jossey-Bass, San Francisco.

Lobitz, G. and Johnson, S. (1975) 'Normal versus deviant children', *Journal of Abnormal Child Psychology*, 3, pp. 353–74.

McAuley, R. (1982) 'Training parents to modify conduct problems in their children', *Journal of Child Psychology and Psychiatry*, 23, (3), pp. 335–42.

McAuley, R. and McAuley, P. (1977) *Child Behaviour Problems*, Macmillan, London.

McAuley, R. and McAuley, P. (1980) 'The effectiveness of behaviour modification with families', *British Journal of Social Work*, 10, 1, pp. 43–54.

McClannahan, L. E. and Risley, T. R. (1975) 'Design of living environments for nursing home residents: increasing participation in recreational activities', *Journal of Applied Behavior Analysis*, 8, pp. 261–8.

McMahon, R. J., Forehand, R. and Griest, D. L. (1981a) 'Effects of knowledge of social learning principles on enhancing treatment outcome and generalization in a parent training program' *Journal of Consulting and Clinical Psychology*, 49, 4, pp. 526–32.

McMahon, R. J., Forehand, R., Griest, D. L. and Webb, K. C. (1981b) 'Who drops out of therapy during parent behavioral training' *Behavior Counseling Quarterly*, 1, pp. 79–85.

Marchant, R., Howlin, P., Yule, W. and Rutter, M. (1974) 'Graded change in the treatment of the behavior of autistic children', *Journal of Child Psychology and Psychiatry*, 15, pp. 221–7.

Marks, I. M. (1978) 'Behavioral Psychotherapy of Adult Neurosis' in S. L. Garfield and A. E. Bergin (eds), *Handbook of Psychotherapy and Behavior Change* (2nd ed.), John Wiley & Sons, New York.

Marlatt, G. Alan, (1982) 'Relapse prevention: a self-control program for the treatment of addictive behaviors', in R. B. Stuart (ed.), *Adherence, Compliance and Generalization in Behavioral Medicine*, Brunner/Mazel, New York.

Mathews, R. M., Whang, P. L. and Fawcett, S. B. (1980) 'Development and validation of an occupational skills assessment instrument', *Behavioral Assessment*, 2, 1, pp. 71–86.

Matson, J. L. (1980) 'Preventing home accidents: a training program for the retarded', *Behavior Modification*, 4, pp. 397–410.

Matson, J. L. (1981a) 'Use of independence training to teach shopping skills to mildly mentally retarded adults', *American Journal of Mental Deficiency*, 86, pp. 178–83.

Matson, J. L. (1981b) 'A controlled outcome study of phobias in mentally retarded adults', *Behaviour Research and Therapy*, 19, 2, pp. 101–8.

Matson, J. L. (1982) 'Independence training versus modeling procedures for teaching phone conversation skills to the mentally retarded', *Behaviour Research and Therapy*, 20, 5, pp. 505–11.

Meichenbaum, D. (1977) *Cognitive Behavior Modification*, Plenum, New York.

Miller, L. K. and Miller, O. (1970) 'Reinforcing self-help group activities of welfare recipients', *Journal of Applied Behavior Analysis*, 3, pp. 57–64.

Miller, R. C. and Berman, J. S. (1983) 'The efficacy of cognitive behavior therapies: a quantitative review of the research evidence', *Psychological Bulletin*, 94, 1, pp. 39–53.

Minkin, N., Braukmann, C. J., Minkin, B. L., Timbers, G. D., Timbers, B. J., Fixsen, D. L., Phillips, E. L. and Wolf, M. M., (1976) 'The social validation and training of conversational skills', *Journal of Applied Behavior Analysis*, 9, pp. 127–39.

Molick, R., Love, B. T., Henderson, P. D. and Pinkston, E. (1982) 'Group Training Parents to Negotiate Behavior Change with Their Mentally Retarded Adult Children', in E. Pinkston, J. L. Levitt, G. R. Green, N. L. Linsk and J. L. Rzepnicki (eds), *Effective Social Work Practice*, Jossey-Bass, San Francisco.

Morgan, R. T. T. (1981) *Childhood Incontinence*, Heinemann, London.

Morgan, R. T. T. (1982) 'The management and treatment of nocturnal enuresis in children', *International Journal of Behavioural Social Work and Abstracts*, 2, (1), pp. 1–16.

Mori, A. A. and Masters, L. F. (1980) *Teaching the Severely Mentally Retarded*, Aspen, Germantown, Maryland.

Neale, J. M., Oltmanns, T. F. and Davison, G. C. (1982) *Case Studies in Abnormal Psychology*, John Wiley & Sons, New York.

Newson, J. (1972) 'Observation and development of conscience in ordinary young children', in *Aspects of moral development*, (Symposium) University of Leicester, September.

Nomellini, S. and Katz, D. (1983) 'Effects of anger control training on abusive parents', *Cognitive Therapy and Research*, 7, 1, pp. 57–68.

Novaco, R. W. (1975) *Anger Control: The Development and Evaluation of an Experimental Treatment*, Heath, Lexington, Massachusetts.

Novaco, R. W. (1977) 'A stress inoculation approach to anger management in the training of law-enforcement officers', *American Journal of Community Psychology*, 5, pp. 327–46.

Oliver, J. (1981) 'The behavioural treatment of a case of obsessional house cleaning in a personality disordered client', *International Journal of Behavioural Social Work and Abstracts*, 1, 1, pp. 27–38.

Orme, J. G. and Gillespie, D. F. (1981) 'Target complaints as an individualised outcome measure', *International Journal of Behavioural Social Work and Abstracts*, 1, 3, pp. 199–204.

Ostapuik, E. and Reid, I. (1981) 'Rehabilitating Offenders in the Community', in J. McPherson and A. Sutton (eds), *Reconstructing Psychological Practice*, Croom Helm, London.

Patterson, G. R. (1975) *Families*, Research Press, Champaign, Illinois.

Patterson, G. R. (1976) 'The Aggressive Child: Victim and Architect of a Coercive System', in E. J. Mash, L. A. Hamerlynck, and L. C. Handy (eds),*Behavior Modification and Families* I, Brunner/Mazel, New York.

Patterson, G. R. (1982) *Coercive Family Process*, Castalia, Eugene, Oregon.

Patterson, G. R. and Hops, H. (1972) 'Coercion: a game for two', in R. E. Ulrich and P. Mountjoy (eds), *The Experimental Analysis of Social Behavior*, Prentice-Hall, Englewood Cliffs, New Jersey.

Patterson, G. R., Cobb, J. A. and Ray, R. S. (1973) 'A social engineering technology for retraining the families of aggressive boys', in H. E. Adams and I. P. Unikel (eds), *Issues and Trends in Behavior Therapy*, Charles C. Thomas, Springfield, Illinois.

Patterson, G. R. and Reid, J. B. (1973) 'Intervention for families of aggressive boys: a replication study', *Behaviour Research and Therapy*, 11, pp. 383–94.

Pedalino, E. and Gamboa, V. U. (1974) 'Behavior modification and absenteeism: intervention in one industrial setting', *Journal of Applied Psychology*, 59, pp. 694–8.

Peine, H. A. and Howarth, R. (1975) *Children and Parents*, Penguin, Harmondsworth.

Pilavin, I. and Briar, S. (1964) 'Police encounters with juveniles', *American Journal of Sociology*, 70, pp. 206–14.

Platt, J. J., Spivack, G., Altman, N., Altman, D. and Peizer, S. B. (1974) 'Adolescent problem-solving thinking', *Journal of Consulting and Clinical Psychology*, 42, (6) pp. 787–93.

Porterfield, J., Blunden, R. and Blewitt, F. (1980) 'Improving environments for profoundly handicapped adults: using prompts and social attention to maintain high group engagement', *Behaviour Modification*, 4, pp. 225–41.

Powell, L., Felce, D., Jenkins, J. and Lunt, B. (1979) 'Increasing engagement in a home for the elderly by promoting an indoor gardening activity', *Behaviour Research and Therapy*, 17, pp. 127–36.

Powell-Proctor, L. and Miller, E. (1982) 'Reality orientation: a critical appraisal', *British Journal of Psychiatry*, 140, pp. 457–63.

Preston, M. A. (1982) 'Intermediate Treatment: A New Approach to Community Care', in P. Feldman (ed.), *Developments in the Study of Criminal Behaviour Vol. 1: The Prevention and Control of Offending*, John Wiley & Sons, Chichester.

Rachman, S. J. and Wilson, G. T. (1980) *The Effects of Psychological Therapy*, Pergamon, Oxford.

272   *Bibliography*

Rathus, S. A. (1973) 'A thirty-item schedule for assessing assertive behavior', *Behavior Therapy*, 4, pp. 298–306.

Reavley, W., Gilbert, M. T. and Carver, V. (1978) 'The Analysis and Treatment of Child Abuse by Behavioural Psychotherapy', in V. Carver (ed.), *Child Abuse: a Study Text*, The Open University, Milton Keynes.

Reid, J. B. and Hendricks, A. F. C. J. (1973) 'Preliminary analysis of the effectiveness of direct home intervention for the treatment of predelinquent boys who steal', in L. Hamerlynck, L. Handy and E. Mash (eds), *Behavioral Change: Methodology, Concepts and Practice*, Research Press, Champaign, Illinois.

Reid, W. and Hanrahan, P. (1958), 'Recent evaluations of social work: grounds for optimism', *Social Work*, 27, 4, pp. 328–40.

Reisinger, J. J., Frangia, G. W. and Hoffman, E. H. (1976) 'Toddler management training: generalisation and marital status', *Journal of Behavior Therapy and Experimental Psychiatry*, 7, pp. 335–40.

Robin, A. L., O'Leary, K. D., Kent, R. N., Foster, S. L. and Prinz, R. J. (1977) 'Communication training: an approach to problem solving for parents and adolescents', *Behavior Therapy*, 8, pp. 639–43.

Robins, L. N. (1970) 'Antecedents of Character Disorders', in M. Rolf and D. K. Ricks (eds), *Life History Research in Psychotherapy*, University of Minnesota Press, Minneapolis.

Rogers, C. R. and Skinner, B. F. (1956) 'Some issues concerning the control of human behavior: a symposium', *Science*, 124, 3231, pp. 1057–66.

Rose, S. D. (1972) *Treating Children in Groups*, Jossey-Bass, San Francisco.

Rose, S. D. (1981) 'Children's groups – an excerpt from ongoing process', *Behavior Group Therapy*, 3, 1, pp. 22–5.

Rothman, J. (1980) *Social R and D: Research and Development in Human Services*, Prentice-Hall, Englewood Cliffs, New Jersey.

Rowe, J. and Lambert, L. (1973) *Children who Wait*, Association of British Adoption Agencies, London.

Rush, A., Beck, A., Kovacs, M. and Hollon, S. (1977) 'Comparative efficacy of cognitive therapy and pharmacotherapy in the treatment of depressed outpatients', *Cognitive Therapy and Research*, 1, pp. 17–37.

Rutter, M. and Giller, H. (1983) *Juvenile Delinquency: Trends and Perspectives*, Penguin, Harmondsworth.

Rutter, M., Tizard, J. and Whitmore, K. (1970) *Education, Health and Behaviour*, Longman, London.

Sarber, R. E. and Cuvo, A. J. (1983) 'Teaching nutritional meal planning to developmentally disabled clients', *Behavior Modification*, 7, 4, pp. 503–30.

Saunders, D. G. (1984) 'Helping husbands who batter', *Social Casework*, 65, 6, pp. 347–53.

Schinke, S. P. (1984) 'Preventing Teenage Pregnancy', in M. Hersen, R. Eisler, P. Miller (eds), *Progress in Behavior Modification*, Vol. 16, Academic Press, New York.

Schinke, S. P. and Gilchrist, L. D. (1983) 'Primary prevention of tobacco smoking', *Journal of School Health*, 53, 7, pp. 416–19.

Schulz, R. (1980) 'Aging and Control', In J. Garber and M. E. P. Seligman (eds), *Human Helplessness*, Academic Press, New York.

Seligman, M. (1975) *Helplessness*, Freeman, San Francisco.

Shearer, M. S. and Shearer, D. E. (1972) 'The Portage project: a model for early childhood education', *Exceptional Children*, 38, pp. 210–17.

Sheldon, B. (1980) *The Use of Contracts in Social Work*, BASW, Birmingham.

Sheldon, B. (1982) *Behaviour Modification: Theory, Practice and Philosophy*, Tavistock, London.

Skinner, B. F. (1938) *The Behavior of Organisms*, Appleton-Century-Crofts, New York.

Skinner, B. F. (1953) *Science and Human Behavior*, Macmillan, New York.

Smith, L. J. (1981) 'Training severely and profoundly mentally handicapped nocturnal enuretics', *Behaviour Research and Therapy*, 19, 1, pp. 67–74.

Spence, S. (1980) *Social Skills Training with Children and Adolescents*, NFER, London.

Stallard, P. N. (1983) *The Shape Behavioural Rehabilitation Programme for Young Offenders: Client Variables and Follow-up Data*, paper presented at the meeting of the Association for the Advancement of Behavior Therapy, Washington DC, December.

Stein, T. J., Gambrill, E. D. and Wiltse, K. T. (1978) *Children in Foster Homes: Achieving Continuity of Care*, Praeger Special Studies, New York.

Stern, R. S. (1978), *Behavioural Techniques*, Academic, London.

Steuer, J. L. and Hammen, C. L. (1983) 'Cognitive–Behavioral group therapy for the depressed elderly: issues and adaptions', *Cognitive Therapy and Research*, 7, 4, pp. 285–96.

Stuart, R. B. (1970) 'Assessment and Change in the communicational patterns of Juvenile Delinquents and their Parents', in R. D. Rubin (ed.), *Advances in Behavior Therapy 1969*, Academic Press, New York.

Stuart, R. (1980) *Helping Couples Change: A Social Learning Approach to Marital Therapy*, Guilford, New York.

Stumphauzer, J. S. (1979) 'Elimination of Stealing by Self-reinforcement of Alternative Behavior and Family Contracting', in J. S. Stumphauzer (ed.), *Progress in Behavior Therapy with Delinquents*, Charles C. Thomas, Springfield, Illinois.

Stumphauzer, J. S. (1980) 'Learning to drink: adolescents and alcohol', *Addictive Behaviors*, 5, pp. 277–83.

Stumphauzer, J. S., Aiken, T. W. and Veloz, E. V. (1979) 'East Side Story: Behavioral Analysis of a High Juvenile Crime Community', in J. S. Stumphauzer (ed.), *Progress in Behavior Therapy with Delinquents*, Charles C. Thomas, Springfield, Illinois.

Suinn, R. M. and Richardson, F. (1971) 'Anxiety management training', *Behavior Therapy*, 2, pp. 498–510.

Sutton, C. (1979) *Psychology for Social Workers and Counsellors*, Routledge & Kegan Paul, London.

Sweet, J. J. and Resick, P. A. (1979) 'The maltreatment of children: a review of theories and research', *Journal of Social Issues*, 35, pp. 40–59.

Tams, V. and Eyberg. S. (1976) 'A Group Treatment Program for Parents', in E. J. Mash, L. C. Handy and L. A. Hamerlynck (eds), *Behavior Modification Approaches to Parenting*, Brunner/Mazel, New York.

Tavormina, J. B. (1975) 'Relative effectiveness of behavioral and reflective group counselling with parents of mentally retarded children', *Journal of Consulting and Clinical Psychology*, 43, 1, pp. 22–31.

Tharp, R. G. and Wetzel, R. J. (1969) *Behavior Modification in the Natural Environment*, Academic Press, New York.

Thomas, E. J. (1977) *Marital Communication and Decision Making*, The Free Press, New York.

Thomlison, R. J. (1984) 'Something works: evidence from practice effectiveness studies', *Social Work*, Jan–Feb, pp. 51–6.

Timms, N. and Timms, R. (1977) *Perspectives in Social Work*, Routledge & Kegan Paul, London.

Toseland, R. and Rose, S. D. (1978) 'Evaluating social skills training for older adults in groups', *Social Work Research and Abstracts*, 14, pp. 25–33.

Tsoi, M. and Yule, J. (1982) 'Building up new behaviours – shaping, prompting and fading', in W. Yule and J. Carr (eds). *Behaviour Modification for the Mentally Handicapped*, Croom Helm, London.

Turkat, I. D. and Calhoun, J. F. (1980) 'The problem-solving flow chart', *The Behavior Therapist*, 3, 1, p. 21.

Tutt, N. and Giller, H. (1983) *Social Enquiry Reports* (Audiotape), University of Lancaster.

Wahler, R. G. (1980) 'The insular mother: her problems in parent-child treatment', *Journal of Applied Behavior Analysis*, 13, pp. 207–19.

Wahler, R. G. and Afton, A. D. (1980) 'Attentional processes in insular and noninsular mothers: some differences in their summary reports about child problem behavior', *Child Behavior Therapy*, 2, pp. 25–41.

Wahler, R. and Fox, J. J. (1978) 'Solitary toy play: a desirable family treatment component for aggressive–oppositional children', unpublished manuscript, University of Tennessee, Knoxville.

Walters, R. H. and Demkov, L. (1963) 'Timing of punishment as a determinant of resistance to temptation', *Child Development*, 74, pp. 207–14.

Watson, D. and Friend, R. (1969) 'Measurement of social-evaluative anxiety', *Journal of Consulting and Clinical Psychology*, 33, p. 449.

Watson, J. B. (1913) 'Psychology as a behaviorist views it', *Psychological Review*, 20, pp. 158–77.

Webb, L. and Scanlon, J. R. (1981) 'The effectiveness of institutional and community-based programs for juvenile offenders', *Juvenile and Family Court Journal*, August, pp. 11–16.

Weisner, S. and Silver, M. (1981) 'Community work and social learning theory', *Social Work*, 26, pp. 146–50.

Wells, K. C. and Forehand, R. (1981) 'Childhood behavior problems in the home' in S. M. Turner, K. S. Calhoun and H .E. Adams (eds), *Handbook of Clinical Behavior Therapy*, John Wiley & Sons, New York.

West, D. J. and Farrington, D. P. (1973) *Who Becomes Delinquent?*, Heinemann, London.

Wheeler, J., Ford, A., Nietupski, J., Loomis, R. and Brown, L. (1980)

'Teaching the moderately and severely handicapped to shop in supermarkets using pocket calculators', *Education and Training of the Mentally Retarded*, 15, pp. 105–12.

Wilson, B. (1982) 'Toilet training', in W. Yule and J. Carr (eds), *Behaviour Modification for the Mentally Handicapped*, Croom Helm, London.

Wodarski, J. S. and Lenhart, S. D. (1982) *Adolescents who Abuse Alcohol: a Behavioral Group Procedure*, paper presented at the Sixteenth Annual Association for Advancement of Behavior Therapy Meeting (Special Interest Group: Social Work Group for the Study of Behavioral Methods) Los Angeles, California, November.

Wolpe, J. (1973) *The Practice of Behavior Therapy* (2nd ed.), Pergamon, New York.

Wootton, B. (1959) *Social Science and Social Pathology*, George Allen & Unwin, London.

Yule, W. and Carr, J. (eds) (1980, reprinted 1982) *Behaviour Modification for the Mentally Handicapped*, Croom Helm, London.

Zander, T. and Kindy, P. (1980) 'Behavioral Group Training for Welfare Parents', in S. D. Rose (ed.), *A Casebook in Group Therapy*, Prentice-Hall, Englewood Cliffs, New Jersey.

Author Index

Subject Index

Numbers in **bold face** refer to complete chapters or sections.

see also cognitive-behavioural
  approaches, cognitive theory,
  operant conditioning-respondent
  conditioning, social learning theory
loss 64, 232
  see also bereavement
lying 194

maintenance see generalisation and
  maintenance
marital problems 14, 38, 66, 70–1, 74,
  76, 80, 85, 101, 132, 138, 179, 180,
  153–60, 240
  see also communication training,
    decision making, family therapy,
    negotiation training, relationship,
    marital, sex therapy
material problems 60, 255
  see also accommodation, financial
    problems, money
meal planning **229**
measurement 2, **81–2**, 86, 102, **112–18**,
  213
  instruments 82, 83, **89–102**, 162
  see also evaluation
mediators 36, 69, 70, 153
  see also change agents
meetings 31, 78, 79, 82, 86, 92, 125, 252
  see also committees
mental disorder (illness) 12, 70, 95, 181,
  251
  see also agoraphobia, anxiety,
    delusional talk, dementia,
    depression, obsessional disorder,
    phobias, schizophrenia
mentally handicapped 12, 21, 67, 125,
  127, 129, 131, 154, 181, **215–30**
  adults **226–30**
  children 166, **215–25**
  and jobs 250, 251
  and sexual problems 160
  teenagers 1, 66
modelling 27, **40–5**, 56, 58, 60, 69, 70,
  129, **140–2**, 148, 157, 158, 162, 163,
  169, 170, 171, 172, 183, 199, 208,
  210, 221, 227, 228, 250
  and aggression 40–5
  and anxiety 45, 239
  of attitudes 159, 163, 243
  covert **144–5**
  see also models
models 44, 45, 107, 136, 141
  'coping' 141, 188

in groups 165, 188, 241
parents as 75
  see also modelling
money 60, 82, 126, **251–5**
  handling skills 129, 227
  see also budgeting, financial problems,
    social security
moods 59, 235, 248
  see also feelings
motivation 61, 64, **65–9**, 71, 74, 108,
  145, 205, 213, 229

National Association of Social Workers
  (NASW) 11, 17
negotiation training **153–8**, 198–201
  see also contracts
non-accidental injury 1
  see also child abuse and neglect
normalisation 226

obedience 68, 74, 76, 79, 81, 82, 90, 115,
  124
  see also compliance
observation 69, 74, **85–7**, 107, 133,
  162, 165, 212
obsessional disorder 145
offenders 137, 160, 197, 209, 211, 212,
  256
  and groupwork 170
  and jobs 250
  sexual 123, 144
  young 12, 107, 163, 200, 208, 209,
    210, 249
  see also delinquency
older people 119, **243–8**
  see also elderly, the
operant conditioning (learning) 26,
  27–40, 41, 42, 50, 51, 58
  and delinquency 196
  and depression **231–2**, 237
see also antecedents, consequences,
  extinction, punishment,
  reinforcement
operant intervention procedures
  124–39
  see also antecedents, altering of,
    behavioural rehearsal, chaining,
    extinction, fading, prompting,
    punishment, reinforcement,
    response cost, time out

paradoxical injunctions 14
parent training 149, 161, **178–86**, 187,
  198, 225